ALBUQUERQUE

Other Books by Margaret Randall include:

Sandino's Daughters
Christians in the Nicaraguan Revolution
Risking a Somersault in the Air
We
Cuban Women Now
Cuban Women—Twenty Years Later
Women Brave in the Face of Danger
The Coming Home Poems
Breaking the Silences
Poetry of Resistance
Testimonio

Translated by Margaret Randall:

Carlos, The Dawn is No Longer Beyond Our Reach,
    by Tomas Borge

Margaret Randall

ALBUQUERQUE

Coming Back to the U.S.A.

New Star Books
Vancouver, Canada

Canadian Cataloguing in Publication Data

Randall, Margaret, 1938-
  Albuquerque

ISBN 0-919573-52-5 (bound). — ISBN
  0-919573-53-3 (pbk.)

1. Randall, Margaret, 1938 -   2.
Authors, American - 20th century - Biography.
3. United States - Social conditions -
1980 -   I. Title.
PS3568.A5677Z54 1986   811'.54   C86-091260-4

First Printing June 1986.
1 2 3 4 5 90 89 88 87 86

New Star Books Ltd.
2504 York Avenue
Vancouver, B.C. V6K 1E3
Canada

Printed in Canada

This book is for Susan Sherman
with love

ACKNOWLEDGEMENTS

Many people have been key in the process of this book. Most of them are recipients of a journal I share with those close to me. They are Floyce Alexander, Russell Bartley, Lanny Beckman, Miranda Bergman, Jane Caputi, Bell Chevigny, Blanche Cook, Clare Coss, Gail Dolgin, Sue Doro, Annie Fitzgerald, Trisha Franzen, Sister Jeanne Gallo SND, Suzanne Gardinier, Dan Georgakas, Elaine Gill, Ruth Hubbard, Judy Janda, Liz Kennedy, Diane Kenney, Marjorie King, Paul Lauter, Jack Levine, Meridel LeSueur, Christina Mills, Marian McDonald, Colleen McKay, Ann Nihlen, Jane Norling, Philip Pasmanick, Stan Perksy, Bobbi Prebis, Elinor Randall, John D. Randall, John P. Randall, Adrienne Rich, Odilia Rodriguez, Susan Sherman, Debra Vetterman, Rhoda Waller, Lynda Yanz, Sylvia Yoneda, and Marilyn Young.

Stan Persky edited the first manuscript draft. Much later in the process, I was stuck, and he got in his little red car and drove from Vancouver to Albuquerque to spend several days helping me figure it all out. Without his love and help, this book would be another—lesser—one.

Barbara Bush typed the first draft, and Elinor Randall proofed the second.

To all of you, and unnamed others, my gratitude.

INTRODUCTION

In September of 1961 I travelled with my ten-month-old son across the United States from New York to Albuquerque. I had been born in New York in 1936, had experienced my childhood years there, and had returned there to write and have a child as a young adult. Now I went to visit with my own parents, still living in the Albuquerque of my youth. Then I headed south, to Mexico.

That was the beginning of an open-ended adventure, a chance to more easily support my son and myself—single motherhood, in the early '60s in this country, was even harder than it is now—and for a long time I didn't stop believing I would be "coming home soon." I didn't come home for twenty-three years. Mexico became an adopted country, the home of a bilingual literary magazine* I co-founded and edited for eight years, the scene of midwifery and political awakenings, a marriage, three more children, and underground escape.

*El Corno Emplumado / The Plumed Horn, bilingual literary quarterly, Mexico City, 1962-1969.

9

In September of 1969 I went to Cuba to live. I had suffered political repression connected with the great Mexican student upheaval of 1968, and Cuba was both a refuge and a lesson. I lived there from '69 through '80, and those years saw a refining of my knowledge of women's oppression and liberation, the beginnings of my affinity for oral history, the first of many books in which ordinary people (mostly women) speak in voices which without my probing (or the probing of others like me) would have remained silenced as they have been for centuries. The Cuban years were also my first experience with a socialist experiment: the joys and problems inherent in trying to change society from the roots.

Shortly after the Sandinista victory of July 1979, I went to Nicaragua to write about the women who had helped fight and win that war. Three months were enough; I was hooked. And so, in December of 1980 I went to Managua to live, accompanied by my youngest daughter, then eleven. The next three years saw several more books, books on women, books of poetry, and a book in which I branched out to explore the Christian experience in the process of change during the Nicaraguan revolution. Photography had also become an intense part of my life by this time. And for the first time I was not the emotional/economic center for my children. They were growing up and moving out onto their own terrains.

On January 18, 1984, I left Managua and came home. I had been away for twenty-three years. I had not planned this nearly-quarter-century as one of expatriatism or exile (terms frequently used by others, but not by me). I often thought of myself as a kind of hybrid, with as much of Latin America as of North America within me, and with values which reflected both cultures. I spoke only Spanish with my son and daughters. But I always thought of Albuquerque, New Mexico as my home. This city of 350,000 where watermelon-colored mountains rise above a wind-swept valley in the east and a desert stretches to the west. Albuquerque, town of military bases, plastic development, and three distinct cultures: the Native American, the Hispanic, and the Anglo. This city where my mother and father live, and my brother runs a bookstore.

So, early in 1984 I came home. And this book is about my home-coming, that re-entry. It is a book about coming back to the United States, and it consists of journal entries, poems, dreams, photographic images, meditations. Its fragmentary character is intentional, conveying, I hope, the texture of this experience, ongoing of course in many ways but it is also a pattern of strangeness-become-familiarity once more—as my senses undergo changes. My eyes are growing old for a second time as I settle back into a remembered, but different, space.

In presenting these impressions of the United States as seen through the eyes of one who is a stranger and yet not a stranger, I hope readers may find themselves stimulated to join me in reflecting on the bent hoop (bent? broken?) of the American Dream: the trivial become created-need, authentic cultures lost (or rather covered but still here), a presidential campaign no longer manipulated by TV but in fact created by that medium, the "economic recovery" in which more and more human beings are starving, a time in which the language of ordinary U.S. citizens and the language of the peoples of the world become, necessarily, less babel to one another.

January

1

If I start in the middle, as you told me last night Floyce, I will have to move forward and back from everyone I see in the streets. I will have to move forward and back at precisely the same time. How can I do that? I am struck by how little I know of everyone behind the masks. Eyes seem covered by a constant film. Metaphors multiply all over the surface of each day. An arm around a grocery bag assumes an angle that infringes on my personal comfort. I cannot imagine what is in the bag. The space between two bodies brings me down five or ten degrees. The young mother playing with her child on the sunny sand of a communal apartment space gives me more time, and recognition cuts through. I begin to smile. But she doesn't. And I move on.

I prepare myself for each encounter: now I will open my mouth and say hello. Now I will smile. Now I will give out a phrase I've heard. Now I will hold the door or open my wallet the way I have seen them do it. And I will try to keep from seeing the corpses. And I will smile again, and then laugh, listening to the rhythms on their tongues, laugh, get through.

When their mouths open, I must listen hard. And imagine. Here in Albuquerque, New Mexico 1984 "hang a left" means to make a left turn. "My phone is working" means it's ringing. Something else, mumbled beneath the surface of sound, wasn't what I thought. It *was* something else. I wait my turn. Everytime I pass the Heights Community Center and think of myself at thirteen, fourteen, full crinoline skirts and tight waist, agonized hopes and sideline smile kept firmly in its place, I think of the old Spaniards I knew then. The ones who spoke about the Spain they'd left after the Civil War twenty or thirty years before, as if they could go back any day, turn a corner and come upon the same flower vendor, unaged, the same lisp and colors. Once in a while I feel like a bit player in a film I myself made—twenty-three years ago.

In 1948 or '49, I remember I once walked from my parents' house in the northeast heights all the way along Central Avenue, to the deep downtown. A long walk. And one that sang inside me then. Central was U.S. 66, the cross-country highway, the big mutha. Today 66 has been replaced by 40, and Central Avenue seems the city's most provincial street. Lined with the familiar old fronts of battered houses, repainted and refinished a dozen times through my absent memories, but always evoking Pine Street,

Floyce

13

Don and Val, good old Liz, a slight pale sister who practiced Bahai and an old Greek who saved all his cut hair and fingernails.

The big streets are the freeways now, straining towards their Los Angeles image, with their own green and white signs and special lanes for entering and leaving. They cut the city through its heart and distribute the pieces in a new order. There's no space anymore between the city and the mountains.

I bring up images of going, as a child, with my parents to near-by reservations to trade old clothes for beautiful Indian jewelry. And I remember a few years later scorning that—in my parents and myself—as colonialist and sad.

And I bring up other images: the volcanoes. And they evoke other memories. Loading a borrowed pickup full of old tires, another distant midnight, driving out along that rutted dirt road, with mountains of tires and cans of gasoline sloshing over the bumps, to throw the whole mess into the largest crater and beat it back, laughing, whooping it up in our teenage glee. Listen to the radio, then, and the almost-evacuation scare, seal our secret pact in serious blood, and swear never to tell, anyone—you hear!—until years later.

2

Then I was on the plane, the Managua-Miami plane, the Miami-Atlanta plane, and—running like hell along escalators, passageways, dragging heavy stuff in both hands on both shoulders, trying (and succeeding) to close the narrow space between a very late arrival and an on-time departure. An old man carried my stuff at one point. I listened to the happy Ottawa-bound and the sad Baltimore-bound passengers dealing with a flight that had to cut out the latter because the entire east coast was snowbound and airports closed—while I waited near the Eastern checkout desk in Miami. I always get close to the check-out point...a way of avoiding the salvationists who walk right up to you and hold out their hand, attempting conversation in their dale carnegie manner.

More travesty of conversation: the Eastern employees—all modern airline employees, I guess—have developed a modified campaign speech in every verbal onslaught. The captains are the worst. Somewhere near the beginning of one flight, the monologue went like this: "Well, good evening, folks. This is your captain Bill something-or-other speaking. My first flight assistant is so-and-so, my second so-and-so...and waiting to make your flight a pleasant one, in the cabins themselves are Sally, Mary, Irene, Jeannette, Gail, Pearl and Linda...This here bird is really something; she can go up there to such-and-such a number of feet, and she'll be veering off a bit to the right this flight, quite natural in jet flying. Now we're going to do everything in our power to get you where you want to go safely, quickly and comfortably, and if you enjoy your flight with us we'd really appreciate it if you'd tell your friends so they decide to fly Eastern, and fill up some of those seats if you look around you'll see are a bit empty tonight. On the other hand, if there's something you didn't like about the flight, we'd rather you didn't tell your friends about that, but tell me instead. I'll be waiting right inside the door to listen to your opinions when you deplane...Well, over to your left, ladies and gentlemen..." and on and on it goes.

Throughout the exchanges with airline personnel and airport people, I noticed again—and as I never have before—how very differently women are treated from men, by civil servants and by public employees. Men are invariably treated better, with greater respect, more fully attended. Sometimes the comparison is right there in front of you.

Finally, it was Albuquerque, and Floyce, my brother Johnny, mother and daddy. It was a cold fourteen degrees getting off the plane, as opposed to eighty-five or ninety early in the Managua morning. Big hugs with the family, then off with Floyce to his apartment. We slept little, talked much, began to realize this love that's been growing through dozens of written letters, long-distance calls, dreams.

Floyce has cleared a spot in this apartment where I can work, put my things...The relationship with him is ripe with much of the wisdom that comes with age, mature, a great deal of passion and need, but respect above all, and space.

3

When I search for the moment of wanting to begin the return, I inevitably come to the moment of departure. That September day in 1961 when I headed for Mexico. With Gregory, who was then ten months old. I cannot see the leaving and returning as separate. Just as I cannot see the twenty-three years away as totally away. Nor do I feel that I have left Latin America. This is almost always clear to me. When it isn't then confusion, and depression, set in.

It is startling to me, and at the same time intensely real, that my woman's consciousness was born long-distance; the force of communal women's thought pounding under my skin, displaced from the events launching it among my U.S. sisters. But I have always felt this as a gain. Strong in my woman's history is Flora Tristan—and even Joan of Arc—as well as Sojourner Truth and Harriet Tubman. Michaela Bastides, Monica Ertl, Crystal Eastman, Lucy Stone, Sor Juana Ines de la Cruz, Haydee Santamaria, Lumi Videla, Lucy Parsons, Nguyen Thi Dinh. . .

Language was a barrier. And then a link.

It is all of a piece now. The divisions are very tenuous. There are poems that come in English (American) and others that come in Spanish (Cuban, Mexican, Nicaraguan, Peruvian). There is love that comes in both. There are four children with whom the words are not of my native tongue. And yet the communication is deeper with them than with many others.

When I left the United States in 1961 I had no sense that it would be "forever." Later, circumstances, legalities, papers, rules—they all got in the way. When I came back to the United States, just a few months ago, it was all very quick. Another move to see where it would all go.

And yet it has also been difficult. Painful. Not the change, nor its implications, but the people I've left. Sisters and brothers. Where they are, and what they face. Wanting to make sure they know at times (and it's *my* need of that knowledge) that I am there with them. Sharing that common fate which is made from commitment, decision, a certain meaning, care, love which is larger than two, larger than a cluster, larger than something held in the hand.

4

I am surrounded by objects, simple in this society, but intrusive on my bearings: the bathroom light automatically switches on a fan which "clears the air," its noise only slightly less than that of the automatic thermostat which charges the air when things fall below whatever they're set for...so that when the heat goes off the silence is something I've come—even in a day and a half—to look forward to immensely! Only one sink in the apartment has a right and left hand faucet, simply hot and cold water. On the others there's this single round knob which gets pulled out, pushed in, turned one way or the other always getting its signals as to what it should produce absolutely straight. It's me who often does not. One cannot even shit in a primitive way these days in modern America. Unless, of course, one lives among the "less privileged" twenty percent of the population.

But how I love this house in the love it floods me with! The strength of Floyce's poetry is something that sustains me and makes me love to *listen*—but more, it engenders in me that long-lost need to write, and I know that in him I have a critic as tough as I am with his work. There is a generosity in his love that shelters me from too many "green machines" or automatic can-openers... an honesty in his assessment of himself and a humility in his way of moving through the world absolutely rare in men of any latitude, class or culture. Increasingly, I have been aware of the extraordinary value of being able to transcend the "male" or "female" in oneself and in the objects (animate or not) that surround us. So few have the courage or capacity.

This is a house of treasures. There is such love in the music, in a hand and a body going around watering the plants. In the place where the empty coffee can holds cooking oil after the cooking, just below the kitchen sink. In the books. Fee Dawson wrote *An Emotional Memoir of Franz Kline* in 1967. Floyce bought it back east, at a second-hand bookstore. But I just discovered it in one of dozens of up-ended plastic fruit bins holding hundreds of volumes: poetry, history, philosophy, camera images, and how to make adobe bricks. And there are magazines and magazine sections and newspapers and journals, all neatly stacked in different places, and filling different needs. In the upstairs bathroom there are several books on drinking or not drinking, on writers who drink

17

or who no longer drink, and there is an old work by Laurette Sejourne: that wonderful *Burning Water*. And there are poems stuck up on the walls, in the hall, in the bathroom, on the front of the refrigerator. Marge Piercy, and "Amazing Grace" written in the Cherokee language...Some of our contemporaries, myself even—who at times in this new venture, exhuberant and excruciating, seems to be nothing better, or other, than my own contemporary. Contemporary. Could that mean the mirror image, set beside? Next to? I want to pull the threads together, but I know it will take time.

Some of my things have arrived. At some point, I don't know when, Floyce emptied some of his drawers, two here, two there, making room for what I would want to store and place. And then he took some of my things and arranged them here and there. On a table I suddenly see a small statue. On a desk a photograph of my parents. Hanging over the corner of a wall mirror, a sash my daughter Anna gave me just before we separated—she off to New York and I preparing my last few weeks before I, too, would travel north.

There is something intensely sweet and caring about the way in which Floyce has incorporated my presence and my needs into this place. Pressure and imposition are totally lacking here. I feel a great love, and respect, as I move slowly to place bits and pieces of myself where I can find and use them.

The house is clean and fresh. The amenities of life are easy, easily taken care of, and several gadgets astound me although I know that what is here is nothing more than the scantiest shadow of what this consumer nation is capable of bombarding us with. Music is almost always present. Work spaces have laid stakes: there is the editing area in the front room, near the kitchen, where Floyce works on the books the University of New Mexico Press pays him to revise and, largely I would suspect, rewrite. There is a room in the back, on the main floor, where another writing surface caters to his real work (the poem). Upstairs, on a broad balcony whose fourth wall is so high that although it overlooks the livingroom it is really a room of its own, is the space where I work. And upstairs, too, there is a bedroom—where we love and sleep.

5

In an article about Willem de Kooning I read today, there is this quote from Bill: "The important thing is meeting myself. If I go to sleep and don't wake up, other people will know I'm dead. But I won't know it."

I look out the window before me. The dry dusty surface of the earth seems to offer strong resistance to the buildings, cars, fences, walls, electrical towers, water tanks and occasional small trees standing against it. The buildings in sight (most of them part of this university married-student housing) are exactly the same beige as the earth. Patches of white snow remain here and there, on roofs and on the ground. Beyond the immediate buildings the land rises and slants down to my right. The horizon sports a dreary collection of nondescript structures. This is the Albuquerque of my youth, but there is little recognition yet. The cold tears at my body, so used to more than two decades of tropic heat. I feel as yet no desire to explore, walk, retrieve.

This morning I woke and wrote the following: "The sound a plane makes grows where the light of this day brings my eyes to search in three directions. One is found in the pages of books. Books or films. Or the film threading and threading its life between my teeth. Was that last year or the year before? The way the face moves brings words in any language. The second turns towards you, coming from sleep beside me, and follows the sky. The wing. The way our bodies move, into each other, silently. The third is the crossline. That point where her mouth no longer is, where no one can go home again, where the letter remains unanswered or the small polished stone is nowhere to be found. Even in dreams. Now there is nothing to say but yes. To begin once more."

6

Last night Floyce and I went to see *The Right Stuff*. I had read the book just before coming up. Karen Brudney, an American doctor who came to Nicaragua several months before I left, had it among her things, and when she saw me with it in my hands I remember she commented, "That's something to be reading just before going to the States!" It is a story of the first U.S. space team, the "kind of men" who take the challenge sort of thing. The book seemed to be a serious spoof on the whole damned business, but you're never sure. The film is quite a bit worse. A few well-drawn characters and situations, a few halfway pokes at the American political setup, and much that perpetuates the whole thing, drawn out, badly put together and hammered home till you wondered why you were still sitting there. But it *was* my first movie this time around, and it was at the Highland Theatre, right behind Highland High where I went to school...memories of hundreds of after-school films in the late '50s...the minute we entered the lobby of the theatre the smell of clean popcorn brought me back thirty years.

In the past couple of days, since arriving here actually, I am experiencing something I've never experienced before. When Floyce and I are about to make a spatial transition, for example from the house to the car or from the car to a store or from the car into the house once more, I don't want to move. It is an emotional thing, psychological I suppose, but its manifestation is quite physical: I simply want to wait a few minutes, absolutely quietly, being very still. It's not that I don't want to do the next thing or be in the next place. And it's not fear. It's simply a strong and apparently irrational need, perhaps to go slower? To absorb things longer?

7

Yesterday we had to go to Santa Fe. The main square is much the same, only the surrounding shops are a bit more modern, the usual gadget-ridden consumerism seeping between the cracks of revamped adobe structures, Native men and women sitting along the front arcade of the old Governor's Palace, selling a somewhat more polished version of the turquoise and silver pieces they've been peddling for years.

We spoke with one middle-aged woman from Santo Domingo. She told us there used to be people from the nineteen pueblos only. Today they come from as far away as Montana, Colorado, elsewhere, and they're not just Pueblos but people of the plains tribes as well. She talked some about her life, her husband and

The adobe walls of New Mexico.

kids, how she used to sell along the old road from Albuquerque, until they opened up the new one. The traditions continue strong, in spite of heavy tourism.

In the streets surrounding the square there are dozens of elegant shops: traditional rugs and pots and basket work blend right in with plastic food and fashion. Walking along, trying to take it all in, with my father's ski jacket pulled around, the hood catching the sharp air before my mouth and throat, suddenly a window caught my eye. It was an art gallery. Inside, the paintings were no more nor less than the usual agile but meaningless landscapes. But in the window were two series of white cloth objects—were they figures?—Egyptian mummy-like in a stylized way, body-bag shaped but with large red crosses at each solar plexis, and they were lined up: a row of larger than life figures and then a row of much smaller identical figures, like grim and sterile dolls. My head immediately split and made room for a film strip of body bags, winding their way home from any current war. Or body bull's-eyes on a target range. Or Egyptian mummies indeed, with all their wisdom intact. It was startling and painful, at one and the same time, perhaps especially in this particular setting. Following Floyce's finger to the bottom and front of the display, I found the tiny U.S. army tank, with its gun mount turned and its long cannon aimed at the shrouds. And then the whole thing fell to pieces. Some statement about war, in the midst of this antiseptic perfection . . . so absurd. I became angry.

8

Around 11:30 we sat down in front of the "small screen" to watch what was billed as a film about Jacobo Timmerman, the dramatized production of his *Prisoner Without A Name, Cell Without A Number*. It was my first look at TV this time around. And something that I know all about—the U.S. penchant for slicing shows with commercials every ten minutes—got to me in a way I hadn't thought possible. The slicing is ribbon-like. The entire image one gets is altered, and one's senses are altered, and one's vision of the world. Unless one happens to have one's own image, brings one along, heavy with history, and the whole thing just suffocates— which is the feeling I had last night. Each time a dramatic scene

22

was truncated (and the film itself was probably not that bad...now that it's fashionable to speak of what has been going on in Argentina for the past decade!) I heard myself making some audible expression of exasperation, and each time I became more irritated—*not* with the makers of this madness (because, oh yes, I know all about why they do it!) but with *myself* for falling into the trap! I guess that's how they engender self-hate and impotence, along with all the rest of it.

9

I am experiencing a strong sense of complexity. In many ways the experiences of these twenty-three years have been based in black and white contexts. Either/or. But not in the way of Kierkegaard. Now I am besieged by strata, levels, degrees. I do not find the kindred spirits nor do I find the rednecks I expected in Albuquerque. Instead I find a bit of both in almost everyone. Everyone is a little of what they are not, and some of what they are. But not conclusively. There is little I find to hold on to. There is so little—at this point—that is sure.

Every time I drive up to the foothills I pass this Paul Bunyon figure and want to make a picture. One day I did.

10

There was so much I identified with in Latin America, *do* identify with—to the extent that when, in 1978, I was being interviewed in Boston for a Spanish-speaking radio station and the interviewer asked me "As a North American living in Latin America, what do you think of (such and such)?", I had to stop and ponder that. I wondered if, in fact, I *was* a North American living in Latin America, or if I was a Latin American visiting the States. There were identifications in both places, questions in both places, absences in both places.

In Latin America, I learned to think in the plural. The *we* of

Driving up to the Sandia Mountains from Albuquerque, just after a light snow.

community. Of shared commitment, sacrifice, and work. There was a way in which that plurality strengthened my singular self, but now I wish to retrieve the individuality (the specific work, the uniqueness of a creative mission) that I feel I can only find here.

In Latin America I learned about the way the world works, the forces at play and the daily effects of those forces—in ways I know I would never have understood had I remained in the United States. Especially because I was not Black, chicana, Native American, poor; and have never understood my female condition as class. Or ethnic.

I realized last night, watching the Democratic contenders for

Inside the Morada.

the presidential nomination, that I have always been acutely aware of being a *woman in the majority*. I have never thought being a woman bore any resemblance to being part of an ethnic minority, a child or the mentally retarded or aged.

It always seems amazing to me when I hear people referring to "...Blacks, chicanos, and women..." or some such litany, list of minorities, ethnic groupings or—worse yet—"women, children, and the old," as if women belong with some incapacitated sector. Women are, in fact, the majority in most countries, and—I believe—in the world. Fifty-one percent is usually the figure. Yet we are destined to be putting up a hell of a fight for the most elemental rights—for at least another hundred years. I don't think it will take much more than that, judging from the progress we've made in the last hundred. In spite of the crap we must hear, still, about fetuses with feelings, the whole Moral Majority line (which, as a bumper sticker I saw recently proclaimed, is neither moral nor of the majority).

My life in Mexico, Cuba, and finally Nicaragua gave me the privilege of being part of a living history. And part of my return has to do with the profound need I feel to bring this encounter with history to the place where my roots took hold, and began to grow.

New Mexico. The desert, the mountains. That is a great part of it. A very strong part, of the past and of the present.

An old gravestone in northern New Mexico.

The Rio Grande River, which is broad and brown where it runs through Albuquerque, is clear and lovely near its origins in the north.

11

Up to my parents' this noon to once again walk the land my father owns next to the lot his own house is built on. He has gotten increasingly excited about the possibility of building a house for me up there, just below theirs. Their land slopes down a bit, and the views are breathtaking. There, on land covered with chamisa, cactus and sage, is a place where a house might grow. A wide arroyo runs through the lot, unfortunately, and in the fourteen years my parents have lived up there, it's run heavy twice; once a three-and-a-half-foot wall of water came rushing down and pulled half their driveway away, supports and all. So today we looked once again at the land, this time with a builder (the same guy, Larry, who built their house) and he said he thought there was a space for the kind of place I need: simple but with room to work. An adobe house, of course. Or something like that. The houses up around where my parents live generally pertain to another world: the affluent four-car garages, or the elegant new rich with their high-ceilinged studios and elaborate solar heating and TV reception dishes. My parents' house is the smallest, and it's more than comfortable. And so, the seeds of this idea have been planted—in all our minds and hearts—and in some strange unformed way the thing seems to be moving forward.

February

1

Let me tell you what is happening between my skin and the air. All the beepers have been silenced. (Notwithstanding an earth-moving machine putting out an electronic noise from dawn till it stops working each evening, across from these apartments).

I began picking up on all the messages. They came from so many directions. In Mexico they sprouted in markets and in parks. Once, in a huge city market I heard myself telling a woman selling onions—when she asked where I was from—that I was Italian. I only vaguely knew why. Still getting through the shame. There were still a lot of blunt edges in Mexico. Those closest to me (Sergio, mostly) pushed me in the wrong direction. I was ready to know things, but had to find out almost everything in the most circumvented ways. So it was mostly a kind of osmosis. Only later putting things together.

In Cuba the lessons were much clearer. Very up-front. So much so that there was too little room for error. To really be able to understand certain things, you must make the mistakes yourself, understand them—and how they have been made—and then go do it again. And again. In Cuba, sitting at a meeting of poets one day (UNEAC,* sometime in 1976), Bladimir Zamora sent a little white paper note over to where I was crying silently, on the inside of my face. He said: *"Si usted quiere leer sus peomas, solo tiene que poner fecha."* ("If you want to read your poetry, just name a date.") He spoke to me using the formal *usted* then, and always thereafter. We became fast friends. And that was the beginning of the contact again, reading to the world. Listening.

In Nicaragua it all came together: place, time, energy. When it happened, there was a sort of natural combustion. And then I knew I had to go home. This is a real homecoming, whether or not they let me stay.

2

These are finally the days for dealing with the end of the honeymoon and the beginning of reality. Some difficult times this week. Floyce has lived, for the past several years, as one of the two managers of this UNM married-student housing complex. A good job, for it gives him a nice apartment, utilities, and close to $300 a month, while allowing a certain flexibility for his editing work and also, of course, for his own poetry—important. Having such a job, though, requires conditions which were met by him when he took it, but are no longer true. I.e., being married, and to a woman who can share the managerial duties.

When Floyce and his wife split up, he wanted to keep the job. And so he never mentioned the split. For a couple of years he lived alone, always allowing his boss to believe that his wife was "around." Then the relationship with me developed. How can one introduce a new wife when the old one has never been removed from center stage? All this, Floyce's way of handling the situation, is foreign and uncomfortable to me. It means he is nervous about my answering the phone, opening the door, that kind of thing—and it means he is nervous with me around his uptightness about these things. *And*, it means my increasing resentment about the status quo in our living arrangement, especially at this point in

*UNEAC, Cuban Union of Writers and Artists.

my life when I need to find my own way in a situation of clarity.

The specifics translate into an irritableness as luncheons with the boss approach—will he be questioned or not about his marriage? Hiding evidence of my existence when the maintenance man or fumigator are due to come to the apartment—after all, they are the "talkers" in this kind of a place. When these things come up, Floyce becomes worried, the anxiety rises from the place where he has pushed it down. And he becomes embarrassed with me. I become confused, at first, as I usually can't trace his anxiety. And as I begin to understand it, I become angry. I would handle this sort of thing totally differently. I feel I would take any opportunity—a luncheon, a meeting—as a time to come clean with my boss. Floyce does a good job, and I don't see why they would fire him. Anything short of honesty, to me, is like allowing people to treat you as a child. This American fear of authority is something I, too, have dealt with in my life. And I hate it.

But Floyce feels coming clean about his situation would automatically mean the loss of his job. He has had enough problems getting and keeping jobs that allow him time for his more important work. He is sensitive to that, and to the increasingly difficult job market in this country, which of course makes all this just that much more complex.

Whatever might be the outcome of such a move, this situation brings up a whole other level of feelings. From fear of my reaction, I suppose, and because he wanted very much for me to live with him here, Floyce was never totally straight with me in our letters about what it would mean for me to live here. He never explained how invisible I would have to be. I even receive my mail at my parents' house.

The situation surrounding my arrival makes it even harder, I think, for me to accept all this. I don't want to be invisible. I need to be who I am, free and open. And the problem is complicated by the fact that we also need to learn how to talk about these things, without signalling defensive responses in each other. It's hard. And at my age, and with these past few years of total independence, it's real hard.

3

Last night we had our first big fight. Dinner at a neighbors', good friends of Floyce's, good people. I had met the woman a few days before, when we ran into one another at a supermarket and I ended up taking her home because she'd locked her car keys in her car. Her name is Gwen Sun; she's from Taiwan. Grew up in an orphanage there, has lived here since she was seventeen. His name is Bill Gordon, he's a lawyer, and they have a wonderful little girl. Gwen works on and off as a nurse, is now studying math and wants to study medicine. Well, she had planned this dinner with great love and care, providing Chinese delicacies as quickly as we could down them. A few others were there: Enrique Cortazar— Mexican poet, long-time friend of Floyce's, his wife Pilar, and a math professor from the Canary Islands named Victor.

Floyce and I had had a wonderful day, working hard, both of us feeling good about our work and about ourselves. Somehow just before we went to this party I had a premonition it wouldn't be good. And I expressed that, though in a very passive way. I focussed mostly on my "fear of new people and places" problem, instead of really trying to understand what I was "seeing." Floyce didn't want to go either. So just before we left the house he opened a bottle of wine and took a glass. Just some good red wine. No problem there.

When we got to Gwen and Bill's, just two doors from our own, the house was smelling of good food. The others came quickly, and conversations got off the ground. Then Enrique asked Floyce if he'd heard from Chihuahua yet. They had both gone to the University there a couple of months back, to give some joint readings, and there is apparently a possibility of a job in English Literature there for Floyce. The job might even involve a Fullbright. Floyce hadn't heard. Enrique said "I'm sure you'll hear soon. I'm sure you'll get the job." Floyce then said he would take the job, especially if it involved a Fullbright fellowship. "A Fullbright on my record...hell yes!" was his way of putting it.

I don't remember how it came up, but at some point in all this Floyce asked me if I would go with him to Chihuahua. Without thinking twice, I simply said no. I don't want to go to Chihuahua. If Floyce wants to go, that's fine. And I don't necessarily see that possibility as the end of the relationship, not at all. I can easily conceive of him going for a year, and being together whenever that's possible. Chihuahua isn't even that far. I noticed a slight twitch in Floyce's face when I said that, he mumbled something about having to think it over, and that seemed to be the end of that. Then he turned to me and said something like "...if I am even supposed to want you to do..." which seemed strange to me at the time. Recalled that sense of unreality in being "supposed" or "not supposed" to want or do something.

Looking back, that was definitely the beginning of it all. Though it certainly wasn't that clear until this morning. Most of those at the party speak Spanish with more ease than English. We often fell into long, passionate conversations in that language. Once in a while one or another of us stopped, tried to switch the thing to English, remarking that neither Floyce nor Gwen Sun understood Spanish. Floyce kept insisting that we speak Spanish, though. I don't even know why. But he drank another glass of red wine, and then another. And then another. When I began to notice he was going off-center, saying silly or meaningless things, I asked him why he was drinking, and I asked him to stop. He said he would, and that the glass he had in his hand—then full—would be the last. A few minutes later he was refilling it. I asked him for the house keys then, and I left.

Floyce came home about an hour and a half later, drunk. Not reeling drunk. Just drunk. I thought we'd talk in the morning, but he wanted to talk then. And we tried. But got nowhere. I made a couple of stabs at telling him how I felt. He consistently twisted what I was saying to fit some pitiful picture of himself. He provoked the hell out of me. I decided to leave. I packed a few things, actually several suitcases, the typewriter, everything I thought I'd need to keep going and working till I felt like coming back for the rest, and after several attempts at getting me to stay he agreed to help me carry the stuff down to the car. Which he did.

Then, somehow, I decided to stay. And we brought everything back up again. It wasn't Floyce's pleading—which was not excessive in fact, nor was he violent. It was something inside me. My love for him, I guess. And the real need to understand what had happened.

4

The other night someone asked me what I most hated about the United States, now that I'd been back for a few days or weeks. I immediately knew what I wanted to say, of all the things I hate—and love—and I began to speak but had to make an effort, raise my voice slightly because by that time not even the person asking the question was really interested in the answer. What I finally blurted out, before the conversation was safely changed, was this: I hate it that the system has created a whole complex world of needs, emotions, frustrations and events about which one finds oneself becoming irritated in the course of a waking day. One is conned into becoming annoyed—or even, often, angry— with trivialities. And so one must struggle against becoming trivial. For white, middle-class, university-oriented, suburban America the real life and death issues are well hidden. They do not exist.

I come from a place where life and death press into you with a daily urgency verging on madness. In Managua, Nicaragua, the last few weeks and months brought several felt deaths a week. *Felt* deaths, I mean the kind you can FEEL. The kind that are part of your own body, even when the person in his or her life might not have been an intimate friend. And sometimes he or she was. That hurt even more. And I remember an overriding feeling there: Why? Why the imposition of this deadly weight? Why can't they leave us in peace to build, to create something beautiful? Something as simple as that.

And of course the "they" is the same; the "they" imposing death in Central America and around the world is the same "they" here in the U.S. cutting any good TV movie up with six commercials every ten minutes. It's the same "they" that has created a university system with as little to do with real learning as is humanly possible. It's the same "they" cutting welfare and telling us the economy has never been better. And on down the line. Making us take constant stock of the trivialities, so we may safely ignore reality.

5

Often I move out of myself, stand some distance away and look long at the precise place I occupy now. In my inner direction and strength I have never felt more centered. In all the outer signs and signals, there is confusion and sometimes a cloudiness or lack of grace. Confronted with Floyce's drunken craziness the other night, I did not feel intimidated, only sad. Some sadness has stayed in my body these last two days, and some of it has settled in my chest. Moments of nurturing identification bring me up; there is strong love and it nourishes me. I know I will not feel completely whole until I have my own space, my own rhythm. It's a matter of patience.

I have not gone out once yet with the camera, walking or driving, leading with my lens-eye as a way of picking up the world. That is beginning to hurt.

6

Not much more than a block away from this apartment where I am carving out a place for myself with Floyce is the Heights Community Center where—when I was thirteen or fourteen—I hauled my anxious body each Friday night, stood with a smattering of other "girls" on the sidelines of a thumping western-music dance floor, and waited. The sense of waiting is what I most remember. As one boy after another, brandishing his own insecurity like a weapon, came and took another of my waiting sisters out onto the floor, my own waiting became tauter, harder, outlined in Roualt black like a ribbon of suffering. The smile stayed put; it was static. The eyes made sure they looked beyond or around, never at. Who wanted to dance, anyway? And I would come back the following Friday for more of the same, waist cinched tighter, crinoline fuller, two sets of straps showing beneath my sheer nylon blouse covering the tenderest of nipples trying to become breasts.

Sometimes, these crisp mornings of almost-spring weather, I drive out (even city driving is my freedom these days), turn left onto Buenavista, and go past the old haunt. They have painted it many times, but the low squat shape of the building front is like a jab in the chest, this chest that feels now so different and so differently. I'm looking for that Community Center.

7

In the bookstore this morning, just talking to my father, picking up mail, puttering around, as I was about to leave, my brother suddenly said: "I guess you know Julio Cortazar died. . ." I didn't. Just as Andropov's death took me by surprise when I opened the evening paper one day last week—something that would have interrupted music programs on the radio in Cuba or Nicaragua, was just another ordinary news item of moderate interest here in Albuquerque.

Julio Cortazar was one of the great writers of these past two decades in Latin America. He gradually reached a peak in his creativity, from a series of extraordinary stories to his "boom" *Rayuela* (Hopscotch), *Manuel's Book*, and others. He signed a protest along with other Latin American writers living in Europe after the Padilla Affair* in 1971, and then—when he began to understand what had happened—was the only one of the group to publicly change his position and support the Cubans. His self-criticism was a profound commentary on real creative freedom, and a recognition of what the Cuban Revolution means in America. In recent years his literary output has been limited almost exclusively to articles and essays about the struggle on this continent, especially the situation in Central America to which he had dedicated more and more of his time before his death.

Dining together that last time—Managua, must have been mid-1983—I remember asking him if it wasn't difficult, now that he was getting older, to have intentionally put a brake on his purely literary production, to devote himself exclusively to a written defense of the revolution in Central America. He looked at me with those large and penetrating eyes of his (Julio suffered from a rare disease, apart from the leukemia that killed him, from which he became outwardly younger-looking as the years went by, and his extremities, including his height, grew continually) and he

*A Cuban poet who was detained for a little over a month in Cuba, and then released. The affair raised the issue of intellectual freedom as understood in two very different types of society.

35

said: "Margaret, if we don't give everything we have to defending experiments like this one in Nicaragua, there will be thousands of potential writers, Nicaraguan and others, who will simply never be able to write anything."

I have many memories of Julio. One I cherish especially, is his enormous frame torn by bug bites, his face a mass of swollen redness, his ankles bleeding, after almost a week with a group of North American peace activists going to make a vigil at Bismuna, in northern Zelaya. The group had gotten as far as Puerto Cabezas, and had to wait to fly into the area where they were scheduled to camp (because of a battle there in which fifty-eight contras had just been killed). Commander William Ramfrez spoke with them and told them straight out: "Any of you who want to turn back to Managua, you can do that tomorrow morning. No one will think any less of you for not going on. I want you to know it's dangerous..." People looked at one another. Then Julio, close to seventy, stood up and announced: "I'm going to Bismuna." No one stayed behind.

About a year before Julio's death, his young wife of several years, Carol, died of bone cancer. Then the Alfonsin government replaced a decade of military dictatorship in Argentina, and Julio was able to visit his country one last time. When I heard about that trip, I wrote:

A man has gone back to his city,
the city some have told him cannot be recognized
in its great new structures, glass and steel
rising where the edge of the world meets his eye.

He thinks of this
coming from where the magic bird has set him down
but the smell of grilled meat at construction sites
stays in the workers' shirts. Tells him he's home...

Later, I sent him the poem. A few days after his death the envelope was returned, unopened.

Tonight, in Al Madan's darkroom, I puttered around with a few negatives I have of Julio, and I printed a couple of pictures I like. If I had been in my own darkroom, I might have spent the entire night with him, bringing him to life again through the images.

Julio Cortazar in Managua. This picture was taken about two years before his death.

8

Today Floyce and I were married. When we left Albuquerque in the early morning the vast mesa stretching out to the mountains on our right, and the snow-topped Sangre de Cristo ahead, cut through an intensely transparent air. Everything was very bright.

We were driving circles around the doctor's house by nine o'clock, wondering whether or not to go in. We had been in Santa Fe the day before, and had our blood tests. He told us to come today around 9:30. For want of a nearby place for coffee, we finally opened his office door, and when he came out with the health certificates in his hand and said he wouldn't charge (". . . it's just a service," he said) I gave him some of my Nicaraguan postcards. Then he opened a bit. Told us he had been in Nicaragua working, several months at Bilwaskarma, "on the Miskito coast," he said. 1971. He was a little shy. Later someone told us his wife is from Honduras.

Then it was over to the County Clerk's office, for the license. The morning was to offer both the best and worst these states can muster up around such events, and when they finished filling out the papers and collecting their $5 over the counter, the young woman attending us reached under it and handed us a plastic bag.

She was blushing. "What's this?" I asked. "A homemaker's kit," was her fumbled reply. Out in the car we opened the kit. It contained:

One small box of TIDE, America's favorite:
Tide's In...Dirt's Out (net wt. 7 oz.).
One bottle JOY, Lemon fresh, spot-free shine (5 fl. oz.).
One small bottle SCOPE, mouthwash and gargle,
$T_2 5^*$ (1.5 fl. oz.).
One sample package TAMPAX, 2 slender regular, 2 original regular, protection and comfort you can trust.
One Massengill DISPOSABLE DOUCHE, specially designed slanted nozzle. For easier more comfortable insertion and use. Completely sanitary and conveniently disposable.
One package MIDOL extra stength menstrual pain reliever, with a muscle relaxant for cramps, 6 caplets.

All this with a postcard bearing the following inscription: "May we suggest...you use this card to note any comments you may wish to make to the Marriage License Office...product sponsors...or others that presented you with your Newlyweds Gift-Pax. They are always delighted to hear from their charming newlyweds. Thank you."

After the laughter—the "home" turns out to be the body, and *it must be clean!*—we went to a great cafe on the Plaza, where we downed a good Mexican breakfast each. Then it was off to the court building, where we had arranged to meet Farber, the lawyer, and a friend of his—Pamela Messer—at just before eleven.

The judge we had picked, of the several he recommended the day before, was the only woman: Judge Petra Jiminez Maes. She was over at the legislature, rooting for some bill that was having trouble making it through the house, but it wasn't long before she was back in her chambers and we were standing before her. I guess we'd expected more of the same, so we were surprised and delighted to get the other end of the spectrum, a sensitive and lovely text which we might have written ourselves.

It was amazing: I felt happy about the affair. Tried thinking back on my other marriages—I had been married to only two of the four men I had lived with for any length of time—and the first I cannot remember anything at all about. In the second, with Sergio, I can remember that the judge was drunk and had to be held up by his secretary.

When dressing this morning, I took great care to wear things I could feel had something to do with the event. I put on a pair of my father's jeans, and felt his presence strongly because of them. I wore a pair of lovely earrings my mother once brought me from Greece, and felt her in them. I put on my own black turtleneck sweater that has accompanied me on so many readings and public appearances. And over it, a red and blue blouse the women in Tejuantepec wear when they marry. Under the blouse and shirt, where only Floyce and I knew they existed, I wore my Ho medal, and a wooden cross which speaks to me of liberation theology in Latin America.

It was the first day of a full moon on January 18 when I arrived in Albuquerque. Today it is the first day of another full moon.

9

Today I went way back, almost into my childhood. I have always had some long black hair growing on parts of my body where I'd rather not have it, and around 1952 my mother took me for the first time to a woman here in Albuquerque named Alice Walker. I remembered her office, with the low table-like reclining couch, and the music she put on an old phonograph to get your mind off the pain of the electrical current travelling through the needle into the folicule of unwanted hair. She was a small woman with white and perfect skin, and long black hair.

Recently I asked a friend to recommend someone who could do electrolysis on me here; the problem has never gone away, and over the years I've had it done one way or another. My friend gave me a name and a phone number, and this morning I called. Slowly, looking at the little piece of paper on which I had written down the information, and then hearing that voice on the telephone, I remembered . . . it was the same woman. Now she is more than thirty years older, her hair is silver grey but otherwise the years have not changed her much. She works in the same small brick house down on Fifth Street, in the west valley. There was a strange excitement in our recognition of one another. Thirty years is a long time. She said she saw "something in my eyes." The process is still as painful as it was, and it's still as much of a relief to have it done.

Driving down to Fifth Street and back, I really got off on the old center of Albuquerque. The "downtown" area which was once so imposing in my youth . . . the streets are tiny and the stores and offices all seem like toys! I drive along and feel I can reach out and touch everything. And I do. Some of the names come reeling back through the years and years of experiences as different from this space as can be. The old Kimo Theatre is now a renovated place for readings and lectures. The old Sunshine Theatre shows films in Spanish. I have yet to see the center of Albuquerque filled with people, crowding across the streets or filling the sidewalks. No, there seem to be few people. As the city has spread out, so has life. The buildings along Central Avenue are insignificant now; not more than a few rise higher than two or three stories. Newer, more modern buildings have been constructed to either side; there's a new city center and several important plazas. Driving up Central to the Heights again, I begin to feel I am really home. Home. Everything is so familiar. As if nothing has changed.

10

Tonight we saw a film that physically assaulted me more intensely than any I can remember. *Star 80*. It was not the finest film I have ever seen. Far from it. It was well edited, well directed and well acted, but *Tender Mercies*, *Silkwood*, and several others we've seen lately have been better. This one, though, spoke to every fiber in my body right at the level of the socialization we have all been burdened with, and as the situation progressed towards its climax the tension mounted in my gut, in my fingers, along my neck, on my skin, even in my hair. My teeth were tense. And my eyes.

Storyline: a pretty young woman working at a Tastee-Freeze in Vancouver is spotted by an entrepreneur who engineers a whole scenario around and with her. His need is on three levels: ordinary male possession, use her and sell her, and become someone himself through his association with her. She (played by Mariel Hemmingway) is candid, fresh, honest, the typical girl next door; with a talent for embodying what one remembers of one's own youthful values and aspirations (if one is a woman, middle-class and white, born and raised in North America). He (Erick Roberts) is all he is in immediacy; he has no past (history) and projects a single dimension to its outer limits. She is wholesome and inex-

40

perienced. No, wrong. She has had the typical experience of most young women of her time. In the scene where he takes her to bed for the first time, her repeated "I think I'm not any good" is memorable. She tells him how she's done it once before, but isn't even sure it really happened: "it was so fast. But then," she reasons, "it must have happened." The football player who "did it" later told the whole school she was a "bad fuck."

He begins taking pictures of her with his polaroid camera (instantaneous, no history) and little by little breaks her resistance to posing nude, doing things she never imagined she would do, and even wanting to do them. "It was so exciting," she tells interviewers in the film's rhythmic flashbacks. The texture of the film is a perfect part of its content.

From the beginning you know "what happened" and "who done it." He pushes her into the *Playboy* world, and Hollywood. She "makes it." They are married but she never fully understands what's happening. He is more and more jealous of her successes and the attentions paid her, becomes seized with spells in which his madness completely replaces any feigned (real?) sanity. And he ends up murdering her, manhandling her even in her death, and then committing suicide. The physical handling of the film material is a modified oral-history technique, reminiscent of that used in *Reds* but much more subtle, more blended into the storyline, expert without breaking any frontiers.

Two things affected me about this film. One, the identification I felt with so many of the situations. Not only, though of course primarily, hers. Also his. As they became more extreme, madder and more surely headed for delirium and death, as they *moved farther away from what I have actually experienced in my life*, they evoked a more intense recognition in my body. As if the glitter, the need to communicate, the insecurities, jealousies, inverted innocence, had their points of departure in my memory, and their exaggerated conclusions in the film branded me with red hot certainty that intention and outcome are closer than we allow ourselves to believe. There but for the grace of god, go I. In that respect it is a masterful statement about the socialization of men and women in a consumer society. Taken by many, I am sure, as an example only of one extreme case. Taken by me as exemplary of the very core of capitalism, and what it does with and to human beings.

The other item of interest is the counterpoint between the high-level, successful, wealthy, powerful symbol of evil portrayed by Hefner (actually called Hefner—the founder of the *Playboy* empire—in the film) and the miniature, failing, lumpen pimp type of evil of Paul Snider, the man who seduces, launches, makes, marries and eventually murders Dorothy. Hefner, in his world of crooked values and objectified women, comes off to the ordinary viewer, I'm sure, as fatherly, sane, helpful, with the girl's best interests at heart. Snider comes off as a sick and murdering madman. So true, on every level, to the way the system thinks of and projects itself, at the expense of all the Dorothys and Pauls, and of their mothers, sisters, brothers, lovers, friends. So true to the way powerful nations rape and control the smaller nations. When you're rich it's called culture; when you're poor it's called crime.

11

How do we begin to recover a society that values week-old fetuses above women and men struggling for their right to live? That objectifies women, and curses men with the terror of not "making it"? That abuses and mocks the most precious values in order to keep us all reproducing its myths—and as cheaply as possible?

Star 80

The man on the screen was going to be someone
using the woman on the screen.
The man on the screen photographed a delectable object
endlessly.
(With me it was always partial, partial.)
The mother knew
but her eyes vanished.
The man on the screen invented and blundered,
then need cruised his body
and he bought a pardon.
(In my life it always seemed more like reality. So subtle.)
The woman on the screen saw herself changing
according to the rules
and travelled an old road. The sun came out. Briefly.
Then the man without a history

bought a gun.
Everything had already happened
as many times as there are pores in my body.
And it happened again.
Pity occupied another house.
The sound was explosive
and final.

I sat very still.
They pushed my head against the seat
hard.
My hands grew cold. Then hot.
In each of my body's pores
memory lit a single candle.
Wax smothered the pore.
Still, I burned.
Pain moved like music
as each receding image filled
with my exact experience.
Everything hurt more.
I felt old
from so much pain.

In my seat I did not want to rise.
I wanted to wait
for the answer.

12

Yesterday, after an interview I had been anxious about, I felt I
deserved a triple chocolate sundae with three different types of
goo on top, and I went to a place called The Hippopotamus to get
one. This afternoon, after another difficult time, I felt the same
need. Back to The Hippo.

Yesterday, as I came out of the cafe, two police cars were pulled
up in front, their large tail lights flashing. Against one of them, a
lean young man was being frisked. A friend who was with me
explained that this was a corner where a lot of young people con-
gregate, that a lot of dope dealing goes on here, and that every

once in a while there's a bust. As we walked away, towards the place I'd parked my car, I found myself looking back, and looking back. I wanted to get my camera out and take those images: the angular fragility of the kid, the sureness of the cops, the flashing lights, the expressions of those looking on.

Today, standing at the counter in The Hippo, a guy to my right suddenly looked at me and said: "That's a nice little doll you got..." He was talking about a seven- or eight-year-old child standing beside me. "She's not mine," I responded, "and she's not a doll; she's a person." Almost immediately I realized I was asking for it. The guy got a schizy look on his face and painfully pushed the words from between his lips: "No...no...no toymaker can...can...can make..." and he never did finish the idea.

I turned away with my triple fudge sundae and sat at a table. The guy walked over to a wall, leaned down and picked up some soggy paper napkins someone had thrown on the floor. With them he began "cleaning" the unoccupied tables, and then the chairs. Finally he centered his attention on a high small table with some coffee makers on it. He spent the next twenty minutes cleaning and recleaning its surface, with the soggy napkins which were shredding into liquid pulp by that time. He never again looked my way. His eyes receded into his head. The sundaes were good both days, but they will forever be inextricably linked in my mind with the hopeless and sick of this society, the outcasts who inhabit its underside, its most brutal pain.

13

I thought (and still think) that one of my re-entry keys might be teaching: sharing with students some of what I have learned these twenty-three years, learning from them what people are thinking and feeling these days in North America.

But how? Without a degree, I knew my chances of breaking into the university community were next to nothing. More and more people without degrees are teaching these days in the arts, writing and dance. But they compensate by having acceptably "big names." Most university teaching has gone in the other direction with professors needing higher and higher degrees to even compete for jobs, which are harder and harder to obtain. The whole system has its own rules: publication in "scholarly" journals, the tenure system, women fighting every inch of the way, etc.

In any case, I designed a course called "A Literature of Identity and Commitment," mostly as a framework to be able to teach some books I think essential (Agnes Smedley's *Daughter of Earth*, Cardenal's *Gospel in Solentiname*, Walker's *In Search of Our Mothers' Gardens*, Susan Meiselas' and others' *El Salvador*, Galeano's *Days and Nights of Love and War*, my own *Sandino's Daughters*). A new friend here took me to see the guy who heads Continuing Education, thinking it might be the department most likely to accept me with my "limitations." (Meanwhile, Ruth Hubbard, in Boston, is telling me on the phone: "Think big...remember you're doing them a favor; not the other way around!") The Continuing Education guy, Oliver, took a look at the course description while I bit the skin on my right thumb, just to one side of the nail. He said something about it sounding interesting, and immediately asked me for my "academic credentials." I said I didn't have any. He said he thought it would be difficult, but then somehow filled the remaining silence with a request for a curriculum vitae with details of other achievements, which might, in my case, be seen as taking the place of a degree.

I came home and got a headache. And prepared a six-page vitae. Oliver had suggested I see other people on campus, "get around," he said, "and maybe someone from another department will be willing to co-sponsor the course."

Yesterday afternoon I saw Helen Bannan, the acting head of Women Studies. It was a wonderful experience...that rapport that renews the knowledge that women have (to a large extent) found a language in which they can speak. She was very interested in the course description, had a few suggestions for changes. (Not thinking in terms of Women Studies, I had originally included Nazim Hikmet, Malcolm X, Esteban Montejo, Crystal Eastman, Domitila de Chungara...too many books, and a focus that could be narrowed—now, for example, I want to save Domitila for a course on Third World women I'd like to try to compete for, in Women Studies per se.) Anyway, Helen took a look at the course description, took a look at my curriculum, and said, simply, "I'm willing to sign for this!" And a couple of hours later, back at the apartment, I got a call from Oliver telling me I was on!

March

1

Almost every morning, after doing some work, I go out to an area some ten or twelve blocks from here, where my brother's bookstore, the post office, a xeroxing place, and a group of heavily frequented cafes fringe the university grounds. The area is a gathering place for students and semi-students—which I'm finding out is another human category here, as it must be at most U.S. universities: the young ones can be identified by their backpacks or because they're jogging; the older ones are craggy around the eyes and exhaustion seems to have consumed them.

The punks are about twenty percent of the student population here now—even in the high schools (or, perhaps, especially in the high schools). People in the stores and cafes are trained in a high-pitched niceness; they are *so* nice that when they suddenly become unhinged and act the way they feel, they become positively angry.

Young people in this country now have a short memory. Their sense of history seems permanently maimed. And living with so

46

many fatal probabilities—lung cancer, nuclear holocaust, AIDS, herpes, muscular dysfunction, madness, Alzheimer's Disease— their adjustment to what each day brings them is totally off balance. They train and train and train—the lucky ones, the ones who get into school, the ones who are middle-class enough and white enough to get accepted, the ones who have "made it" that far—and when they are spewed from their centers of higher education, they can't get jobs. Men and women with Ph.D.s are selling electrical appliances and life insurance.

Religion is big. The born-again Christians, the Yogis, the Hari-krishnas, the Charismatics, and the rest are still looking for what the variety of political movements of the '60s and '70s didn't end up giving them. The older ones are coming round a second time; the younger ones have no sense, even, of their own history. The punks are saying, with their strands of pink hair and their pur-poseful "ugliness" that they are rebelling, rejecting, protesting. But no one cares. The world stares back at their empty faces, with its own huge emptiness.

I can remember a time when every gesture had its shock value. We dressed in '20s garb bought for pennies at the Salvation Army,

Salt of the Earth Books is run by my brother Johnny, and a lot of other people who feel like a bookstore should be a place to gather. At this particular event Charlie Clements speaks about his experience as a doctor in El Salvador's liberated zones.

we smoked and designed our own eyes and worked as much or as little as we wanted at whatever we saw fit. We had our own morality, and new ideas, and babies. And people were shocked! Today no one cares. The rebellion falls flat because no one gives a shit.

Along Cornell and Central, off and on campus, I see men and women of all ages who look as if they haven't focused their eyes *on* anything for years. They are filthy and lost, dream-like and sad. People are removed, even as they are formula-nice. Until they break and the anger seeps through—and then it retreats once more, and again they are only ugly, dirty, lost, alone. But they are all alone together. Talking to Nelson Valdes today he mentioned McLuhan's "medium is the message," and it occurs to me that the whole surface of the nation has become a message of its own listlessness. Of course the other world, the world being made by the so many who are working, creating, producing, believing: it exists, and it exists against this background making it shine and glow even more.

2

Last night I sat down to watch a TV news program for a while. I couldn't work; I was restless. A "perfectly groomed" man and a "perfectly groomed" woman (no, they are not yet the shabby, wretched, loosely fitted beings who roam the streets near the university) came on to make their presentation. They spoke about what they had "in store": two drug combinations which seem to be responsible for kidney failure in people taking them in overly large amounts; a possible California state law to provide for arrest of AIDS victims who will not co-operate with authorities; a "surprise" in the New Hampshire Democratic primaries (Hart beat Mondale, though it's just a momentary thing); ex-diplomats from Iran and Iraq talking about the war which has flared there in the past few days; large screens permitting people in one city to be interviewed by TV journalists in others.

I sat there on the couch, eating a bowl of chile. The news caught my attention, but I kept wanting it to be different. What did I want? I do not know. It is a gnawing feeling of absence, of longing, of dissatisfaction. Knowing it can only be as it is, yet wanting something else. The faces on the large screens within the small livingroom screen I was watching seemed larger than life. Every muscle twitch could be noted, followed, taken into account. The TV people—especially one Black interviewer—looked *up* at their interviewees. As if they were having them and being had, at one and the same time.

3

Out of the window before me a smattering of lights still flickers across the mesa. The reflection of my studio lights mingles with those way out there, and the design is lovely. The two planes move and come together, separate and expand. I am filled with a feeling of intense sadness. Dissatisfaction. Yearning for my kids. Longing. Nicaragua. A world where sadness and happiness, fear and tranquility are emotions which correspond simply and completely to the events of every day. It is all so big, and I remember well the frustrations. But it seems—from this vantage point— within one's control.

Anna in New York. Ximena in Mexico City. Sarah in Havana. Gregory in Paris. Floyce is sleeping loudly in the room across the hall. My parents in the mountains. My brother and his family nearby. Karen and Tony and Flor in Managua. Alex and Grandal in Havana. Susan in New York City. Lynda and Chris in Toronto. Stan in Vancouver. Jane in Santa Cruz. Marian in Oakland. Diane in Kansas City. Jeanne in Boston. Jack in Philadelphia. Felipe in Palo Alto. Roque, Rodolfo, Jose Benito, Carlos...dead.

Where is the living wire of my life? I am filled with questions. And memories.

4

Perhaps—it occurs to me as I write this—one of the things I fear is finding myself depleted by it all. As if there were no room left for further feeling. And feeling itself is dulled. And then knowledge is dulled, capability, possibility. It was an experience I had often in Managua these past two years: first the inability to feel, then the desire to feel again, then the inability to remember, linking mem-

49

ory to a possibility of future—if the past disappears, what will happen to the future?—then, once more, the new opening, the possibilities returning, moving once again, energy coming back and with it, memory. The trip, the realization of my need to come home. Another chance. Is that it?

5

A late night news program seems to be among the current windows I'm trying to open to make my way into this other sense of things: the American sense, or the U.S. sense, to be more accurate. Last night the interviewer made a stab at assessing the current controversy over the excessive amount of perverse violence in the rock videos that sweep the nation. We, the passive viewers of the discussion, were first informed that hundreds of communications companies offer these programs canned each day. One program reaches 20 million viewers. And we are given glimpses of the content, those of us perhaps not as familiar with it as others: a dressed-up S/M, grotesque thrills, a totally pervasive sexism, and the use not only of women but of all human beings as objects whose only expression is a meaningless misdirected rage. Chains, plenty of them, chains and boots, whips, knives, blood, eyes that jolt and bore instead of see, movements aimed in on the maker, or aimed at another with too little individuality to be thought of as "other."

A semi-articulate hyped-up member of the group called Kiss said he was proud of everything he did. That its release meant the group stands behind it. And he went back again and again to his assertion that "everything on TV has the same violence value: the news reporting, footage of some country out there where thousands of people are being killed every day . . ." etc. Once it's on television, he claimed, it's all the same. The same meaning, the same effect on the viewer.

The professor, at one point, appealed to Kiss's conscience, suggested he soften or tone down. Kiss referred to his opponent as "button-down" and spoke of their "costumes" as appropriate to their respective stances, but both still costumes. The professor tried to be "good-natured" about it all. In short, what attempted to pass for a good democratic discussion, both sides of a vital question, obscured—for me—the real point. And I sat there wondering if I might be able to evoke it at some later date—as I felt myself falling off to sleep. The medium *is* the message. Once it's on television it's all the same.

North Americans are fed Vietnam, El Salvador, or Lebanon; and they are fed the white white surface of a female throat spurting open to the slash of a knife plunged by a black-leather-clad figure with dulled electric eyes. Then those things become one, inseparable, their meanings distorted and linked, both messages transformed.

My mother and father, out among the chamisa and cacti. My father holds the plans for my house.

6

My father owns two small lots, one on either side of his and my mother's home up in the foothills of the Sandia Mountains. He bought the three lots years ago, and built that house of adobe that becomes a part of the land—the sandy expanses, rocks, low desert shrubs, and extraordinary mountains above. Their home was the ninth one built up there. Now there are 900. But it's still a beautiful area, filled with solitude, another set of relationships, openness, quiet.

My father wants to give me one of those lots, and with some money his brother left him, help us build a house there. Yesterday they finally came up to get the level of the land; the first real act in what may turn out to be the history of our home. I took pictures of them measuring, and my heart almost leapt from my body!

7

My friend Bell Chevigny in New York is doing a book, with Jean Franco, about literature in Latin America, including a section on "The Vision and Voice of Women." Bell has long wanted to do an interview with me for that part of the book, and in order to give me something to begin thinking about, she recently sent me some questions about my life as an American woman writer living and developing in Latin America:

In New York I thought of myself as a poet. I was close to the Beats, but perhaps even closer to the Williams root (through Creeley and some of the other Black Mountain people) and Deep Image (Kelly, Rothenberg, Economou). I took the craft—what I had of it then, and what I hoped to get—seriously. I remember Paddy Chayevsky, whom I met only briefly at a party, telling me that the way to learn to write dialogue was by standing on the corner of a place like Forty-second Street and Broadway for hours, *without* a notebook, and then go home and practice recreating what you'd heard, conversations, fragments, accents, syntax. The manner of speech. And I actually did that.

The Beats despised women—all contrary assertions notwithstanding—but so did most men I knew back then. The establishment was up for re-evaluation, but not patriarchy. We women who were starting out back then, who were trying to learn how to be poets (and human beings) were reduced to groupies more often than not. Those of us who resisted that still believed that to "make it" in a man's world, we had to make it by being like the men, writing like men, loving like men, going after the same things and in the same ways. In the world of poetry—back then—we were few, and we went various ways. Our journeys through that and out of it have also been varied, and some of us have come to a feminist perspective through very different routes—but that's a later story.

Waitressing one summer out at Amagansett, Jack Kerouac came in and sat down at a table along with others in his group, a couple of whom I knew. I was working on my first novel at the time. And I had the audacity to go get a chapter and show it to him. He read it right there, or pretended to; what choice did he have? And I took the suggestions he made to heart. That was the way I was in those days.

Milton Resnick, the painter and a dear friend, once told me that if I couldn't write, I should sit at the typewriter and just pound out anything that came into my head. I'd get so bored with writing trash, he said, that eventually I'd be forced to write something with meaning. Years later he denied having ever said that. But I know he did say it. And I followed his advice. Discipline was the most important thing I learned in the New York years.

By the time I went to Mexico, in late 1961, I was beginning to imagine a voice for myself. Falteringly. And was meeting poets from other parts of the Americas. We gathered at Philip Lamantia's apartment on Hudson Street in Mexico City. It was a time that pried me open on many levels. Perhaps I still thought of it as an essentially literary experience. But, without fully realizing it, I was being affected by the ways in which people from different class and cultural realities see the world, and see their (our) place within it.

El Corno Emplumado was born out of the need we felt to share what we were doing, to create a place where the works of the young Latin American poet and writer (later also the thinker, and activist) could be read by his and her North American counterparts, and vice versa. In 1961 our group was not particularly developed politically. And as a woman I did not yet think of myself as engaged in a feminist struggle. My feminist consciousness—although long latent, I think—was underdeveloped. I was romantic about poetry. I believed it could change the world. In a very literal sense.

We began to make the magazine: Sergio Mondragon, Harvey Wolin, and myself. Harvey soon dropped out—around the second issue, I think—and Sergio and I continued. No one really believed we would produce a magazine that would appear like clockwork every three months, that would present the best new writing being done on both continents, and that would find its way around the world. But we did. Because we were young and filled with energy and possessed of more than one dream. We really thought *El Corno* was important. And because we thought it was, and worked hard at it, it became so.

When I went to Mexico my Spanish was adequate street talk (I had studied a bit in school, and had lived in Spain in 1955 and '56) but I didn't have a literary knowledge of Spanish. From the beginning Sergio saw himself as editor of the Spanish side, and I edited the English.

In 1962 we were married. Sergio was a man who had been in the Communist Youth Movement, who had participated in the big strikes of 1958, and whose political vision seemed to be what I was moving towards after my New York experience: the Catholic Workers, Spanish Refugee Aid, the great event of the Cuban Revolution, Fidel's trip to New York City and the tragedy of the Bay of Pigs. And living in Mexico, a Third World country, beginning to understand the relationship between the U.S. government and the lives of people in the countries which it influenced and controlled, pushed me further in the direction I had begun to move. But Sergio moved differently. Around the time our first child—Sarah—was born, he began doing yoga. He became involved with a Fiudjof group, became vegetarian, and eventually (after our divorce, seven years later) went to live for a couple of years in a Zen monastery in Japan. The basis of our rift was ideological.

In January 1967 we were invited to Cuba to commemorate the hundredth anniversary of the great Nicaraguan poet Ruben Dario. My first trip to a socialist country. We already had contact with the Cuban poets. We had published them, along with graphic artists from that country, in two issues of the magazine. But the experience of going to a socialist country was essential to my growth. Sergio returned to Mexico right after the celebration. I stayed on two extra weeks, travelling around the country. Between that trip, and another I made in 1968 (to attend the Congress of Intellectuals of the Third World), I left Sergio.

And it was at that Congress, at the beginning of '68, that a Spanish poet named Jose Angel Valenti told me that while *El Corno* was important to many of the young poets on both continents, there were also many who were disappointed with it. They were the ones at the forefront of the cultural struggles in their respective countries. Valenti made me see how the Spanish side of the publication was a let-down to those who deeply believed that the written word, if it were truly alive, must be more consistent in taking the side of life. I came back to Mexico, Sergio left the magazine, and I did the last issues by myself, and then with Robert Cohen, a North American poet who came onto the Mexican scene. I ended up living with Robert for as many years as I'd lived with Sergio.

The problem of the politics or ideology of writing, of course, wasn't limited to the magazine. That was relatively simple. What was much more difficult was my own perception, vision, need and conclusions—in my own work. As a human being, as a woman, I was ripped apart by conflicts of all kinds. I was still trying to find out where I belonged in terms of a "national" identity. My gender and nationality made me an outsider, and yet it was hard for me to understand that. Life in Mexico taught me the external relationships. Internally, it wasn't so easy. I used to talk about "remaining in Mexico for the rest of my life" and indeed I became a Mexican citizen, out of economic hardship at the time. I now see whatever ideological content some have given that—for I never gave it any—as shallow, as shallow as its apparent opposite, when, during the early Cuban years, I would speak of "returning to my country" as a political exile might speak of that—without ever really having been such. Both were narrowed stances. But there was no way I could have had another, more authentic, one. Because I didn't yet know that much about myself, really. I spoke about freedom, but in my relationship with Sergio I was locked into a tight, petit-bourgeois prison. In the magazine, I forged ahead with a developing vision, almost oblivious to what was happening in its Spanish-language section. As I woman I was extraordinarily oppressed. Culturally, I was confused.

During this whole period there was something else, intimately related to the confusion yet always more difficult to speak of. The language itself. I wrote in an English which was becoming more and more distant (although I continued to read "everything" coming out of the States, I almost never had the opportunity of reading my own work in a group, or of hearing others read. And I was no longer moving through a world where English was what you heard, primarily, if you stood on a street corner and listened!) But I didn't begin to write in Spanish. For one thing, Sergio made me believe I would never be able to. (The first poem I attempted to write in Spanish was one that burst from me in Lima, Peru, in 1973; on a job that put me in daily contact with women's oral histories, and in a man/woman relationship in which the languages spoken were Spanish and Portuguese.)

This problem of being a woman who functioned in Spanish but still wrote primarily in English went from only slightly unhinging me to becoming a deep frustration. It came to a head somewhere in the middle of my eleven years in Cuba. Throughout most of the Cuban experience I was living with Robert Cohen. We spoke English and of course there was the added dimension of our both being writers, but I continued to speak Spanish exclusively with my four children, I worked and read increasingly in Spanish, and those were the years in which I began to become involved in oral history projects in Spanish. The fact that I could not share my most intimate expression—my poetry—with those closest to me became more and more painful. In this context, Bladimir Zamora's invitation to read my poetry at the UNEAC was an important event.

I was changing. I was gaining confidence, as a woman, as a human being, and as a writer. Most important, however, was my increasing commitment to people's voices, testimony, oral history.

The research project which led to the writing of *Cuban Women Now*, was the beginning of that. While still in Mexico I had done a book on women in the United States, on the incipient women's movement, trying to present its multiple facets to women in Latin America.* Almost as soon as I came to Cuba I wanted to understand what a socialist revolution could mean for women, what problems it might solve and which leave unsolved. I presented this project to the Cuban Book Institute; it was accepted, and I was involved in that project for two years.

Travelling around the country, speaking with (or listening to) hundreds of women, old women, young women, peasant and working women, professionals, leaders, women who were barely adults, taught me a great deal about women's lives under the Cuban variety of socialism. What it took me longer to realize, was how essential the human voice was becoming in my experience, how my vision of the world was coming from the way that ordinary women (and some men) verbalized or articulated their

*Las mujeres, Siglo XXI Editores, S.A., Mexico, 1970.

experience. I've always been a pragmatist. I didn't then think of myself as a historian, even as an oral historian. In fact, I had no idea such a category existed. I had read none of the literature on the subject. As with almost everything else I've done in life, I just forged ahead. Making lots of mistakes, correcting them, learning as I went along.

My own poetry also began, simultaneously, to make use of people's voices. Poems like "Attica," "Wounded Knee," "Catching Up with Moncada," "Carlota," and even "Motherhood."

Because of the particular way in which women have been oppressed and largely silenced throughout history, the explosion of oral history projects with women has been particularly important. I'm thinking now essentially of Latin America, but I'm sure this is true for other parts of the world as well. These projects have given us women's vision of themselves, the world, and history, for the first time. This is particularly true of peasant and working women. What record did we have of how a Latin American peasant or working woman, or a Latin American Indian woman, sees the world and herself, before the testimonies of women such as Domitila Barrios, Manuela La Mexicana, Doris Tijerino, Gladys Baez, Rigoberta Menchu, Lima's domestic servants, the Cua women?

One of the more obvious implications is that literature becomes public property, no longer reserved for an elite. The magic of the verb is everywhere. No one has an exclusive option on it. One can sit and listen, spellbound, for hours, to a woman in the hills of northern Nicaragua. It's not simply what she says that's fascinating; her use of language is precise, magical, evocative, often astounding. What she is creating on your tape recorder is the very first draft of a wonderful story. At the same time she is revealing to you what she as a heretofore unheard country woman in a repressed but fighting culture feels, thinks, has experienced, remembers, knows. It is a precious gift. And you have the responsibility of providing an adequate vehicle for this voice to reach the world. You know that it's important on two levels: as the absolutely unique creation of a single human being, and as a window revealing a vision shared by hundreds of thousands of peasant women in northern Nicaragua. And beyond that: the effect this experience has on your own work (mine), your life (mine), your vision of the world (mine), and on your growing impatience with so much that passes for new and innovative literature (my impatience).

In Cuba I found a world engaged in frenetic creativity. The revolution was already ten years old. Some of the big errors and tough problems were becoming apparent. It was a time of great creativity and—beginning with the failure of the 1970 sugar harvest—a time of profound introspection and self-criticism.

Havana, 1979.

The Cubans had largely dealt with their ideological/literary problems during the 1962 discussions, culminating in Fidel's speech "Within the Revolution Everything, Outside the Revolution Nothing." During the years I was in the country the youngest generation of poets was moving towards a much more internal search. These were men and women born in the revolution, not "affected" by it. What they wrote simply *was* revolution, whether it was about love, fear, death, life, or a flower. They didn't have to wave flags or use tractors and raised fists as symbols.

The revolution itself became older and more confident, and so, less defensive about those writers and artists who had left. There is still a sense, in Cuba, that he or she who deserts the revolution is guilty of a sort of treason. But in the more sensitive circles, at least, this has become less extreme.

Women, who with few exceptions had never been particularly

A group of clowns during the 1979 Carnival, Havana.

outstanding in Cuban letters, moved to the forefront then. Suddenly most of the important poetry prizes were being won by women, and it was becoming clear that women were not only writing better poems than men; they had something qualitatively different to communicate. It was the logical recording of a social and political leap—rooted in, though not limited to, an economic one.

Each revolution learns from its predecessors. And this is particularly true of revolutions as historically and culturally linked as the Cuban and the Nicaraguan. Nicaragua, as I see it, has been a further moving towards that difficult and extraordinary place where artistic expression will become a part of our nature as important as eating or breathing.

In Nicaragua I continued to work intensely in oral history. In the slightly less than four years I was there, I completed three books based in people's voices: *Sandino's Daughters*, *Christians in the Nicaraguan Revolution*, and the book I have just finished on Nicaraguan writers.*

Risking a Somersault in the Air: Conversations with Nicaraguan Writers, Solidarity Publications, San Francisco, 1984.

59

Women in Nicaragua have made a qualitative as well as quantitative breakthrough in their social participation, their leadership and influence. And the role Christians have played in the Nicaraguan process has also been historic. This latter has had particular importance for me. As a nonbeliever and someone with little contact with the Catholic or any other church, Christianity was almost an unknown for me. And I confess to having approached it, at first, from a totally sociological and political point of view. It seemed necessary to "understand" the role Christians had played, and were continuing to play, in the Nicaraguan process, particlarly in light of the fact that so many Latin Americans are Catholic. "Understanding" has never, for me, been the product of outside observation, or academic research. Getting close to Nicaraguan Christians opened a whole new world, and helped break down a series of prejudices and preconceptions. And I found that it wasn't just important to understand the role of Christians vis-a-vis the Nicaraguan revolutionary experience, but also to understand the position held by the revolution vis-a-vis its Christians.

In Nicaragua I participated in a revolution in which the big questions of artistic expression were still being battled out. In Cuba that had taken place long before my arrival; in Nicaragua I

Singing the "purisima" at one of hundreds of neighborhood altars. Managua, Christmas 1982.

was part of it. Concepts of form and content, the responsibility of the artist—in Nicaragua we had big public discussions about these, in the daily papers, in the cafes, in the streets, and in the Ministry of Culture and the Sandinista Cultural Workers Association.

The revolution quickly and emphatically placed itself on the side of complete artistic freedom—as had the Cubans—but at a historic moment and with international solidarity that allowed their attitude to be less defensive than the Cubans. Artists in Nicaragua paint, dance, write, sculpt, act or sing whatever comes out of their individual and collective need; and they take what they do to the front lines where men and women still die daily defending a country under continued attack from north and south.

It was a poet (Leonel Rugama) who, in 1970 when the house in which he and two others were hiding was surrounded by the National Guard, kept firing till he ran out of ammunition. And when the head of the National Guard called into the smoking house: "Surrender!", Rugama replied *"Que se rinde tu madre!"* which might best translate as "Up yours!" *Que se rinde tu madre* has become the official slogan for Nicarguan cultural workers. In the great parades, on May 1 and July 19, artists and writers from the Ministry of Culture or the artists' unions march behind great banners bearing that phrase.

Nicaragua is a country of poets like no other country I've every known. The word "poet" has become a title, like Doctor or Attorney. The importance placed on cultural and artistic expression—even in these war-torn times—surpasses one's imagination.

I want to speak about photography. I was forty-three before I started making pictures. A good friend, Judy Janda, who is a wonderful photographer, had come to Cuba to make the pictures for my *Cuban Women—Twenty Years Later*. Judy didn't speak Spanish, and so I took off and went around with her. I had recently bought my first camera, but I don't remember knowing I was going to be a photographer when I bought it. I was just spending some of the money I had earned on something I "believed I should have—as a journalist." By that time I was doing a good deal of cultural journalism for the Cuban Ministry of Culture's magazine *Revolucion y Cultura*, and I was often with one of the publication's two photographers: Gory or Grandal.

When Judy came to Cuba and we worked together, I found myself wanting to tell her "why don't you take a picture of that . . ." or "why didn't you take a picture of this other . . .", but I didn't say that. I had too much respect for her as a person and as a photographer. And Judy is careful, meticulous, a very different kind of vision than my own. The minute she left Cuba, I took out the camera I'd bought at least six months before in the States, and began experimenting with it.

Grandal was, and is, a good friend. I asked him to teach me photography. I consider him one of the best, if not the best, of the Cuban photographers. He's also a very macho man, pragmatic (good for me) and overbearing (bad for me). He needed a darkroom, I had a tiny bathroom that could be converted, and we began fixing that up and sharing it. Everything I knew about photography, until I could begin to call myself a photographer, I learned from Grandal. Mostly from watching him. I would stand beside him, though he smoked and I had asthma, for hours, in that tiny darkroom which was barely big enough for one, let alone two. And I'd watch and learn.

Because of never having gone to college, I've always been pretty sure I don't learn well from books. Most of them I can't even read. But I learn well from watching. I learn everything. Grandal had his own very definite ideas about photography. He'd tell me to go out with nothing longer than a 28mm lens and shoot with that, to make me conquer my shyness with people on the street. And I'd do it.

One night—I was working on the anthology of Cuban women poets*—I decided to print the whole set of portraits of the women. I worked all night. I had never printed before. When Grandal came around the next morning, he found the pictures spread out on the dining room table. I was asleep. His shout woke me. When I remember those prints today, I remember how bad they must have been. But they were excellent for first prints. And that was the way it was: fast.

When Ernesto Cardenal invited me to come to Nicaragua to do a book on Nicaraguan women I accepted immediately. I'd been doing photography for some four months. I had hardly printed

*Breaking the Silences: An Anthology of Cuban Women Poets, Pulp Press, Vancouver, Canada, 1982.

more than those pictures of the Cuban women poets. And I hadn't developed more than a dozen rolls of film. Grandal told me to take thousands of pictures and send all the rolls back to Cuba. He'd develop them for me, and send me contact sheets so I could "see how I was coming along." His offer was made out of kindness, and a real fear I'd fuck up (this once in a lifetime opportunity). I told him no thanks.

I went to Nicaragua, stayed three months, made 4,000 negatives and developed all my own film. I ruined a couple of rolls. I made a deal with an old man who worked as a photographer for the Ministry of Culture. Zamorita was his name. He had his tiny darkroom set up in a commercial publicity house. He lent me a key, and I'd go there every morning around five. I'd develop all the rolls I'd taken the day before, hang them up to dry, and in the evenings after I'd finished a day of interviewing I'd go back, make contact sheets, take them home and study them to see what I was doing wrong (or right).

Sandino's Daughters (which is the English title of the book that came out of the project) has my text and images. But the interesting thing to me now is *how* I worked with both, the process. I did all the interviewing, photographing, and research in Nicaragua. I had the tapes transcribed, and I brought the typed transcriptions as well as the negatives and all the contact sheets back to Cuba with me. Then I spent six months writing the book. What I found myself doing was working on a particular interview during the day, say on Dora Maria Tellez, and then I'd go into the darkroom that night and work with images of Dora Maria.

The written testimony influenced the way I'd print a picture— by that time I had more control over my printing—and the physical image began influencing the way I would edit an interview. An interaction between word and image began taking place which has been important to me ever since. And which I've consciously tried to develop.

I have often thought that one reason I was attracted to photography was that it transcended my problem between two languages: English and Spanish. The photographic image is another language altogether. Photography is not "the truth" for me—it is not a picture of a static reality but tells a more complex story. There's no denying that it crosses barriers of language; the images can be seen by people of many places, and their responses depend

Comandante Dora Maria Tellez, the legendary "Commander Two," just after
the end of the war. Nicaragua, 1979.

much more on class, gender, history, culture, sensitivity, feeling, than on words.

But if that was, in fact, one of the reasons I became involved in photography, my involvement quickly went beyond a defensive stance. I am a strange photographer. I hold the camera badly, I use my left eye against the view-finder (although I have recently learned that my right eye is the stronger). I am shy in public. And I like being in the darkroom much more than I like going out shooting. But making pictures is, today, as important to me as writing.

On December 14, 1983, I was sitting in my livingroom in Managua, with a friend and journalist named Paul Goepfert. The last couple of years in Managua, in a semi-war situation, had been rough. I was leaving. I believe that it was not the war alone, but my age, my tiredness, a longing for my own land and people, and the feeling that after twenty-three years I was ready to bring what I had learned to a new dimension of energy and creativity in the United States.

None of this was easy. There was a lot of death.

One of Paul's questions was: "If you have come to know what you must write about through the route you've travelled—Mexico, Cuba, here—now that you're going back to the U.S. and hoping to devote more time to writing, mightn't you find that you no longer have anything to write about?"

I thought, and talked, about many of the things I've mentioned in these pages. And then I said: "Nothing to write about? Why there's no distance at all anymore between what I have to say and what I must do in order to be able to say it."

8

Calm? Dispassionate? Shit! This will not be a calm dispassionate analysis. This is for you, Floyce, and it's for you Karen. After watching Stanley Kubrick's *A Clockwork Orange*.

I watched the film without any feeling at all. I wasn't disgusted when disgusting things were happening on the screen. I wasn't frightened—me, who cringes at any horror film with eyes half hidden behind opening and closing fingers. I wasn't angry or incensed or annoyed. The rape scenes seemed like ballet to me. The faces, masks. The violence, like looking through a child's kaleido-scope and watching the little pieces of colored glass form patterns always perfectly symmetrical. I identified with none of the characters at all, not a single one. There was no suspense.

I caught myself thinking about other things—not often, but occasionally. Once I got up and went to the kitchen and served myself a plate of chocolate ice cream. I continued looking at the screen through the open room divider, neither entranced, nor anxious about missing anything. Just having decided to see it out. Like a class assignment.

Every person in the film is unthinkably rotten. The young man, his friends, the representatives of law and order, the government, those from the opposing party aspiring to be the government, the man's mother, his father, the representative of the Church, women, men (and I was almost going to say children. But there wasn't a single child in the film). The subversive writer was as evil as the representative of the system. The victims as bad as those who victimized them. No one displayed any believable human feeling.

What is Kubrick saying with this film? My first answer was: the system is rotten, in all its parts. But after talking about it for awhile, I came to the conclusion that he is not making a statement about a particular system, but about all systems. Perhaps about all things. Nothing is salvaged, or salvageable. Total nihilism.

I immediately remembered the TV program I saw the other night with the "debate" about video rock and the violence in these packaged programs. And the member of the rock group Kiss, who argued in favor of his videos, saying that once violence is por-trayed on television, it's all the same, that the very fact of the medium equalizes news footage and theatre, that a man with a ten-foot chain beating a half-naked woman has no more or less value or meaning than "thousands of people getting killed in some country out there."

Precisely the same message seems to be Kubrick's in this film. He refuses to take sides in the condemnation of violence; indeed, there is only one kind of violence: all-pervasive and at the same time unreal.

It is McLuhan's "medium is the message." It equates the criminality of the sickest dictator with a people's decision to be free at whatever the cost. It is the grossest over-intellectualization of life.

Strange, I began discussing the film with Floyce, and I was completely calm. I had no feelings for what I had just seen, simply a dry contempt for the message. Or the message as I interpret it. (It seems so preposterous, that I still wonder if I might not be completely wrong.) I saw the film as excellent in its movement, acting, direction, photography—the separate parts of its art. Art, of course, is much more than the sum total of its separate parts.

As I began to try to understand why I felt so detached from the film, why I felt so dispassionate, why I had just watched rape scenes ad nauseum and not felt any anger at all, I began to cry. I didn't cry uncontrollably, I didn't cry a lot, but I cried enough. More than I have since being back in the States.

And I began to think of my reaction to a rape scene in a film I saw years ago, in Cuba, a film about two French families at a resort where one father tries to rape his son's girlfriend when he finds her sunbathing out in the hills. She struggles with him, and he forces her head back, "accidentally" killing her. The film is actually about racism, the relationship between the French and the immigrant Algerian workers, and the rape scene is almost incidental to the plot.

It affected me tremendously at the time, and when I emerged from the theatre and began walking down the hill towards home, a guy in a parked car said something to me—one of those comments Latin American men frequently make to women on the streets—and before I knew what I had done I'd lashed out and punched him in the jaw with my fist. Later I wrote a prose piece about the whole event. It is called "Anger."

Although that was certainly an extreme response, rape always evokes in me anger, outrage, resentment. I wondered why the rape scenes in *Clockwork Orange* produced no response at all in me. Then I began to cry.

One might end the whole thing right there.

But there are certain moments in this film which strike me as "concessions" to life: the use of Beethoven's Ninth Symphony; the capacity of the old drunk in the first scene, when, greeting the young men's clear intent to beat him silly, he gives a very articulate speech welcoming death; the totally off-key responses of the boy's parents who simply *never* confront a situation as they should and yet are always somehow "doing the right thing"; and the scene in which the representative of the government is forced to feed the hospitalized and incapacitated young man, morsel by morsel, and the young man receives each spoonful of food with a grotesque snapping of his mouth—which sets the stage for everything that will happen from there on out.

These are moments in the film which stand out, brilliantly delineated within a kind of Rouault black line, as if to say: yes, it means exactly what you think it means, but...what about this? And this? And this? The unanswered questions.

9

The many-tentacled squid (me) is preparing for the trip east, trying to get immigration forms in shape, still attempting to secure a couple more university courses for the fall semester, and today went bowling for the first time. Shanti, my twelve-year-old nephew, is a quiet kid, at least around people he's not very familiar with. He is a deep kid, thoughtful and bright—runs with a track club, plays the violin and piano, is in seventh grade. His problems are probably similar to those of many young people in this country, whose home life is a window on what the world could be, and yet they must deal with what life is like, *now*.

I had no idea how bowling would strike me, and I really liked it. It seemed both a challenge and physically interesting. Shanti was very thoughtful about teaching me the basics, and very supportive of my clumsy, awkward, amateurish, piss-poor showing. We played three games. I could have kept on going, and wanted to, but he had to be home! Shanti made 100 points or more each time. On his second game he made one point less than his best game ever (150). I, sadly, did 54, 54, and then 67. But I hope we can go again next week.

10

I am more and more fascinated (and often awed, or repulsed) by television. There is an ad, a commercial, for example; every time it comes on I rivet onto it as if mesmerized, knowing what the next scene will be, and the next, previewing the monologue and dialogue in my mind. An extremely well-dressed woman (she is all our model must be: slim, simple, elegant, driving her own $20,000 car) is at the wheel. She drives through a landscape that evokes Kentucky breeding country, there are arches of well-kept trees on either side of the road and one wouldn't be surprised to see stallions grazing. Except it's evening. The dusk outside the car emphasizes the glow around the woman, who is revelling in how much her girlfriends loved the diamond her husband gave her. In the last scene of this "tasteful" commercial we have the woman, in an attitude somewhere between demure and radiant, come home to her husband's arms and tell him: "Oh, they all loved it!" "I know," he answers with a fatherly and self-satisfied smile, "Jane's husband already called." Diamonds are still a "girl's best friend." If your social aspirations are absolutely at the top, diamonds still represent love on the free-world traditionally American scene, and buying one for your wife or getting one from your husband still brings with it a promise of everything insinuated in the ad: total oblivion to what's happening in the world, safety, protection, comfort, status, untouchableness, the white American dream . . .

My own dreams are pressing in. The waking dreams. The bad ones, where the hand that reaches out always comes within inches of touching, where something stiffens the chest, the voice that is supposed to say yes says no, the mirror image flashes again and again and again. And complex papers are tossed by winds that just don't stop. It's a dream that's recurred for years, since 1969. Today I tell myself: you must not let the dream become reality. And if it does, you must face it with dignity. Even the slightest crack in that dignity means they are winning a little and you are losing—a little. That's one of the dreams. Then there is the noise dream, and the cold dream, and the wrapping-paper dream— where I fight to emerge from huge amounts of suffocating brown wrapping paper.

Strange, whenever I think of paper like that, I remember years ago (I must have been twenty-seven, or twenty-eight), modelling for an art class at this same university where today I am attempting to get work teaching. Standing naked in the middle of a cold room, the students concentrated on their anatomy task. Elaine de Kooning was the guest professor, and at one point, during a break, she tore a great piece of brown wrapping paper from an enormous roll the students used, held it out to me, and said: "Here. Try it yourself. It's fun!"

11

One of the big differences between the United States in the early '60s (when I left) and today: degree. What many of us saw back then was considered an exaggeration by those we tried to convince. The connections we made went too far. The conclusions we arrived at, gross. Now, it seems a lot of catching up has been done. It's as if whole aspects of the society have caught up with themselves.

Today not even the CIA (or the State Department, or the spokesman for the president's office) would deny U.S. involvement in any number of sticky schemes, from offing foreign heads of state to reversing revolutions, changing governments, stacking foreign elections, or outright invasions of anything from privacy to territory or the future.

12

When I was young and lived in this country, we blushed at a *Playboy* centerfold. The really heavy porn was sold under the counter at a series of small shops along New York's Forty-second Street. Today magazines like *Hustler* are sold on any newsstand. And magazines, as a medium, are now pale and second-rate. Today it's the rock videos, with S/M, violence without a cause, the most brutal kind of sexism and racism, black leather/white skin/red blood.

Years ago *Soldier of Fortune* was something that came in a plain wrapper. It wasn't easy to get. One knew there were cults of killing, and that men sold themselves to fight wars. Today the recruiters work openly in any city in this land. Ads are up on campuses and in "respectable" media. Just like the classifieds—for a long time now—begging partners in love, sex, perversion, and other games.

I remember when many of us were shocked because the New York *Times* gave almost a full page to an interview with the head of the Ku Klux Klan. It was like reading about the dean of your local agricultural school. The Grand Master explained, in a very articulate way, the Klan's history, reason for existence, accomplishments and dreams. Today such an interview, in such a place, would shock no one.

Today a member of Kiss can get on TV and tell the public there's no difference at all between "thousands of people getting killed in some country out there" and the violence canned, sold, and presented on his rock videos. "Once it's on TV, it's all the same." The medium is the message. We are horrified (I speak for myself) but he's right. That's not the way it should be, but it is the way it is.

Years ago (how many years?) I was driving with my mother and father; we were travelling, and my mother and father were having an argument. I think I remember my mother objecting to the American Civil Liberties Union defending freedom of expression for a fascist or racist organization. My father objected too, but defended the ACLU's position on the grounds that freedom of expression, *even in the abstract*, must be safeguarded.

We've all gotten older and wiser. Today the lines are much more specifically drawn; we know enough to understand it is no longer a matter of "principles," of abstract discussion. There are always two sides, and today it is a matter of life and death.

Is it all just a matter of degree, though?

The same things are being done, in the name of the same people. More of those people see through the facade; more are openly against it all. And perhaps more are indifferent, used to it. It's done, and it's done more thoroughly, "better," with more far-reaching results. The exposes are conclusive. So now we have experts in doing it right out in the open, refining mechanisms through which being candid itself becomes an attribute.

13

I often end up in front of the small screen. Some of the late movies are good. Some of the corniest serials attract me for what they say about life here, for what they want people to *feel* about life. And the presentation of the news is always interesting. As are the commercials. I've already mentioned a few. One that's really bugged the hell out of me this week, is a Bimbo Bread ad. It starts out with a home scene so "real" you're not even sure it's a commercial. It might be a preview of some coming attraction. A father plays with his kids. A mother prepares a snack (naturally). Everything is very very white, pastel tones of greens and blues and yellows at most. And over and over again the phrase: "we do things right here," "we live right here," "we eat right here," and then, finally, "we eat Bimbo Bread!"

It's not even the bread (rotten and sawdust-like as it is) that gets one about this ad; it's the insidious image of "well-bred, white, affluent, upper-class America" totally identified with "family, love, comfort, happiness...HERE." Certainly not the "here" most people in this country know.

Since my return to Albuquerque I've thought a lot about the bilingual, bicultural, Anglo-Latin nature of this city, of this state. Without a word of English, a Spanish-speaking person can do just about everything: shopping, theatre, schools, many jobs, services of all kinds. What was a rather spurious label of "bilingual state" when I grew up here in the '40s and '50s (a sign in Spanish somewhere, haphazard translation in Congress and courts) is today a reality. When I went to highschool in this town, there were two highschools then, the downtown school was mostly Hispanic, and in those days the word "chicano" hadn't been invented. Hispanic people were "pachucos" or even maybe "spics." Both terms, needless to say, derogatory if not insulting.

In my uptown school, there were 1,500 or so students in my last year, maybe six or seven were of Latin origin. They were anomalies. And they wouldn't think of speaking Spanish, or even admitting they spoke it at home. Society taught them well to be as white as possible.

And except in specific and working-class sections of Albuquerque, you wouldn't find a shingle advertising the services of a lawyer, doctor, architect or other professional of Hispanic origin. The services offered by "pachucos" were those you could get from a neighborhood plumber or the guy at the corner gas station.

Today more than half the powerful state politicians, architects, doctors, professors, planners, lawyers, state commissioners, senators and representatives, the governor—they're all Hispanic names. Hispanic culture has become a part of the overall culture of this state way beyond the confines of the Old Town plaza. And wherever you go you hear people speaking Spanish, fully, proudly, out loud. It's a particular Spanish. It's New Mexican.

Walking out of our apartment door, going through the courtyard of this married-student housing, going to the post office, getting gas at a gas station or applying for a driver's license, I fall as easily into Spanish as into English. And no one thinks twice about it—except Manny, a chicano who works at the post office and speaks Spanish with just about everyone but me! It's been thirty or forty years since I was in school here. A long time for a Hispanic growing up and bucking the kind of discrimination that was the bread of every day back then. But not so long if you think about racism as a phenomenon, and how deeply rooted in this society it is, how necessary to the system.

14

Last night my father took me to a basketball game. What interested me was the world there, the attitude of the people, the mythology of the cheerleaders (more objectified, if that's possible, than when I was in school), the way people dress for this kind of event, and the kinds of people who go.

Sports, especially college or other nonprofessional sports, are in a world of their own which plays a specific role within the larger one. A whole system of playing ethics is worked out in this context, and people who remain racist, exploitative and basically blind as regards the world situation, relate perfectly to a group of young men trained to maneuver a ball—be they Black, chicano or white—and they are able to function on this level without making any connections at all to the greater world. Yet basketball, as are other sports, is a lovely game, with real skill and energy, and it's not hard to see how these things become an important part of life.

15

Daily life is so easy here, so smooth and comfortable—as long as one has what amounts to a modest job, a way of getting by, the basics.

Since daily life has these attributes, it's hard to keep in mind the rock bottom, gut level problems plaguing humans under their skin, all the time, every day. I am brutally reminded on two separate occasions recently: one, when I ask Johnny what he thinks may be bugging Shanti beneath it all, and he tells me that one of the problems Shanti—and others his age—has, is a gut fear of war, destruction, oblivion. Living with the threat of nuclear war. With the threat of a death so big no one can comprehend it. An end so total there's no way of getting a grasp on it.

73

The other occasion was over dinner with my parents last week. They were speaking about their lives, what monies they have been able to save over the years, and they both mentioned the possibility of one of those old-age diseases which middle-class people can struggle with for years—at the rate of hundreds of dollars a day. Of course the poor have it much worse, and when these things happen to them they die at home (like Antonio's father, with stomach cancer, in those terrifying hills above Caracas) or in the still-infamous state institutions.

But the problem for the middle class in a country like this is that their fears fall into some impossible grey abyss: they are not eligible for poverty level help, so they spend years in increased anxiousness about their future. Will they have enough? What will happen? The triumphs of modern science extend their lives—but can't resolve this anxiety. And as science moves forward, it seems to reveal, as well as the several cures, more of these feared diseases, almost as if it has become a self-engendering monster. Which, of course, is not totally untrue, under capitalism.

The holocaust is certainly as real to young people in Central America as it is to those in the U.S. At first glance, most would say much more real. While kids here fear an unknown and almost unimaginable future demise, kids in Central America live surrounded by death. They see it when they wake up in the morning, they go to bed with it at night. Their friends have been murdered; they have lost members of their families. And many of them, at ages one no longer wants to repeat (because it seems to only add to the mystery, the unbelievability of it all) they are required to kill—and be killed. And yet the fear of death for a young person in Central America seems very different from what it is for a young person here. I'm not saying it doesn't affect kids—and everyone else. It does, and powerfully. But you can trace your fear very directly, very specifically, very well. Death is a known element in most parts of the world, not an unknown element.

I'm not, of course, making a case for death anywhere. Living with it as a neighbor in Nicaragua, and beginning to see what it does to people here even in its most futuristic, invisible, state, are simply two more, among many, reasons to struggle against it, wherever. But thinking about Shanti's fears, and those of so many like him, actually seeing those fears take the distorted shapes they do, is an interesting lesson.

The other is easier: the confidence one should be able to feel, as

Children at a new peasant settlement in Chinandega, Nicaragua. People are forced to move away from the northern border because of continued contra action.

one grows older, that one's basic human needs will be met, somehow. People talk about the rationing in Cuba, about the hardships beginning to weave themselves into the fabric of every-day life in Nicaragua. I've experienced them. But knowing you're taken care of if you're ill, knowing that medical help is available to you for however long you may need it, knowing your kids will be treated if they're sick—and none of it costs you anything; knowing there's no one waiting to rip you off around the basics, that no one's going to sell you an expensive coffin and a plot of ground when a family member dies; knowing you've got shelter, food, health, education, relaxation, culture, spirituality, assured: that's worth a lot.

Sure, a middle-class person in the United States enjoys a much higher level of provision in all these categories, and perhaps a broader variety of choice as well, than the across-the-board population in a place like Cuba. And that's how the comparisons are usually made. What's interesting here is seeing the anxieties of the traditionally poor creeping into the lives of those who have never worried before.

Meanwhile, Reagan seems to need no competition for the Re-publican nomination to the presidency, and the Democratic contenders play their various games across the country. It's on TV, in the papers, and on everyone's lips, every day. I liked McGovern, and he's out of the running. Jackson is doing something wonderful, and he's out too. Mondale and Hart (the two main runners now) talk respectively of a "marathon all the way to California" and "new ideas." One finds oneself looking, almost desperately, for a shadow of truth, hope, something to grab onto.

16

Last night's "Nightline" was almost exclusively devoted to a discussion—not of capital punishment per se, but of whether or not an execution should be shown on television. The talk of the day. A killer in Texas was executed yesterday morning, by lethal injection, and he had requested his execution be shown on TV. His request was fought for in some quarters and eventually denied.

So last night we had the Texas attorney general arguing for a public display of this terror, and others arguing against. The ideas bandied about touched on whether or not people thought the sight would be a deterrent (though it was never quite clear whether a deterrent against crime or a deterrent against capital punishment was meant, if indeed it were either), and the value or weight of this type of death versus, say, scenes of war, rape, police brutality (even the word incest was mentioned once or twice). The only thing I come away with after witnessing this discussion, is that those involved have a totally distorted idea of the meaning of death—or life.

17

Between Santa Fe and Taos there is a series of back roads with small towns, some of them more accurately villages, and Floyce and I took off very early this morning to drive through the area, something we both needed immensely. I know I needed it almost like air. I hadn't used my camera since arriving here, hadn't made a single picture or looked with the lens' eye. We also hadn't taken a day to relax, just to be together, laugh, talk, share some new experience.

In the small towns and villages along the old road from Santa Fe to Taos, in northern New Mexico, where people speak Spanish, from the time of the conquistadors.

Santuario of Chimayo.

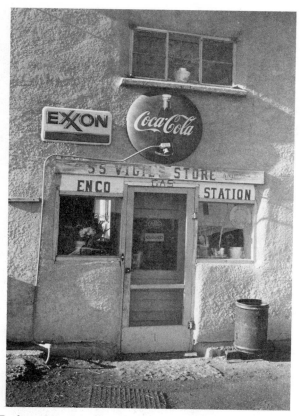

Back road between Santa Fe and Taos, northern New Mexico.

For me, it was like evoking a time thirty years back. And yet also new. The immensity of the land, its toughness and durability. The sage and chamisa and cactus, the pinon with its scent that is everywhere. The great valleys and mountains always just off to one side. Today the sun was bright, casting deep shadows. The air was clear and blue as the distances lengthened, the earth baked and hard, the villages polished clean. The same signs over and over again: churches with sparse outer lines (most of them closed tight); small graveyards with a dozen fascinating tombstones, and a strange profusion of plastic flowers arranged over the stones or wooden crosses, sometimes even stuck through branches of real shrubs; lots of bright yellow school busses parked in crazy barns or garages; all-purpose stores—one in every village—with their mad collection of ads and signs; ruins with "private property—keep out" on them; occasional home windows with the flourish of a lace curtain and an arrangement of plastic flowers behind the scrubbed glass; runty dogs with curling tails; ancient automobiles in varied states of decay.

Through the valleys and across this land other cars came, their drivers always waving at us and at each other. Many are topped with complex racks which turn out to be loaded with skis. Occasionally we'd stop and talk to someone. I heard more Spanish than English.

Santuario of Chimayo.

The land I came home to. In the junked car and the vast pinon-covered land is my memory and my future.

Northern New Mexico.

18

Yesterday was raw with the death in El Salvador of *Newsweek* photographer John Hoagland. Floyce saw it on TV early in the afternoon. A CBS crewman who had been near Hoagland (Nickelsburg from *Time*, and a few others were also there) said the tragedy had taken place during crossfire between the army and the guerrillas. From the testimony it seemed likely it had been the army that hit Hoagland—in fact it seemed purposeful—and that the guerrillas had brought the body out and laid it on the road. The CBS crewman clearly said he thought the soldiers were firing at the journalists. By the time I got home in the afternoon and Floyce gave me the news, there was little on any of the broadcasts (TV or radio). I had to get the dead photographer's name by calling the *Journal* newsroom.

The great thing on the news here is the weather. Weather reports take up at least a third of the news space. As Floyce says, it's the most important thing for people to find out, so they'll know what to wear the next day, what to wear and where to go. The rest of the news is divided between sports, human interest stories (the latest premature baby struggling for life, the latest kid with a rare or incurable disease), and financial reports. There's always a bit on local news, and international reporting is limited to the very top items, almost never followed up in any realistic way.

I knew Hoagland. Not terribly well, but I knew him. I probably spoke with him dozens of times this past year, mostly in the lobby of the Intercontinental, sometimes on trips to the border. I know Nickelsburg too. I didn't stop searching the TV screen or scanning the dial and papers for some rendering of this incident. But by today's news, the word is "it was probably the guerrillas," and that seems to be that. And of course my temptation (desire?) is to see it move like another Bill Stewart story.* If only it would do that kind of good! Even if simply among the major press people

*Bill Stewart was a U.S. newsperson, working for ABC; he was gunned down in broad daylight and at close range (obviously intentionally) by Somoza's National Guard in Managua, 1978. The incident brought renewed attention to the atrocities committed by the Somoza regime, and gave the international press increased motivation for accurate reporting about the situation in Nicaragua. It was a kind of turning point in the war coverage and helped put the Sandinistas in an offensive position.

themselves, for they wield a good amount of power. But who knows if it will do any good. I felt this death. I feel it.

19

Last night I had a real treat, a treat and an important experience. Important in terms of my coming trip. Holly Near came to Albuquerque, along with Nina Golden—pianist, singer, and composer—and they packed the Kimo for a benefit for Judy Pratt. I had never heard Holly live, and she's extraordinary. One of the most beautiful singers and loveliest stage presences I've heard in a long time. But most of all, and important for me just before my tour, she gives so much to the audience. She just gives and gives, out of a real need to give, and that comes through, strong. I took hold of that, and will hold it—for I so often close off to an audience when I'm tired or irritated by something.

At intermission I wanted to meet her, so went back stage and sent her a note. In a couple of minutes I heard her calling: "Margaret!" and we were embracing one another. It was wonderful talking to her after so many years of admiration (mine for her), and never meeting.

20

Johnny came over around noon to ask if I'd like to go down to take some pictures of the sendoff for Judy Pratt. She's walking around the state (well, driving actually, from city to city and town to town, and walking through each place, through the neighborhoods, talking to people, explaining her ideas, policies, and dreams. Talking to working people, women, people who struggle for survival). It was a pretty sorry turnout, fifteen or twenty in all. The weather was cold and dreary grey, and that probably accounted for some of the slackness in the crowd. But not all.

That was the beginning of the day. Then we went bowling. We had picked up Shanti at a friend's house and I was delighted. We played nine games—Johnny, Shanti, and I—and I could feel myself improving. I made 100 once, and then 108. But my consistent scores were still in the 80s, with a couple of 90s. The thing I liked best was getting better, understanding the game more, controlling the balls better. Why do I love bowling?

I've never liked any team or competitive sport. I can remember in grade school keeping to the edge of the playground, engaging friends in confidences, stories, ideas. Never much physical play. In junior high the sports problem came to a head. I frequently found ways of getting a doctor's excuse for not participating in gym. I had my period more often than anyone I knew. When there was nothing else for it but to give up and drag my feet through the ordeal, I was never chosen for a team. One side chose and then the other, and I was always left last on the field, dubious addition to whichever side got last choice. Then there was nothing to do but suffer it through—with the added glory of knowing how much I had been wanted.

As an adult I swam, I rode horseback occasionally, I became a fairly good shot (with bow and arrow as well as with a firearm). But never another team game. Never that competition.

So, what is there about bowling? It began when I asked Johnny to tell me what kinds of things Shanti likes to do, in hopes one or more of them would overlap with what I like to do, and that through doing something together we might become friends. Shanti's list (as told by Johnny) included golf, playing video games, riding his bike, running, playing the piano, and bowling. What choice did I have?

I like bowling because it's a challenge. I like the way it makes my body feel. I like doing it with other people because I've never felt I was competing, except with my own best score. I mean I don't feel I want to be better than Shanti or Johnny. I want us all to be good.

21

It is early morning, well, eightish. I'm sitting before a sun-filled window with plants, lacey bits of cloth, driftwood, dried starfish and sea shells—all the semi-living-breathing items which people who live on snowy tundra, who are constantly looking out at a web of stark black branches against white snow, place between themselves and the world. This is the home of a couple of the

Women at the Foot of the Mountain—a St. Paul theatre group. Martha Boessing welcomed me late last night, worried about the profusion of cats, solicitous of my needs.

Yesterday began too early. Two hours before the alarm was set to go off I was listening to the loud sound of the planes flying low over the airbases.

The flight showed commercial planes at their worst, giving that sense that, as a woman using these services, one is somehow either completely invisible—or considered a very young child. One requests something as simple and basic as going to the bathroom, or else just gets up to go—not imagining that one needs permission. And it all hits, suddenly, when the stewardess informs you that the pilot has not yet turned off the fasten-seat-belt signs so would you please return to your seat (grim smile). "But I have to go to the bathroom . . ." And she comes back with her readymade reply—for women.

What really gets to me is that this attitude is not used with men. If there was a real reason, applicable to all, the chagrin and then anger wouldn't be so pervasive. So, it was cheerful Frontier and United all the way, with their meaningless snacks and reassuring drinks (that you pay for). Then, finally, down in Minneapolis-St. Paul where everything was snow, biting cold, yesterday's TV promise made good.

By the time I descended I had ripped pages from as many current *Newsweek*s, *Fortune*s, *U.S. News and World Report*s and *Business Week*s as I could. One, for example: "You can help put kids in their place!", tells us when we "work with Junior Achievement, we get a chance to turn kids into giants. Giants of industry like the National Business Hall of Fame laureates you see before you. Selected every year by *Fortune* magazine . . ." And there before us we have 103 tiny photos of laureates stretching back to the last century. Even good old George Washington is there. Among the 103, there are two women: Olive Ann Beach and Lila Acheson Wallace.

Katherine Kocy was holding up a copy of *Sandino's Daughters*, so I recognized her right away. We had to hurry, to drive through cold northern Minnesota to St. Johns, which is only for men; and St. Benedict's which is for women. We made it just in time for dinner squeezed tight up against the reading. There were a dozen or so of Gary Prevost's students at dinner, interested in asking some questions before the formal activity. In the student cafeteria we were surrounded by long-robed monks, barefoot except for their crude sandals, students in modest apparel, and a table full of ROTC fellows, their camouflage suits like a strange garden in the gloomy hall.

Walking across campus to the auditorium was an effort; too cold up here, and even with my newly acquired warm duds I was far from adequately clothed. Maybe 100 showed up for the reading, students from the two colleges, their faces largely impassive. Towards the back, a young monk in his black robes held something bright and red on his lap (it turned out later to be a ski jacket). As I read, I felt there was a red and black flag, waving at me from the rear of the hall.

They wanted fifty minutes of poetry to allow time for discussion. (The women had to make a last 9:30 bus back to their campus.) So I cut the formal material a bit, and left time for talk. And good talk it was. This was a surprise: 100 students at a small religious college in northern Minnesota, asking what turned out to be the most complete, in-depth and supportive questions I've heard in a while. Every single question came from a place of support for the Central American people, with emotions ranging from anger to perplexity at what the current U.S. administration is doing there. When a young man in a ROTC uniform raised his hand, I thought to myself, well, here it comes—but this guy was, perhaps, the most sympathetic of all. After the meeting he came up to me wanting more information about Nicaragua's foreign policy. He will be representing that country at a mock UN meet next month.

Later, in the car with Gary and Kathy, we talked about these students. Gary has been teaching at the college for several years. He spoke of their contradictions, the different forces that pull them, and their concerns. And we drove through the cold night back to Minneapolis. To this house.

22

Gustavus Adolphus was a Swedish king. The college at St. Peters (eighty miles from the Twin Cities) is named after him. An old Lutheran school, lots of Swedes and other Scandanavians; Robert

Bly went here I am told, and lectured here on occasion, but no one I've met remembers. In a dorm window: "Reagan-Bush." The country (stretches of perfect farms, exquisite shapes, perfect repose) smacks of conservatism. Most of the farmers sell to Green Giant, the huge monopoly (packers, canners) whose employment practices, and the living conditions of its workers, caused such a scandal in these parts several years back. The man who drove me to St. Peters—Kurt, a very nice fellow from the Twin Cities Nicaraguan Solidarity Commitee—says nothing has changed since that struggle.

We arrived in the late afternoon, and drove around a bit, hunting for the home of Ruth Mason, head of International Relations at the college, and our host for the evening. My event was to culminate their series of Central American Week activities, which had included programs on El Salvador and Guatemala, films, the appearances of other speakers. I suddenly got into one of my fearful funks, not wanting even to find the house, dreading the "intimate" meeting with interested students beforehand, I wanted to see the slums of this clean Minnesota town. There aren't any, I was told. The idea of kids growing up in a place like this, without even the *view* of poverty, was something I chewed on for a while. But our second swing past the front door of Ruth's place brought her out smiling to greet us, and there was nothing to do but go in.

Actually, it was a lovely gathering. Ruth turned out to be an extraordinarily warm and knowledgeable woman, whose husband also teaches at the college (comparative literature) and whose kids immediately made me feel at home by being kids. And the students arrived, one by one. A guy from Bangladesh, a woman from Bolivia. Another from Holland. Several who had lived in Mexico, Nigeria, Liberia, Spain. I began to get a picture of each of these young people, how they think, their vision of the world. The woman from Bolivia spoke to me as if she had found a long-lost sister—she seemed desperate to speak Spanish, in this snow. Slowly, my fears diminished, and by the time we got ready to go to the college, I was feeling fine again. (Memories of Tony, telling me not to make a tour this year: "You're not ready for it. It will take too much from you even if you don't think so. Wait a year or two. Rest." Several times, even over the scant time that's passed since I got on the Albuquerque plane, I've thought of those words. It's true. But it's also true that I think I can make it, if I take it one day at a time.)

23

Four years ago today, in El Salvador, the death squads downed Monsignor Oscar Arnulfo Romero, the country's archbishop. He had increasingly spoken out against the officialized terrorism that still batters that nation, and he was saying mass in the chapel of a cancer hospital when they got him. Last night, at Minneapolis' Cathedral of St. Paul, close to two thousand people gathered in his memory. Scattered Latin Americans could be seen throughout the huge basilica. But mostly it was people from this cold, snowy, northern U.S. place, moved by the message of a man and a people, moved by a struggle so many miles to the south. The service was ecumenical, of course, the confessions offered by Mary Foster (Interreligious Committee on Central America, of the Twin Cities Metropolitan Church Commission), Reverend Richard Podvin (priest at St. Stephen's Catholic Church), and myself. The readings were by Rev. William Teska (Holy Trinity and St. Anskar Parish), Tamara Rosberg (St. Luke Presbyterian), Jorge and Virginia Rodriguez (our Lady of Guadaloupe), Rev. Philip Anderson (American Lutheran), Joan Lubinski (Maryknoll Missioner) and Rene Hurtado (a Salvadorean refugee).

Those who offered public confession before me had their words down on paper. I didn't. I had no idea at all what I was going to say seconds before I faced those two thousand people. But I knew I would say something from my heart, something connected to the Central American experience. After whatever it was I did say (for I have forgotten, completely) I led the prayer: "Lord God, forgive your Church its wealth among the poor, its fear among the unjust, its cowardice among the oppressed. Forgive us our lack of hope in your reign, our lack of faith in your presence, our lack of trust in your mercy. Forgive our worship of death in our longing for our own security, our own survival, our own private peace. Lord, restore us to covenant with all your people. We affirm with hope your presence in the world. You see the broken, the tortured, the disappeared in Central America and say: These are my brothers and sisters. Lord, inspire us with your hope, challenge us with your truth, empower us with your strength, to live for life in the midst of death, to translate our vision and hope into action. Amen."

24

Minneapolis and St. Paul are cities with a solid working-class history. The Democratic party here is called the Democratic Farm and Labor party. You can feel the strength of workers' struggles, and the strength of that history. And resistance. The giant Honeywell company, the one that makes the cluster bombs first used over Vietnam, rises in brick red along one of the freeways. The Honeywell Project (men and women who oppose that death) began twenty years ago, and was strong throughout the Vietnam War, fading out a bit afterwards. But recently it has been revived, and a couple of years ago 500 people stormed the gates in opposition to what the company does. Six months later there were 2,000, and 360 were arrested. These are people who move from one level of struggle to another. They are to be seriously reckoned with.

25

What we do for our children. What we do to our children. What we do in spite of our children, and to them in spite of ourselves. What we do with them. What we and they do. How we make it, each of us, in spite of . . . I have been thinking a great deal about all this in this house, with Martha and her three children, who are no longer children, but growing, almost grown, old enough that their character says something about how they have lived, how they have been "raised." Curtis, who is twenty-two, is by Martha's first marriage. Rachel, a light black woman just ready to go to college, was adopted by Martha and her second husband, Paul. And Jenny is Martha's and Paul's daughter.

I used to say about my own kids that the reason, or one of them, that they all seemed to be doing o.k. was that we loved them, and—no matter what else was part of the picture—that was the important thing. But I now feel there is something else. Not simply the love we've had for them, but also their experience of our values. I cannot imagine why I never saw this before. I have known for such a long time that almost all the values people are forced to carry are wrong, they don't fit, they have little to do with our gut feelings and needs. They are created by a consumer society in a madly competitive world. Strange, how we can do this, and still feel uneasy about giving our children different lives, different values.

Today was my "free" day in Minneapolis-St. Paul. Marilyn Lindstrom and I went bowling. Did my best game so far, 125. It was great at the alley: a team of blind bowlers and several deaf mutes. Plus the usual collection of ordinary working-class people of all ages. Next to us a young couple alternated between rolling the ball and listening to their favorite tunes on a Walkman with one set of earphones.

26

Yesterday was illuminated by "Las Gringas," the play the Women at the Foot of the Mountain have made about invasion, personal and public. The play was partly based on testimony from *Sandino's Daughters*. I had met some of the women when they were in Nicaragua several months back, and had heard good and bad reviews of the production. I didn't know what to expect. Martha and I went over to the theatre early, so I could watch or participate in the entire process, including an affinity circle and warm up.

The experience of the play really affected me. I've never felt tongue-tied facing a crowd before, and I did when—once the performance was over—they introduced me and asked me to say a few words. I was, literally, speechless. Six women play a total of eighteen characters, between the "gringas" and latinas. They have collectively taken the histories of Dora Maria, Zulema, Nora, Julia, Amada Pineda and Yaosca, and written twelve more: North American women including a black lesbian carpenter, a Washington D.C. call girl, a Wisconsin dairy farmer, the wife of a college professor, the wife of a conservative U.S. senator. These weave in and out of one another, working expertly with music, dance, song, a Greek-chorus-like transition, Spanish, English, readings, poetry, storylines which neither dominate the experience nor get lost, and audience participation which grabs the public hard and pulls them into the play.

Before entering the theatre people are given a sheet of paper with a list of questions which they are requested to answer anonymously. You are asked if you have ever been raped, molested, mugged, assaulted; by strangers, acquaintances, family members; if you trust your community leaders, city leaders, leaders in Washington; if you have ever felt discriminated against because of sex, race, sexual preference, being "different" etc. Then, during the play, we are informed (by one of the characters, a news announcer) that "internationally, on the eve of elections in El Salvador, the Senate is asking for $93 million to bolster that country's tottering dictatorship, while here at home, fourteen persons present tonight admit to having been the victims of incest, twenty-eight say they have no confidence in their leaders in Washington..." The connections between personal invasion and the invasion being suffered by our sisters and brothers in Central America are made brilliantly clear.

27

One of the things I have been noticing on this tour is how the English language has been stretched, in the years I've been away, to include words and expressions needed to denote concepts which were not part of people's life experience before. For example, when the dentist flicked on a tiny TV just in proper viewing position so I could lie back, grit my fists and try to get my mind off the scaling job he was doing on my soul, he described Ralph Nader as a consumer advocate. I didn't want to say I didn't know what a consumer advocate is. Could it be someone who advocates consuming? Sounded like some kind of lawyer, to me. Here in the Twin Cities, I have heard the phrase "inadequately parented" to refer to someone whose family context did not offer all the love and support generally considered necessary to a healthy growing up. And, rather than say "this is my husband, lover, comrade, friend, mate" or whatever, the term recently coined in this part of the world for the woman or man who shares one's life is "significant other." "S.O." for short. "Better than S.O.B.," I heard someone laugh. Then there's "state of the art," "printout," "data bank," and so forth.

28

Iowa City. Again, the neat, beautifully arranged collection of barns and silos surrounds a farmhouse every two or three miles along the road from the airport at Cedar Rapids. This city was once the state capital and now cannot have more than 80,000 people, between its student and town populations. The downtown is nothing more than a couple of streets, one elegant shopping mall, some trees being supplanted by the building of a Holiday Inn. The university student population is mostly middle America, conservative and desperately job-oriented. And yet, here too, the signs are everywhere: the women's, and especially the lesbian, community seems extraordinarily active. They are working with the solidarity people, and all sorts of joint activities have been described to me.

There is money here, and it's being used for progressive TV. Preparations are being made to welcome 200,000 at a peace event in the near future. Holly Near was here recently; and Odetta (remember her? from the '50s and '60s!) is coming in a couple of weeks. Where there is community and consciousness, to this extent, there is always a lot of hope. I am trying, here, to say something I've been feeling since I came home: sure, it's a downbeat time of general political conservatism (how else could a Reagan have been elected and be, today, on the threshold of re-election). But the real American dream is not dead; the seeds are everywhere.

29

Wanting to write about what I'm experiencing, inside. The exhaustion and the fear. The moments, sometimes during readings, when everything goes blank, white, empty. As if I am invaded by absence. But an absence of what? I do not know. I remember first experiencing something similar in 1978, at the very end of that heavy three-and-a-half-month lecture tour which took me to more than seventy universities across the country. Then, I ascribed it to being tired. Worn out. What else? I guessed I had simply pushed myself too far.

I especially remember one incident, speaking before a group of radical sociologists. The white spaces seemed endless. Afterwards, friends came up, congratulating me. When I managed to ask about the spaces, no one knew what I was talking about. No one had noticed. "It was a fluid presentation," was their response. That didn't make me feel any better, though. Oh, maybe it did momentarily. Yes, I knew I hadn't "fucked up." But added to my fear of the whiteness was my fear that I myself was experiencing something, or seemed to be experiencing something, which had not in fact happened. The fear of going to pieces, complicated by the fear of misperception.

But it went away. And I returned to Cuba. I had "done a good job." I was tired, but would recover. Much more recently, in Nicaragua, the spots returned. That was a period of such intense work, so much of it, such long hours, being more tired than I could ever remember being. The spots were not in public performances, but sometimes while driving my car through the city. And with them came a time disorientation—even of the century I was in!

There was Ana Maria's death.* And there was simply the war. And I started going to see Tony, and she explained the spots and taught me how to handle them. I began to think about coming home. Lots of things began falling into place. My life, once more, took a new turn.

When I arrived in Albuquerque, especially during the first weeks, the spots were frequent. I didn't talk about them much, except with Floyce, and I just mostly stayed inside. My inclination was to go as slowly, approach this old/new world as carefully, as I could. At first I only saw my close family. And, little by little, I began to make my way out into the world once more.

The constraints at not having a darkroom, at not having a proper place to live and work, were getting to me. And that was a solid sign things were progressing! I began trying to find work. I

*Comandante Ana Maria (Melida Anaya Montes was her real name) was second in command of the Salvadorean liberation forces. When she was not on active duty in her country, she sometimes came to Managua to meet with representatives of other liberation movements. It was during one of these stays in Nicaragua, while asleep in her home, that she became the victim of a particularly brutal and cruel political murder. She was found with the marks of extreme vengeance on her body, and her throat was slit. It was later discovered that she had been assassinated by forces inside her own organization who opposed her strategies. The incident was a terrible shock, especially to those of us who happened to be living in Managua at the time.

began speaking to people I knew only slightly or not at all. Only a couple of times did I really feel the fear: once when I went to a totally meaningless meeting with a member of the photography faculty at UNM, and I sat there staring at him and wrecking a necklace I was wearing, picking at the strand of beads until they split and scattered on the floor; once in a supermarket; once when I had to go to a friend's darkroom to work and it seemed especially difficult to have to face his particular brand of sexist "teaching." The incidents were isolated, controllable. I continued to prepare for this tour. And then I started out.

The first few days in Minneapolis-St. Paul were truly miserable. I felt a heaviness and a loneliness almost all the time. I was surrounded by supportive people, and the activities did not go badly. But each one of them required a tremendous effort. And I found myself ticking them off, as if saying to myself: "O.k., today you have this and this and this. And if you can just get through the first, then you can think about the second, and then the third, and before you know it you will have done them all, and night will come, and you can go to sleep."

It was that Saturday in the Twin Cities that changed everything. The previous night I had taken part in the service at the Cathedral. There had been two thousand people, and it was an awesome sight. I was wearing blue jeans (my father's, which I always think give me a special kind of emotional support) and a sweater, so I kept my poncho on so as not to look too out of place among the women who were wearing tailored suits and silk stockings. I got up to speak, and I felt good. But immediately afterwards I didn't know what I had said. I remembered the strong, steady timbre of my voice, full, confident, but couldn't remember the words. There was the blankness, the whiteness, again. I was more curious than afraid that time and the next day I bought a newspaper in order to find out what I had told those people.

On the Saturday, I had gone bowling with Marilyn in the morning. I felt relaxed. And at night I went to see "Las Gringas." The theatre experience was cleansing. That night I felt, for the first time, wholly good. Complete. I was only mildly puzzled by the fact that when I had read in the paper the rundown of the Cathedral events, including a summary of my participation, I had recognized nothing. It was fine, but I didn't recognize my words.

Later, I experienced that twice again, the whiteness, the silence, the space, invading me at particular moments—suddenly—and then leaving as unexpectedly as it had come. Both times I was afraid again. Uneasiness. But again, both times must have been infinitely tiny, for when I asked people afterwards if they had noticed, no one knew what I was talking about.

I am afraid that the spots will increase in frequency and even in duration. That they will begin to get in the way of my work, production, performance. And then, I am bothered, too, by the apparent discrepancy between what I perceive and what others evidently see. What does it all mean?

April

1

I'm in Cambridge, Massachusetts, sitting at a small desk in a room in Ruth Hubbard's and George Wald's home where I have been so graciously received since yesterday. Hella is Ruth's ninety-two-year-old mother. She told me this morning: "Why are people leaving Cuba? What is wrong? They say such terrible things about the Soviet Union. Why is it like that? You know, Stalin did a lot of harm. Some say history will prove him right. He had to pact with Hitler, he would have pacted with the devil, because he needed time. But I don't know . . . You have a bad cold; you must drink some hot tea! My mother was a great admirer of Napoleon. She read a lot of Stendhal. But when I was nineteen I read *War and Peace*, and I wrote to my mother: 'I have been reading what Tolstoy has to say about that friend of yours, Napoleon.' She wrote back: 'I am in good company too, with Stendhal!' I don't know. We were Marxists, but Stalin came along. The world is a funny place to live in." (There's no other place to live, I interject— but she goes on; she does not hear.) "My husband was a doctor.

My friend Ruth Hubbard and her mother, Hella, in Boston.

And I was an independent woman, I was a child prodigy in music, and I went through the Vienna Conservatory. Then I decided to study medicine, and I became a doctor. My husband and I were both doctors. In 1948 he had a heart attack and had to take it easier. So we would work for four months and travel for two; work for four and travel for two. But we never went to Cuba or Nicaragua. I wish we had. Now I would not go alone, because I am old and deaf. We went to Switzerland, to Austria. I had two children of my own: my son, and Ruth. But then I adopted a Polish lad, a year younger than my son. When Hitler came to power we worked over here, we worked for the children. But I always thought U.S. Jews were selfish; I never thought they did enough. They talked big, but they could have done more. So I told them, money isn't enough. You should be taking a child into your home. I said yes. My son was eighteen then, and he was studying, in California. Ruth was away from home as well. I took this Polish boy, seventeen years old, the only survivor of a Polish family. His mother, father, brother, sister: all victims of Hitler. He had lived in a death camp from the age of twelve to the age of seventeen. When he came here he didn't know a word of English; only Polish. And he hated all Christians. The only good Christian is a dead Christian, he would say...well, he had suffered a lot. But he learned English, I taught it to him, and he went to school. And then he wanted to go to Harvard. I told him why don't you try another school? Harvard is too hard for you. What will you do if you flunk out? Study on my own for a year and try again, he answered. So I got him into Harvard. And fortunately, he was very good at soccer. And he studied hard. So he did well. And he married a Christian, a woman named Maria. But I always say she is the only Jew in the family. She observes seder, everything. I have to laugh! The world is a funny place to live in. My mother used to say that fashion is like an old trunk, you just keep filling it up with clothes, and if you turn it over every twenty years and start wearing the old clothes again, you will be right in style. But I think it's the same with everything—just the same with everything!"

George Wald

2

The dreams. They are coming back. Last night and the night before last. I only vaguely remembered those from the night before, and only this morning, after trying to assimilate last night's into waking memory. As if the accumulation was what

97

made them insistent, unflinching. And I do not remember the details. But they all have to do with death. With death and with fear. In part of last night's, there is a scene repeated and repeated throughout: a young man, a soldier who was a neighbor of ours in Havana many years ago (who is still a neighbor, there on Linea Street; it is I who have moved away) lay down on his coffin again and again. He would get into the box, and then he was dead. But he would "awake" or remove himself from it, and he was alive. For some reason his two small daughters (twins, whom I have used in an image or a series of images, my "Diane Arbus period") were connected with this ritual. They were clearly being shown with their father, dead. Why? I do not remember. But it had to do with danger. Danger and fear.

3

This morning I was downstairs at seven, reading the Boston *Globe* and the New York *Times*, and waiting for Teresa who showed up promptly to initiate me into the mysteries of painting on silk. I had dreamed, in among the fear dreams, about the banner I would make for Johnny's bookstore, how the lettering would be, the colors. I wanted to make something like those watercolors I did years ago when I first read Agnes Smedley's *Daughter of Earth*: the browns and ochres and reds and oranges of the desert, the dull greens and pale pinks, the intensity of New Mexico's blue sky. And so I did. Teresa spoke to me of her childhood (chicano father, Irish mother, in California) as she taught me how to melt the wax and use it with a brush or small hollow instrument to draw the letters. Later the wax is melted away, leaving the white silk showing through. She taught me how to mix the pigments and paint the stretched fabric, and I moved into it as I revelled in a world of such movement and color. I loved it and ended up doing the banner, and another large rectangular surface which I cut into three long scarves, one each for Sarah, Ximena, and Anna. I learned how to stretch the silk, paint it, dry it and then roll it in newspapers and steam it on the kitchen stove (so that the colors would set). Later we unwrapped the pieces, washed them well, and hung them up to dry once more.

Twins of a neighbor. Havana, Cuba, 1979.

4

At this time twenty-one years ago in Mexico City it was bright and clear. I worked around the house, and made lunch. In the early afternoon I went to a nearby street market, looking at some pots for plants. When I returned to the house, and went to the small downstairs bathroom, I noticed two tiny drops of blood on my panties. Without any pain at all, we got my things together and went to the hospital. Sarah was born less than an hour after we got there. I took her in my arms, and walked out of the delivery room with her warm body wrapped in blankets. Twenty minutes later I took a cold shower, and eleven hours later we were home. Sarah was a strong woman-child, though slightly cross-eyed and with only a whispy smattering of hair (she was to come together, as the beautiful woman she is today, at about eight months). She is, of all my children, the one who is most brazenly like me (inside). I miss her intensely—especially on a day like today.

5

The dreams again last night. This time Floyce is always just around the corner. We are in a large resort hotel of some kind. I see him up on a balcony. I see him in the distance. I imagine he is over there, or over there. I have him paged on a public address system, over and over again. The sense of anguish increases, I need him, and his presence is always elusive.

6

Today was my toughest day to date: four activities, beginning with an interview at a radio station, then the Boston Theological Seminary reading—Jeanne picked me up there and we headed straight for the University of Massachusetts—then a quick dinner and off to the Boston College (a Jesuit school) reading. I was wiped out by the end of the day, barely able to make it through the last cheerful "informal" commentary.

My friend Jeanne Gallo, a Sister of Notre Dame in Boston, next to a picture of herself when she used to wear the habit.

7

I'm at Jack Levine's and I'm finally feeling good. The readings are hard because they cause me pain now, reading these poems, these pieces of lives and deaths, over and over again. And I put my whole self into it, exert myself each time, and just try to get through it. And again. And again. And so, between reading and reading I am thinking about that, waiting for it, waiting to get through it, or waiting (during the reading itself) for it to be over. I both love and hate it. I love giving what I'm giving. And I hate thinking I'm going to fuck it up, the blank spots coming, coming over me, overtaking my sight and my sound. Sometimes I hate reliving what the poems mean. The meaning seems to translate into the white spots, and when they happen—several times to-day—I feel that I'm fighting with what they're made of, actually fighting them, until it all goes away and the printed page and the lights and the people and the place and the actual physical time comes through again, comes and takes back its own shape, out of the whiteness.

8

When I got here I was suddenly faced with the prospect of all these reporters: radio shows, news interviews. And I refused to do them (learning to say no), all except for one. Carol thought the *Inquirer* interview was important—for them, mostly—so I said o.k. I'd do that one. The woman came to Carol's house. She seemed nice enough. But the first thing she did was take a piece of computer printout from her purse and put it on the table. "Look at this," she said. "I fed the name Margaret Randall into the computer down at the paper, and this is the only thing they could come up with for me..."

The sheet started out with "Requested -05 04/05 170611 Database name -N78, User Name -Inq. User Account -Beth, Query -'Margaret Randall'." It turned out to be a story published January 8, 1979 by a guy named Jimmy Breslin. "Author: Rich-Aregood. Section: Editorial. Daily News. Page 21. Title: 26 MINUTES FROM MIAMI." It's a very "cute" story about flying to Cuba and meeting some crazy old CP-type woman on the plane and the conversation that ensues, which the author of the story presents as absolutely indicative of "what Cuba is like." There is the line: "On the plane, the woman across from me introduced herself as Alice Miller. She was in her forties and wore jeans and no makeup..." There is talk of a series of Communist Youth Conferences and other international gatherings where this woman thinks she may have met this reporter before, and she rambles on—again, in as cute a way as the writer can project it all—about her friends in Cuba. At one point she is quoted as saying: "I'm seeing another old friend in Cuba. Margaret Randall. She ripped up her U.S. passport years ago because she did not want to come back to the States. Victor Rabinowitz just got it back for her. In my opinion Margaret Randall is a farout lefty."

Well, I cannot remember ever having met a woman by the name of Alice Miller. I never ripped up my passport, neither years ago, nor more recently. Victor Rabinowitz never got it back for me, either. I sat there reading and re-reading this data-bank information which was supposed to give a reporter on the Philadelphia *Inquirer* background information on who I am. And I must admit it was painful. How much incorrect trivia actually passes for fact, once it gets authenticated by the solidity of a computer? It somehow reminds me of the sensationalist headlines—72-YEAR OLD WOMAN HAS CHILD FATHERED BY 12-YEAR-OLD BOY; WOMAN EATS HERSELF TO DEATH; WOMAN MARRIES CORPSE, etc.—I always notice at checkout stands in grocery stores. You know the stories aren't true, but seeing the headline in black and white gives them a kind of gnawing credibility.

Actually, this reporter seemed to be as amused by the message as I was appalled. She didn't believe a word of it, which is why she'd brought it for me to see. But I wonder how many reporters on the Philadelphia *Inquirer*—or elsewhere—who feed the name Margaret Randall, or others, into a computer, believe what comes out?

9

I have recuperated a part of myself by working in Jack's darkroom much of today. I entered gingerly, everything was unknown (Jack had to mount my film on his reels because they are the plastic kind, different from the stainless steel ones I use). But as I began to understand each of the instruments I began to feel at home, until my whole body changed. I seemed to be standing straighter, holding myself differently, moving into each step of the developing and printing as if it would reveal to me something of what I have seen these past three months. Developed the nine rolls I've taken since Managua: some mother and daughter stuff—Hella, Ruth and Debbie; Jeanne and her mother—the trip Floyce and I made along the back road from Santa Fe to Taos just before I set off on my tour...

In the early afternoon we went bowling. At a real funky place, in the black section of town, shoddy balls, a reset mechanism that shook the whole lane and made a symphony of noises as it resettled itself, a real nice guy behind the counter and a few young kids who came in almost as we were leaving. A real neighborhood place, with high betting listed on the walls. In spite of the lump on my hand (from using balls that don't really fit me, all across this country!) I came back up again, cracking 100 my second game after a very low score on the first. Jack is a natural bowler, like so many with whom I've bowled on this trip, people like Brooke and Marilyn, who don't bowl often, but know how their bodies work.

Yesterday Jack and I were talking about this journal. He is one of the twenty-five or so women and men whom I regularly send it to. Jack asked me whom I write for. For myself (as most journal writers do), or for those with whom I share the pages? I told him I write mostly for them: those eighteen or twenty women and four or five men to whom it travels. They are my closest friends. Family. The journal is a way of communicating with them, as I would if we all lived in the same place, and could speak to each other about what means most to us.

The journal, to me, is communication. I do not share the most intimate part of my being, not those really intense or floundering bits and pieces one shares only with oneself, or with a lover, a daughter or son, one very close sister or brother. No, it is not that kind of a journal, not written in a notebook never far from my side, not "one of a kind." It is an articulation of myself (this is what I am now, here, this is how I feel, what concerns me), where I am (the sharing of the physical place), an attempt to try out certain ideas (many of them only half formed), loves, needs, fears...

10

On the plane leaving all-women's Wells College in the village of Aurora, New York, I was treated to a return to the "modern world." I found myself one of a cozy group of four, the only woman among three very different men. The polite questions began coming one after another: "Are you going to Dayton...? Columbus, maybe? Do you live in Syracuse?" And before I knew it, we were talking.

To my right, a man in his fifties, casually dressed, a kindly face. Almost as soon as we sat down he poked through the selection of magazines lying on the table before us, and voluntarily picked up a *Better Homes and Gardens*, which surprised me. "I always look at this magazine," he said, "and dream." Slowly he fingered pages of elegant homes, interior designs, fine place-settings. "It's a big dream," I responded, not knowing exactly which way to take the thing. Then he went on to tell me that he drives trucks. "Big ones. I work for International Harvester, and I just brought a big one into Pittsburgh. I live near Dayton. Going on home now."

The man directly across from me perked up when he heard the words International Harvester. He began telling us about his father, back on the farm in England. "My father never won a thing in his life," he confided, "until just the other day. Then by golly he won hisself a $60,000 tractor. International Harvester, it was!"

Next to the Englishman (who was selling coffee mugs, and travelling today to show some samples to a prospective client), was a guy in his forties, more the businessman— in dress at least— than the other two. He had a dark blue suit jacket on. And a black briefcase.

The man to my right asked me what I did, and before I thought much about it I told him "I'm a poet." Surprised looks from all three. Then I went for it, and told them I was on tour, reading poetry at universities. The Englishman began talking about reading. "People don't do much of that anymore. TV's taken over," he said. "And video games. Why it used to be you at least played games with the family, monopoly, like that. But now you play with a machine. You don't even play with people."

I agreed that people don't talk enough anymore. And the three of them began discussing the whys and wherefores of that. By that time I was more interested in what each of them would say, and limited my comments to affirmative nods or exclamations of one kind or another. The mysterious businessman diagonally across from me began talking about Galway Kinnel's poetry. "I actually heard some of it by accident," he admitted, "on a TV show."

"You lose your education altogether," said the Englishman. "All I know about now is coffee cups. But I've just had a little girl. My daughter's twenty months old. I believe I'll be educating myself again as she does, and I like that idea." I was warming to the Englishman. He seemed nice. And even more interesting when he began quoting Sartre!

But then it happened. One of them asked me where my home was, and I made the mistake of telling them "Albuquerque, but I just came back to this country, after many years away." "Where?" was the immediate question. "In Central America, most recently," I said. "In Nicaragua."

"I was in Nicaragua in 1949," the truck driver offered. "You know, we told those people back then what was going on. But they wouldn't listen. I was in Guatemala, too, with the Service.

And there were hammers and sickles all over the walls! Even back then! And now look what a mess they've gotten themselves into!" The Englishman said something about Nicaragua being in the papers today. "I guest the CIA's behind the mining of the ports," he said. I neither nodded assent nor denied his statement. I just sat there, being as noncommittal as possible, trying to figure out where the three of them might be coming from (though the truck driver seemed clear enough). Only the guy diagonally across from me said nothing. Looking, as I did, from one to another.

The Englishman mentioned the papers again. And Senator Barry Goldwater's letter. "Those guys are mad as hell," he said. "Reagan's really put his foot into it this time." I wondered which foot he meant. The one you fuck up with when you simply play your cards wrong. Or the one that doesn't belong to you in the first place.

Suddenly the truck driver fairly crushed me as he leaned across my seat to gesticulate through the window on my side: "Look," he said, "down there! See that big building on the right side of the highway? That's International Harvester. And parked over there are the trucks I drive. See them?" We all looked and saw, and made appropriate comments. We were getting ready to land, coming down fast. The businessman said, "Good luck with your poetry." The Englishman said, "The last poetry I read was John Donne. And that was a *long* time ago." I told them all to have a nice day.

11

It's warming up across America. Across North America, the sun is coming out. Floyce says, on the phone, that it's still cold in New Mexico. That the spring winds are blowing, and with them the sand off the desert. I think of the tumbleweed. I wake up each morning surrounded by memories. Whole chunks of life crowd against my skin, asking for acknowledgement or assistance. Bits of day intrude upon the night. Bits of night black out portions of the day. Clouds burst behind my eyes.

A terrible cycle takes place in my body. I have only recently begun to see it as a cycle. Now, perhaps, I am beginning to see and feel it as something not totally automatic, something over which I might take control. I feel my body and say to myself: I am fat. I fit tighter and tighter into the few clothes I have. I breathe with a difficulty I would not encounter, were I thinner. I want to eat less, for reasons of asthma and general health as well as for any aesthetic considerations. And so I vow I will stop eating the bagels, cream cheese, black olives, rich quiches, onion soups, chocolate mousses, with which I have been stuffing myself across this country. But the vow lasts only until the next meal. That is, I am filled with the luxurious contentment of having decided to really curb my eating—until the next opportunity to eat presents itself, and then I invariably do so, greatly.

12

A day not recorded in this journal becomes, for me, a day without a soul. A day lost.

13

In Liz Kennedy's study, in the house she and Bobbi Prebis have lived in since Christmas—books everywhere, a good feeling, clutter, and love. Liz came out earlier than many lesbians in academia, and did so with such courage and principles that her outstanding position at Buffalo managed to survive it all. She, herself, of course, bears intimate scars, among them a bad back. Today she is a full professor, tenured, honored, across the country and in many parts of the world.

I met Liz for the second time at the Berkshire Women's Conference in 1978. She came up to me on that staid Mount Holyoke campus and asked me if I remembered her, the slim young woman who had come to my Mexico City livingroom with her husband in 1961. We immediately became friends again, and she invited me to Buffalo where she organized that city's part of my 1978 tour. By that time she and Bobbi were living together, and I came to love them both.

Bobbi is from a steel family. Her father worked in the mills, her uncles and brothers as well. She has been laid off innumerable times these past years, and has occupied more than eighty different jobs in the industry—to the point where this small, stocky, strong, gentle woman is now considered a pro. Last year, after sixteen months off, she was called back to a dwindling work scene. Steel is on its way out here. The mill that used to hire 20,000 now employs about 3,000. Men on the job forty years are afraid to buy a car; they never know when they're going to get the axe.

14

Language. I remember, in the early days of functioning in Spanish (especially in Mexico, but also, to a certain extent, during those first years in Cuba) I would *think out, think through* a phrase or sentence—or even a group of sentences—before uttering them. That was necessary, or at least helpful, because it was the only way that I might say them out with the ease, intonation, emphasis I wanted. I remember this was particularly true when I was arguing, the speed necessary for prompt rebuttals, not to be overrun because I couldn't come back with my thoughts or arguments fast

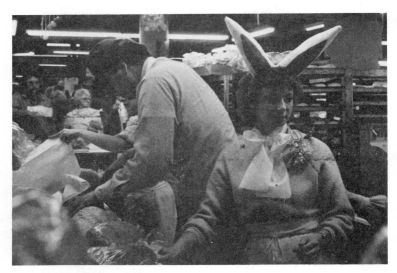

In the big Polish market in Buffalo everyone was dressed up for Easter.

enough. Humor, the punch-line of a joke, those were things that had to be rehearsed.

The most painful part of that history has to do with my verbal relationships with my kids. Kids who had grown up with Spanish as their only language. And a mother whose first tongue was something else, who wrote in English, whose deepest expression was in a language we couldn't share. Having to think out a piece of language before speaking with my children created a distance I never wanted.

On this tour there are times when I design phrases in English, arrange them in my mind before speaking. The comparison with Spanish came to me this morning. As I lay beneath a down sleeping bag, over a pile of covers, blankets, quilts and a sheet, coming to the consciousness that I was reasonably warm, waking up in Buffalo, New York.

15

The anxiety came from *hearing* only Spanish during the Mexican/Cuban/Nicaraguan years. And when I had to speak it (out of my root English, no matter how fluent the Spanish was) the echo wasn't right, the resonance was off. The same, in reverse, is true today: *hearing* English, being surrounded by English, reaching down for the root, which is there (here/within), but now it's the process that's off, or at least, rusty.

16

I dreamed that one or both of my parents called me to "come over and see our new house!" I went. Slowly, in dream tempo, I was taken through an absolutely ugly, very large, somehow unfinished house. It was the antithesis of any home my parents would ever want, need, or have. It was very modern, but that characterless modern, where all is square, spacious, half empty. We walked through room after room, bedrooms that resembled slightly shabby once-elegant hotel rooms, fake fireplaces, small "bars" stuck to walls, vistas of swimming pools and tennis courts out of standardized picture windows. Everything was large and once-elegant, and somehow also dark and tacky.

As I was taken on this tour, I felt I was expected to respond to my parents' obvious excitement at having bought this monstrosity, and I began, dutifully, telling my mother and father that it was "very nice," "very pretty," "fine." All as I searched my memory and current common sense for some reason for this strange event. Suddenly, as we were walking through, my father excused himself. I found him when I opened one of the upstairs hall doors, and came upon a very small, shabby room, the kind of room an old man or woman might live in alone, sadly, in poverty. The room was self-contained: a hot-plate in one corner, bathroom fixtures, a cot in another corner. Because the shower was inside the room and without a curtain everything was wet, covered with glittering droplets of water, like an object that sweats—but it was a cold sweat. Damp and unpleasant. My father had retired to this space; it was clearly what he preferred.

I felt a kind of fear, but I left my father in that strange room and continued walking through the house with my mother. She was showing me room after room. And now I began noticing the unfinished aspects even more: a wall that had not been completed, an unpainted door-frame, a window that had not yet been put in. Once in the dream I returned to the small room where my father was, and found him in his pajamas, sitting before a sweat-beaded TV, and a small boy with him, four or five years old, also in pajamas, also watching TV. When I opened the door of the room, the little boy ran out, and down the hall.

Towards the end of the dream (which seemed slow, and long) I asked my parents how much they had paid for this house. "It must have cost a lot," I said. "Yes," they nodded, "more than a million dollars." "How much more?" I asked (all of this in a kind of monotone). "One million ten thousand," was their droning reply. Suddenly I thought about my own house, the adobe one my father is planning to help me build in the foothills of the Sandia Mountains, next to their own. "I guess this means that there won't be any money for my house," I half-ask half-say, sadly. "I guess not," my mother and father say, in unison. "Unless you want to pay for it yourself." "But I have no money," I say. And they just nod their heads.

17

Liz and I went to her undergraduate cross-cultural women's class, where they had been studing *Doris Tijerino*, and I was going to be their guest for the session. It was an inspiring hour and a half. Liz seats her students in a circle, there were maybe twenty of them, mostly women, and three men, and right away you could tell that the relationship among them was something special. Taking a class from Liz is something special.

Last Tuesday, when Liz came back from the previous session of this class, she mentioned how astounded she had been that several of the class members had found it easier to identify with Nisa (a !Kung bush woman) than with Doris. So we started off this session by reiterating that astonishment, and then I spoke about how I had stopped lecturing, temporarily at least, precisely because I thought you couldn't really get an identification with the Central American people that route, how I had begun reading poetry and oral history precisely in an effort to close the distance. So I was, as well, somewhat shocked that they hadn't been able to identify with Doris through her powerful testimony.

Immediately several of the students took the challenge and went deeper into what they felt. One woman, heavy-set and slightly older that the others, said: "Well, I think it has to do with class. It's hard for me to understand how Doris, being from a monied class, could have developed such a class consciousness. I'm a waitress in my 'other life' and last night I was at the restaurant and the other woman who waitresses with me there literally didn't have enough money for her kids to take to school today. She earned what she needed last night. But if she hadn't of earned it, her kids literally wouldn't have had money to eat with, today at school. And yet that woman thinks of herself as 'middle class.' She's not middle class! No way! Yet most of us white workers think of ourselves as middle class in this country. We have no class consciousness at all. Even about ourselves! So it's hard for us to identify with someone like Doris, who was born into money and yet understood the class situation in Nicaragua."

Another woman said: "For me it wasn't class. For me it was a matter of 'feeling.' I understood everything in the book, all the things that Doris did, everything that happened to her. But I couldn't *feel* what she went through. How *she* felt about it. She describes the torture and all—but wow, what did she *feel*? I never know."

They set me to thinking. And I shared with these students my own ideas about the book. The period in which it was written, Doris' own particular situation—having just found out that Ricardo had been killed, weeks before we began work on the project—the way she always held everything in, seeming a paradigm of calm and control. And I spoke about how she went to pieces after the victory, and had to get help, and how she's finally managing the damage they did to her mind and body. We spoke about the way that people who are fighting often have to postpone their human responses to events and anguish, in order to get through. But how inevitably it takes its toll. *If* the person is lucky, it eventually comes out. Because there are those for whom it never comes out.

18

New York. I am filled, constantly and again, with her magnitude, her maladies and anguish, her immensity in my own life, and her immensity in general. As Anna said yesterday, walking out of a store called Unique: "If you don't find what you're looking for in New York, it doesn't exist." And you start to understand the level of frustration present—from before birth—in people who live in a place like New York and don't have enough of anything. Not only of the commodities they force you to believe you need, but the basics: shelter, food, education, health care. It's a tough place. Strangely, I feel good about Anna being here. I remember what my own experience in this place taught me. It's as if everyone should have a time of it—eventually, I hope, in a less sheltered way than Anna presently has with her grandparents—in order to learn what one needs to know to get through life. Especially a woman.

19

Adapting. From one city to another. One way of life to another. Because cities are that: whole orbs. Orbits. Not static spaces, where all things wait for one to contemplate them, and take them in hand. No, the movement of each space is different. The rhythms are different. The whole space, with—and especially with—its people, is different. Its own. Old friends and faces come up from behind my eyes. From far behind my eyes. The images are accompanied by bits and pieces of my feelings from those times. And the package crashes against what I am now, and how I move. Going up to that, touching it, taking it by the hand, talking to it—and listening—is an exciting experience. But also one which requires a great set-up, a great deal of energy sustained by loving care.

The reflections. New York City.

The people are what make this city, so many, of so many different types and inclinations, doing so many different kinds of things, radically moving in whatever direction they choose (or is chosen for them). Walking from Ninth Avenue and Forty-second Street down to Second and Sixth Street this afternoon, there was a continual life-tape moving before my eyes: young jazzy kids bopping along with enormous radios blaring, or with Walkman headphones securely in place, oblivious, even to the ordinary street sounds. The wild pink and green and blue lacquered locks of the

113

punks, the wonderful dreadlocks of many Blacks. Old men and women of every possible ethnic origin. Mothers or fathers with their young children in carriages and strollers. Disinfected businessmen, comical in their suits and ties. Stiff people. Loose people. Young women dressed—as we did, a quarter of a century ago—in flapper clothes from the thrift shops. Workmen. Drivers. Peddlars. Peddlars selling every conceivable kind of begged borrowed bought or stolen goods. Cops, helping those who ask instructions and then, perhaps, following the prettier of them. Drunks. Women and men doped into their own private worlds. Pimps. Whores. Children—wise and wondrous. Dogs, many with raincoats and elegant collars. People coming to and from work. People in a hurry. People ambling. My camera was always travelling some imagined distance between bag and hand, but I was too loaded down with items of all kinds to ever take it out of its hiding place and use it.

20

There is an article in the Arts and Leisure section of today's *Sunday Times*, which tries to deal with the important and exciting commitment many artists have been making lately *in their art* around issues as troublesome to the establishment as nuclear disarmament and Central America. The piece, by a Michael Brenson, is called "Can Political Passion Inspire Great Art?" The intention is clearly that the reader come to the conclusion that it cannot. "Political passion," once more, separated from any other kind of passion (passion for truth, passion for life, passion in love) as being somehow suspect and susceptible to all kinds of corruption. The "political pamphlet" held up as warning, as if society did not bombard us daily with all manner of pamphlets passing as innocuous advice: TV, advertising, the very use of invention.

Brenson is supremely clever. He moves, early on in his article, to block any possible remembrance of great political art of other times. He says: "Since the road to first-rate art has never been paved with good intentions, or good theory, alone, the first question is what makes for good, or great, political art. Historically, examples of such art are surprisingly rare, testifying to the difficulty of transforming political outrage or themes into work that has anything but the most perfunctory effect. It is a telling paradox that the most enduring political art has probably been made by those who were not primarily political artists. When Goya etched his 'Disasters of War' and in 1814 painted his 'Third of May 1808,' whose theme is the savage reprisals of the occupying French forces to the Spanish resistance, he was more than sixty years old, with a lifetime of art and the broadest experience of people behind him. Picasso, like Goya, was steeped in the history of art and concerned throughout his life with the entire human condition. When he painted 'Guernica,' he was fifty-six, and all that he had lived and painted and thought up to then went into it. 'Guernica' and the 'Third of May' remain such huge moral statements—such strong reminders of the need for a vigilant political conscience—because of the human and artistic wisdom that went into them."

This paragraph deserves a great deal of attention. The skill with which Brenson removes such obviously great artistic statements (so obviously great that they cannot be ignored by an essayist like himself) from their real political context, and the artists who created them from their sustained political commitment, is interesting—and infuriating. Not to mention Picasso's lifelong involvement with a concrete Communist party. It is very much like the dismissal which has characterized the English translations of Cesar Vallejo's poetry: the critic or translator simply takes what he can understand and deal with (and wishes for his own political reasons to project), discarding the rest, leaving his audience with a fragmented window on the artist and his art. Vallejo as Catholic mystic, but never Vallejo as Communist or, more interestingly, as *both*.

Brenson goes on to massacre the agitprop tradition and says, among other things: "The work of George Grosz and, to a much greater degree, Otto Dix and Max Beckmann, has aged well because of its independence and the artistic intelligence behind it." Automatically "artistic intelligence" is inextricably linked to "independence," and of course we all know that one cannot maintain one's independence in allegiance with any cause—except those the establishment informs us are worthy of our alignment, safe. Artists of the stature of a Kathe Kollwitz, of course, are mentioned nowhere in this piece. And Brenson's dealing with Social Realism remains on the surface of any attempt to say anything important about that school, so complex and surely as wrought with negative as with positive elements.

"The 1930s also produced American Social Realism," he tells us, "which was, in part, a response to the oppressive political and social conditions of the depression. Artists such as Ben Shahn, Raphael Soyer and Jack Levine wanted their work to be an indictment of society and an instrument of social change. They tended not to preach but to try to use their realistic technique to convince the public of violence or power and the plight of the common man. Social Realists considered realism the language of hard truth, and with it produced a body of modest but admirable work. However, a very similar style was used for very different purposes in Soviet Social Realism, which followed in the wake of agitprop, but which remains the epitome of art serving a monolithic state ideology."

The most interesting thing here, is Brenson's inability to see Soviet artists as product and part of their society—just as their North American counterparts. "Ben Shahn, Raphael Soyer and Jack Levine wanted their work to be an indictment of society and an instrument of social change." "Soviet Realism...remains the epitome of art serving a monolithic ideology." There is ignorance of the central truths of both these movements.

Someone like Brenson can authenticate and even condone Shahn's work because what it calls up in its viewers is still safely beyond our reach. The Russian Revolution's society-deep attempt to make that "better life" of which the American Social Realists could only dream, is not part of this analysis. Soviet failures, as always, rise out of proportion to their gains. Nowhere is it acknowledged that both eras, in both nations, produced bad and good art, and that where the artistic statement succeeds it does so because of the artist's ability to understand and integrate his/her sociopolitical context with his/her particular aesthetic magic.

Brenson takes particular pains to deal with feminism as a threat. "A major impetus for political art now is feminism," he writes. "Feminist artists tend to reject existing political and artistic systems and, as a result, to produce work in alternative artistic media [sic]. Perhaps the most prominent feminist art depends heavily upon photographs and words. In part in an attempt to expose what is seen as this culture's ideological brainwashing through advertisements and the popular media; in part to create works that are not beautiful and therefore less capable of being 'co-opted' into the art-world gallery, museum and commercial system. One of the assumptions in the commercial-art based work of Erika Rothenberg and Barbara Kruger is that what goes on in advertising is as instrumental to the repression of women and to the national tolerance for such events, let's say, as the invasion of Grenada or the mining of Nicaraguan ports."

These "feminist artists," according to Brenson, *make assumptions* about women's repression and "such events" as the invasion of Grenada or the mining of Nicaraguan ports! Tell me, please, what assumptions can we make about those historical facts, separate from every breath we take, every moment of every day, the way we see and feel and understand everything? As women, the understanding must become recognition, commitment, a statement which may be artistic (we are artists) but which moves in a space much broader than any of these categories. But it would be too much to expect a Brenson to understand that.

When he deals with current political events, he really moves into troubled waters. "The claim of one prominent political artist, Hans Haacke, that 'so-called political art is scrutinized much more carefully' and that it is much harder for political artists to 'get away' with mediocre works is patently unjustified," he says. "There is no better evidence of this than the high visibility of his own factual commentaries. His 'Isolation Box,' displayed at the graduate center of the City of New York Mall as part of Artists Call, is an eight-by-eight-by-eight-foot wooden box with a sign on it saying: 'isolation box as used by U.S. troops at Point Salinas Prison Camp in Grenada.' This kind of simplistic piece tells us far less about troubled United States Caribbean waters than the searching nonpolitical paintings by Eric Fischl which use *a black-white tension in the Caribbean as a starting point for an exploration of turbulent emotional and sexual currents.*" (My italics.) As Susan so aptly pointed out, when we began fuming about this article this morning, people like Bob Morris—and scores of other minimal artists—make boxes all the time. As long as they don't have embarrassing or accusative signs on them, they can be safely looked upon as making it or not in the arena of "real" art.

The crux of Brenson's statement is the point he reaffirms towards the end of his piece: "The best political art has always been art first and politics second." Of course. Again, we must somehow avoid recognition that in the best art the elements work as a whole, the divisions between so-called form and so-called content are broken down, must be broken down for a work to even *be* art. The divisions, the divisions always and forever. The best insurance that we will continue to fragment ourselves, our sensibility, our knowledge. Brenson ends his piece with a truism which could seem to belie all his arguments: "It is only from a synthesis of immediate observation, craft and the lessons of time—from the testing of political facts against one's own experience—that convincing and forceful political art can emerge." But isn't that the only way convincing and forceful *art* can emerge, political or not? Again, he must maintain the divisions. Especially where the "overtly political" is concerned.

Elaine de Kooning and I had lunch, and it seemed like the twenty years had been twenty minutes. Then she took me to her gallery and showed me what she's painting now.

21

I caught a cab, and right off the driver asked me: "What are you, a musician?" "No," I said, "I'm not." "Well, what are you then?"

"I'm a poet," I said, wondering what he'd make of that. "You are! Well, that's really great! You make your living at it or is it just something you do in your spare time?" And so we began to talk about being a poet, what that means, and how one more or less does make a living from related jobs, although never really *as a poet*, how books of poetry aren't exactly on the best-seller list or anything like that . . . the conversation was getting more and more interesting.

Suddenly, heading down Fifth Avenue, he turned around and asked me: "Ya wanna hear a poem? If you say yes, you have to promise to criticize it. But I mean with all your honesty and esteem" (his words). I promised, he kept driving, and he recited: first one poem, then another. They were rhymed poems, song-like in quality, and he told me a friend of his was putting a couple of them to music. The one line I remember as I write this: "there was thunder in the sky/when we said our last goodbye."

He reeled off one, and I told him some of the things I liked and didn't like about it. Then another. By the time we got downtown he'd recited four of them. He told me he always asks people who get into his cab if they're musicians. "It's my opener," he said. "Then they can tell me they aren't, and they can tell me what they do! I've been driving in New York for thirty years," he said, "and you're the first poet I've ever had in my cab! It's made my day!"

We'd pulled up in front of the Marxist School by that time, and I was reaching in my purse for the $4.80 on the meter. But he was asking me where he could buy my books, and I realized he was serious. So I reached in my other bag first and brought out a copy of *A Poetry of Resistance*, which I explained and then gave to him. He was so pleased he said, again, that I'd made his day. And he refused to take my money! I rode up in the elevator, amazed and delighted.

22

It occurs to me that never in my life have I had to turn such intense and complete concentration on such diverse parts of my life, and in such quick succession. I am giving my all at a reading, hugging my wits about me to make a jumble of public transportation and get somewhere in record time, going into

Colleen's darkroom to print up a storm, making myself all eye looking through the camera lens in Washington Square Park, feeling the intense closeness of friends who are extraordinarily dear to me, being with Anna who is so charged with joy and also with pain, pulling up pieces of my life coherently—as I did this morning in the first part of the interview Bell is doing with me—worrying about my future in this country. Bowling today—this afternoon, with a friend, a wonderful woman named M.J.—was good, finally there was physical release. I bowled eight games in succession, with a high of 124 and an average of 102.

May

1

Anna has her own mind and life. She wants to stay in New York. It isn't really, or even mainly, the glitter of the big city. I sense it has more to do with making roots. Her desperate need to establish them—somewhere. "Why do you say you are coming home?" she asked me the other night, in front of some people we were with. "Because this is my country," I told her. "I was born here. And this is where my roots are, no matter how many wonderful, valuable years I spent in Latin America. No matter how much that Latin American time is also in me." "Then is Mexico my home?" she asked. "Well, I guess not," I said. "You were born there, but you only spent your first three months in that country. I should be surprised if you thought of Mexico as home. Perhaps you think of Cuba as home . . ." I added, tentatively, interested in her response. "No," she said, quickly. "I don't think of Cuba as home. Or Nicaragua. Or the United States. I don't have a home."

That says a lot. For many reasons Anna feels she has no real root space. And she is searching for that, as she searches for herself. I respect that search immensely. And can only sense how difficult it must be for a woman at fifteen.

2

On our way back into the city, I persuaded Bell to drive into Scarsdale. Once more—this happened to me in 1961 as well—I was overwhelmed by the estates, the huge houses, the sloping grounds. The seemingly little-changed village. The wealth. We asked one after another of those we saw along the roads—few people out of doors—where the Edgewood Grade School or Roosevelt Place were. For a while, no one knew. Then finally we found a man who was able to give us pretty concrete directions. We found the names of presidents on street signs. But, again, we were lost. Finally, a young man offered to get into Bell's car and show us. And he did just that, leaving us a couple of blocks from my old school. And then, there was little Roosevelt Place, and house number seven: old grey stucco, green trim, the familiar fire hydrant by the front curb (only now it is painted yellow and red instead of the grey and red I remember). I used to sit for hours astride that hydrant. It felt good.

As we drove up, a woman was coming out of a car recently pulled into the driveway. I jumped from our own car before she could disappear into the house. "Pardon me," I said. "I lived in this house almost forty years ago. Can I take a picture of it?" She looked at me suspiciously. But said yes. And then quickly vanished behind the front door, closing it securely behind her, before I could go on with my questions.

A very young girl was playing by the side of the house. But she, too, shied away from any advances I might have made. I photographed the front of the house, the hydrant, the school. I saw the garage in back, and was reminded of the many times birds flying south came up against the door at night, falling dead before it, and the serious funerals we neighborhood kids held, burying them in cigar boxes with quartz tombstones.

Over the back hill, I knew, was the old Briggs' house. I strained to get a glimpse of the hill. It seemed so much smaller than my memory of it. To the left, if you faced our house, was the red brick where the Dohertys lived. To the right the white clapboard belonging to the Miltners. The playground out back of the Edge-wood Grade School brought up memories of the time Miss Ben-field made me get up in front of everyone during recess and sing out loud. I wet my pants and ran home. Towards the village, a sign pointing to Saxon Woods called up the time I got lost there. I wish the woman now living at 7 Roosevelt Place had been nicer. I would have loved going inside.

The house where I grew up in Scarsdale. And the fire hydrant where I'd sit, rocking back and forth and watching the people go by.

3

The experience at the International Center for Photography (ICP): again another world. A world I do not know and have no idea how to inhabit. Do I wish to inhabit it? Yes, I admit I do. But on my own terms. Jack had arranged for me to meet with one of the people there, to show her my pictures. When I arrived—five minutes early—she wasn't in. I went up to the third floor to wait, and a secretary told me to make myself at home in a tiny library through the next door. There was an elderly librarian, floor to ceiling books and magazines, and two people studying at a small table. I felt that I didn't fit anywhere. Surrounded by books I would love to pour over in calm and quiet, I read nothing. I simply waited.

When twenty minutes had gone by I returned to the first office, to ask if the woman had been heard from. Just as the secretary was telling me she hadn't, the elevator door opened and she emerged. "You must be Margaret," she said. "There's a library through that door; wait five minutes and I'll be with you." The library again. Another ten minutes. And she came.

We sat down, finally, on plastic chairs that seemed too fragile for a person's weight. I placed my portfolio before her, but she seemed more interested in talking first. "Albuquerque...? Oh, I have a good friend there...use my name..." She seemed a friendly person, a woman with feminist consciousness. She is, in fact, teaching a course in women's photography (for the first time) beginning this week. But she also repeatedly took her attention from my visit, whenever something or someone more to her interest appeared.

When she went through my pictures, I could read almost nothing on her face. I waited for her to say something. I showed her the Nicaraguan images. Then a few from Cuba. I wasn't sure if she wanted to keep looking or if she would be interested in several I had from Canada as well. At one point she asked if I had ever studied photography. "No," I said. "Would you like to?" she asked. "Well, yes...in a way," I said.

Her verdict on my work: the Nicaraguan and Cuban pictures are "full and interesting" but "it seems to me you've gone as far as you can go, without some training. The images are what one might expect from the part of the world you've lived in: journalistic, strong, but articulate more for what they are of than for what they say in photographic language." She liked the Canadian pictures better: "I see what you're looking for more," she said about those. If I was coming to New York City again sometime I should let her know. "We can probably use you in a seminar, or to speak about making pictures where you've been working..."

I felt that I was regaining a hold on the real world when I emerged into the crisp air of Fifth Avenue and Ninety-fourth Street. The park. The people. Susan is right when she says that it's a political matter; anything with social content is photojournalism, and a one-person show must necessarily be "something else."

124

I'm unsure how much I accepted what the ICP woman said out of a lack of confidence—for I do believe in what I'm trying to do, and no amount of knowledgeable patter can shake that—and how much is simple culture shock. But I didn't feel the trip to ICP was a waste, not really.

4

Last night's affair was jubilant, electric, warm, profound and long-lasting! Some of the *Ikon* women came over early, and with Colleen hauled eight large bundles of magazines, and my books and post cards, over to the school where they set up the tables. Everything was organized perfectly. Nothing left to chance. The women at the door were great. The admission price was $4 more if/less if, and there were undoubtedly lots of "less if" people who came. But everyone got a small white card to fill out, to be put on the *Ikon* and Madre group mailing lists.

Susan and I went around seven. By that time a line was forming outside the front door. I don't know how many people eventually came. Susan says the auditorium holds 450. It wasn't packed, but there weren't many seats left empty.

I, who have had so much trouble over the past few years remembering the names and even the faces of the people I know, suddenly found myself looking into the eyes of friends from twenty-three years ago, friends from six years ago, people who have physically changed quite radically—but whose souls are the same. And saying to them: Hello, Rhoda...Hello, Marilyn... Hello, Grace...Hello, Ruth...Hello, hello...!

Hettie Jones was there, and Clare Coss and Marty Fleisher and Paul Lauter and Jane Creighton and Zoe Anglesey. (I had met Zoe up in New Hampshire; during the reading I spoke about her having sent me the anonymous Guatemalan poem, and I didn't even see her tear-streaked face until after the reading was over.) Kathy Engels was in charge of the Madre part of the evening. Perhaps eighty-five percent were women, but there were many men as well: old friends, poets, movement people, and public. Anna had called from Riverdale an hour or so before we left the house. She wanted to come but hadn't been able to find anyone to give her a ride back home when it was over, and she didn't want

125

to ride the subway alone, out to Riverdale, that late at night. I realized how very much I wanted her to be there and offered her money to go home in a cab. And she arrived just before it started, radiant and wonderful in her Palestinian scarf.

Susan took charge of the event with her usual warmth and wit. She was nervous about every detail, had been for days, but she was extraordinary. First there was a short but moving contribution by Rosa Escobar, member of Madre's executive board, an older woman from the Bronx. Rosa is an organizer, a community worker and leader, Puerto Rican, a woman who has struggled with the Bronx gangs and believes that "every child saved is a future liberation fighter!" She spoke for a few minutes, and then recited a poem, in true Puerto Rican recitative tradition. Then Susan introduced me.

For the first time in my life it was hard to begin. I looked out from the lectern, and couldn't see anyone. The lights were on me, not them. So I asked for the house lights, they went on, and the reading began. I don't think I've ever read so well, with such love and feeling, with such knowledge of the connections. Again, I made certain changes, spontaneous and immediate, as I went along. Everything called for by the moment. This has happened to a certain extent, all through this tour—and others. But never like last night. Last night it was perfect.

I read the words Haydee had spoken to a group of Cuban students in 1967, then Nancy Morejon's "Black Woman." Then I read the poem by the anonymous North American woman living in Guatemala.* And followed it by Dionne Brand's poem about Grenada. Then I read several of my own poems: "March 6, 1982 (for Anna)," "Yes, Tony," "Before the Homecoming," and "Star 80." And I ended with two selections from *Sandino's Daughters*: Carmen's story, and some of the testimony from Dora Maria's interview. There was a standing ovation.

After a fifteen minute break, in which people could loosen their bodies, go out into the front lobby, look at the stuff on the literature tables, and share a bit, almost the entire crowd came back

---

*Across Canada and the United States I read a poem sent by a friend and shared simply as "anonymous, a poem written by a North American woman living and working in Guatemala." More recently, in Milwaukee, I learned that this poem I have for so long read as "anonymous" was written by Jan Carroll and it is called "How Hard it is to Sing."

into the auditorium to listen to, and move with, the best musicians I've heard in a long time. Casselberry and Dupree are two black lesbian women, strong, filled with life, talented beyond imagination, singing out of a place that is rooted in New York, in California, in Africa, in the connections so many are making, finally, today. They've been together fifteen years, someone said—god knows why they aren't storming the country's concert halls by now—or more accurately, we do know why that's not happening. They sing an amazing combination and variety of music: gospel, love songs, history, outrageous lyrics and music of a versatility hard to describe.

And they addressed themselves to some of what I had done, certain of the poems, specific pieces, making connections all the time, tying the thing together. I sometimes feel that what I do—although I know it moves people, makes them think and feel, gives them a gift—is too hard. Too painful. Too difficult for people to assimilate who haven't lived something of what I am describing in the work. Casselberry and Dupree took that reality, and without obliterating a single work—and basically without changing their own program—brought people *up!* Women were moving and standing in the auditoriuim, so in touch were they with what was being sung.

Later, we were elated and exhausted at the same time. Helping the sound man haul an untold number of heavy pieces of equipment, saying goodbye to our friends, packing up the unsold books and cards. None of us could just go to sleep, so we brought all the bags and boxes to Susan's, left everything as is, and went out to get something to eat. It was midnight then. We were Susan, Colleen, M.J. Sullivan, Clare Coss and myself.

5

I saw Hettie Jones at a party that Susan and other women gave for me last night at Joselie's. There were about thirty people there, and dozens of good conversations, at the end of a very heavy day. But the one that moved me most was with tiny magnificent Hettie—a woman I've known for twenty-five years at least, and never really known at all.

Hettie was married to LeRoi Jones in the '60s and late '50s, when

I was in New York City. We did little more than pass one another in the bars and streets of those years. We were—as were all the women in our circles—pushed to a position of "groupie" among the intense Black Mountain or Deep Image male poets of the era. My way of eventually rejecting that status—which I didn't even understand, of course, at the time—was by leaving. Hettie's way of rejecting it was by staying, plodding determinedly through her life, raising her kids, learning herself and others. Perhaps the more courageous of the two ways.

LeRoi's recent best-selling autobiography ignores her completely. Last night we spoke of the years during which their children saw their father damning all whites on TV. And about how a sustained relationship with Roi's family helped those kids never lose their center, their blackness, their identity.

Hettie is a poet, and only now, with those years behind her, and with the strong lessons she's reaped from them (*and* her children grown and off), is she able to write her own work. She is working on a book about those times, and it will be a deeper, more compassionate, and more real, more alive testimony than his. Talking long and hard with Hettie was a wonderful experience for me. It helped put a lot in place, in a matter of minutes.

6

Yesterday Kathy Boudin was sentenced to twenty years to life after a terribly drawn-out two years of pretrial anguish and a hard bargain struck between the defense and the prosecution. Ruth Hubbard, Debbie, Brooke and many others were in town for the sentencing, and in the later afternoon Ruth picked me up and we went over to Jean and Leonard Boudin's for an hour or so—I wanted to give them a hug in this painful time. And spend a bit more time with Ruth, who has become such a fine friend. Leonard wasn't there, but Jean gave me her book of poems (some quite good ones) and her brave and wonderful face: talk of raincoats, her sharp wit. She is admirable in the dignity and humanness she projects through this whole ordeal with her daughter. On TV we watched what the press wanted to record of what these people had been through earlier in the day. Excerpts from Kathy's and

Leonard's statements. Some attention to the families of the Brinks robbery deaths.

Weather politics has, for many years, seemed distant and uprooted to me, but I feel deeply for Kathy Boudin as a woman who fought relentlessly for the best ideals and who, even and especially through this long night of punishment, has never once betrayed her ideas. About how many can that be said? She will not be even eligible for parole until 2001—at the age of fifty-eight.

7

The situation in Nicaragua is very bad. Spoke briefly with Michael Ratner, who just came back, and also read a long letter from Karen. Michael brought me the letter, as well as the first copies of the Nicaraguan edition of my book on Christians in the revolution. Karen says war ships with 30,000 U.S. soldiers are "playing" off the coasts of the country. The U.S. Army is already securing 50,000 hospital beds in health centers across the U.S.— for casualties—as well as cemetery space! Sandinistas are dying in increasing numbers, Karen says more in the past six weeks than in the entire previous year.

8

Sometimes I walk in New York City, today, yesterday, these past two weeks, and suddenly I hear a siren. It gets louder. It's an ambulance, or a fire truck, or one or more police cars. And as it comes closer, is almost upon me or passes by, it sends a terrible chill through my body. I have wondered why the sirens in this city disturb me so. They tell me there has been an accident, someone is sick or dying, there is a fire somewhere. (Or, as Susan said when we spoke of this today, maybe it's just a cop who wants to get somewhere fast. She has seen them use their sirens and stop and buy a paper, or a sandwich.) But I hear them and am immediately transplanted to Managua, to Nicaragua, where the war *is* beginning. I cannot remember hearing sirens in Nicaragua. But when I hear them in New York it pulls me back, fast.

9

My last day in New York.

I went out in the morning and walked all over the lower east side. My old places. Making pictures. A strange building near the corner of Houston and Lafayette, with a huge gold-leaf figure of a paunchy little man holding what looks to be a mirror in his hand. Then over to the park. And several hours there, making pictures of people: women, kids, joggers, parents with their kids, crazies. People in New York are everything.

On Houston Street, in lower Manhattan, a fat little man bathed in gold wears a top hat and holds a mirror in his hand, high on the corner of a building.

10

I want to tell you how I feel about the images returning. I want to share this harsh discovery: things were bad—and now I know how bad they were because things are becoming better. I wasn't fully aware, before, of how irritated I would become when I would share with people my fears at the white spots, the experience of meeting people I knew and not remembering their names, and then not remembering their faces, or only vaguely. People were always saying "That happens to me too," or "Don't worry, that happens to everyone." And it was always well meant, aspiring to comfort. But it did not comfort me, and although it was rarely patronizing, I did not believe it. I wanted to respond with "You don't know. You may have experienced something similar, something that reminds you of this. Or you may simply be trying to make me believe it isn't serious. But it is." Then that kind of a response always seemed too pretentious, especially with friends. Did I really know that what they thought it was was not what it was? Yes, I did.

And I got through it as I have learned to get through things: day by day, a bit at a time, making sure I remembered the reading I was to give that day, what I was going to do, why I was going to do it, and then doing it. And I combined will, aminophyllin, the strength of others, love, desire, and anything else I could find to pull me through. And if the white spots came I would fight my way through them. And that's exactly what it felt like every time: a battle. And if I didn't recognize people I would laugh and make some kind of general comment, until a context had been created right there in the present. And I could find my place in that context, move in it, respond to *it*. Something close enough to be safe. Present enough to be safe.

Now that it is receding, it is a physical joy. One I can touch with my fingers, with my eyes. And the very distance I have from it now gives stature and credence to the experience (for there is the tendency, when surrounded by those who deny in order to comfort, to deny oneself, to say "that's true . . . it *isn't* really as bad as I was making it out to be . . . it's all in the imagination." As if the imagination were not real!) Regaining memory, a certain ability to link ideas with form, ways in and out, the messages of the mind, this process now situates the confusion of the previous state. It gives it another, more ample, dimension. And it engenders a tremendous rush of emotion about the future: there will, somehow, be time to work, space to work, peace in which to work. The work will be done.

11

I want to remember all of it. Every piece, every sound, every sight, the pain, the depth and years. And sometimes, to move through this space and time—the United States, now—I must forget everything. All of it. The places, the sounds, the sights, the pain. Forget in order to remember. To be here first, and then to be able to remember.

Strangely, this all came together this afternoon when Floyce and I—after an erratic day being fitted for and buying bowling balls (I looked at an eleven-pounder that was a strange purple and said, "I believe in magic; this one's mine!") and my going through a very thorough physical exam for my immigration hearing— decided to escape to a movie. There wasn't much playing. In fact, there was only one film in town that we could even consider see- ing: *Greystoke* (the Tarzan story).

But as I emerged from the theatre, I realized the tears were hurting to free themselves from my eyes. In spite of the bad ending and stereotypic bungling, I had identified more than I could have imagined with the trauma of those two worlds. The gulf between what is taking place (what is being built, what is being fought for) in Central America, and what one must fight for here to stay clear, avoid the suffocation of bitterness or pessimism (yes, Karen, it is a struggle)—that gulf widened and closed and widened and closed like the movement of a giant tide. I felt inundated by it all. (Phrases from Reagan's speech last night were battering my eardrums—every sentence was a well-modulated, apparently sensible plea for death, to combat "the spread of communism in Central America.") Images of light and darkness. Images of holding on.

I remember the births I have handled and seen. The pelvic bones separating and coming together, separating and coming together, separating again and coming together again but always just a little less together, just a little more apart, until the head, that wet mass of black becomes a circle and a larger circle making its way down and out. Those pelvic bones: they separate and close. Retreat and advance. It is the only argument against the cyclical interpretation of history, against those who say "Yes, but the gains are lost. The movement was enormous. And look what we have now: conservatism again." True. But it is not everything. For someone like me, who has been away for almost a quarter of a century, the strength of the women's movement (the impelling creativity of feminism), Third World peoples in this country, young people so much more in touch with their feelings and needs than we ever were—all that sings to me, overshadowing money machines and cyclical conservatism and trivia made important (or imposing). Just a little more open with each thrust.

12

"Take off your shoes," the woman with the German accent said. She indicated the doctor's scale and I stood on it. All the while she was talking about her own experience. "I came over from Germany," she told me, "thirty-five years ago. And I went through the same thing you're going through now. Citizenship. Been working for him," she pointed in the direction of the doctor I had yet to see, "for twenty-seven." She smiled. "Five-foot-four!" I had thought maybe I hadn't heard right. Or maybe it was her accent. "I'm five-foot-five-and-a-half," I offered, smiling. "At least I've always been five-foot-five-and-a-half." "Well," said the woman, writing down my height and weight and preparing to take other vital statistics, "you're not anymore. You're five-foot-four now. I used to be taller too. Happens to all of us. See, you can feel where I have the metal rod..." (for I had climbed back onto the scale in a hurry, hoping to retrieve my lost inch and a half). "I want my inch and a half back," I said, with as much confidence as I could muster. "At least an inch..." (I felt like I was bargaining for a piece of pottery in a Mexican market.) But the doctor's assistant was adamant. "Five-four," she repeated, and closed the book. On this return to the United States, I had somehow gotten shorter.

13

Today's horoscope in the good old Albuquerque *Journal* announced: "Sagittarius (Nov. 22 to Dec. 21): A wonderful day for making investments, buying property or changing your residence. A job interview will go well." And, indeed, at two this afternoon I had the interview with a five-member committee from the UNM Women Studies Program that was considering my application to teach the Third World Women course.

While I was waiting to be called into the interview, and I sat in the small women studies library thumbing through a magazine, the department secretary came in to talk. Before long I understood that she was trying to put me at ease, and at the same time signal to me some of the questions she thought they might ask. It was an unexpected and moving gesture. When one of the committee members came for me and we walked along the hallway to the room at the end where the interview would take place, I felt like Susan Hayward walking to her date with the electric chair in an old movie called, I think, *I Don't Want to Die!* (Or maybe it was *I Want to Live!*) As we passed the open door of the secretary's office she shaped the words "good luck" silently; I had the feeling she wanted me to get the job.

Orange and Blue

> *"something that remains in my body after thought has gone to sleep."*
> —Anya Achtenberg

Overwhelming sirens and imminent planes
throw me back to where sirens
are smaller, older, wind.
Only their echo.
Here New York streets and Albuquerque skies
torn by this shrieking wail
signal nothing more
than a one-car crash
or the temporary use of an alternate memory.

On the tender side of my own memory
silence as well as sound
conjure death in large numbers.
And those numbers lacerate our years
twisting and crushing them in shared wounds.

If your body turns
or you light a fire in the middle of the street
you will lose control.
If sound is allowed to grow behind your eyes
you will be immobilized by its heat.

134

14

Seattle. The great northwest. Between where I sit at a lovely oak table and the dense shades of green, trees sloping down to the immient shore of Lake Washington, is only a large clear window. Plate glass. Floyce left me at the Albuquerque airport; Kuaya and Dale greeted me at the Seattle airport—with flowers in their hands. And we were off to this small paradise, the home of a friend of Red and Black, the bookstore that invited me here. The friend would be away for the weekend, and loaned his house. It's a cottage, tiny, elegant, spotless, hospitable, loaded with fresh food and wine, remnants of his life (a stethoscope on the table, a Harvard medical school magazine on a chair). And dear Stan sitting in his little red car, smiling and waiting as we drove up.

The idea that creation (invention) comes out of forgetting. Stan and I talked about this. I was reminded of Elaine's claim that creativity is born in the mistake: "...when the computer makes a mistake," she said. And Stan: "When the computer forgets..." There is a connection, I'm sure, with Floyce's insistence that I must explore the white spots—not *why* they come, but *where I go in them*, what they are. When I forgot the names and even the faces, was it so I could remember to live, to continue? To find

Stan Persky

135

(create and hold) a present context? And now that I am beginning once again to remember the names, the faces, what will be retained and projected into the future?

15

A very precious aloneness before the reading last night. That, too, is something the Red and Black crew know how to offer. After interviews, bowling, adequate food and all kinds of other amenities, I had several hours to write, think, be with myself immersed in this idyllic setting: the movement of water (which is with me now again, as I write this morning) and green. It had finally stopped raining. And a sullen sun emerged. I went off into it.

No white spots. The atmosphere was conducive to deep contact. I read as I wished to, quietly, intensely, speaking to my friends (old ones, and those who would be). I felt better and better and sensed that the 300 or so in the audience were also warming to what I had to give (what so many had to give, through me). Afterwards there was a good question period. Out in the lobby I sat at a round table covered by a rich woven cloth of some Latin American origin, and was handed a purple pen with which to sign my books. A very young woman—she must have been in her early twenties—approached with an older woman who seemed to be urging her on. She waited for others to wander off, and when I was finally alone, she knelt down beside the table and took a deep breath. Then she began to speak:

"I live in San Francisco," she began, "but I came up when I heard you were reading here. I'm from Nicaragua, I was born there, in Corinto, but I've lived here most of my life. My mother left in the early '60s, and she brought me with her. I've grown up with a different story of my country than the one you tell; my mother's distortions came to me every day, in all sorts of ways. She accepted the *Good Housekeeping* vision of this country, and that's what she wanted me to have." (I was looking intently at this young woman's face, especially at her lips and at the skin around them. Her lips moved almost as if she had set them on a course, and left them to do what she had bid them out of great determination.) "When I read *Sandino's Daughters* it changed my life. It was the first evidence of something different, something that spoke to me, out of a history I had never been told. It just felt right. But when I gave it to my mother—just before she died—she flipped through it and then threw it across the room. 'Communist trash!' she told me, because she knew no better. My mother died of alcoholism here in this country; this culture and its visions destroyed her. And now I have this conflict inside, I need to know, I don't know what to do..."

The young woman was not crying. Her face remained as solid as when she had begun to speak. All the passion was inside, intact, in a place so deep I felt it might take weeks to tap. I took her hands—lying on the table-top to steady herself as she knelt—in mine and I told her: "Don't let your situation get the better of you. Don't let it. You're in a unique place, look at it that way. You can be a bridge; you can be what many can't. Go to Nicaragua to visit. Go to your mother's city. See for yourself. Don't be afraid. But you are also of this country. Don't close any doors. Open them. Don't be afraid." It was as if a wave of relief spread across her features for the first time. She began to smile, faintly, from somewhere very far away. *"Hasta luego, entonces..."* she said. *"Hasta luego, hermana,"* I answered.

I Don't Know You...Do I?

Why did you leave, why come?
What are you asking (about yourself)
your eyes, each book
alone and unrepented
(only the holocaust
cloning these shelves)

Sun
bursting along the edge
of such broad glass.
Greens moving. Water.

Why did you leave (rebuke
or question), why
did you open or close your mouth,
extend or take away your hand?

137

Why
are you here, not there,
retrieving scattered cells,
holding a door
slightly away from its frame?

Tighten the pressure
from fingertips to leaden surface.
Look up and see
an explosion of faces and seed.

Why did you leave, why come?
Would an armful of dark
and wild flowers be enough?
Or a sprig of pussy-willow
soft and small?

16

Pieces of my life run to catch up with me. The picture of the mother and daughter standing before the church door (no one knows it's a church door, only me) in San Pedro Norte, Nicaraguan-Honduran border. Is the village still intact? And the people? These particular people, this woman and her daughter, pride lighting the mother's eyes, total self-knowledge occupying the daughter. I want to get on with my pictures of mothers and daughters. I need my darkroom. I want the time and the space between now and the having of that, to collapse and disappear. The people here in Eugene, Oregon, have produced a lovely poster for my reading. On it is this picture of the mother and daughter.

17

I touch day in another strange bed, and sit upright. "I want to know more about every woman and man whose eyes I hold," I say, as I flip on the bedside light. "I want to know them, before it's too late." In the nearby bathroom, a hot shower is strong and comforting. Downstairs I hunt for real coffee, resist the instant, stand my ground. A young seventh grader is finishing his breakfast and preparing to go off to school. A large black dog plods around the room. Tony, a man I met last night when I came in, is engineering a work of art made from bananas, fresh strawberries and cheerios doused with milk in a bowl.

How deep can I scratch, with my tired fingernails, the lives of these friends? How little or great an indentation will my presence make on the ordinary fabric of their living, on the way they walk through whatever it is each must do in his/her skin, heart, house, city, history? Where, right now, is the place where—years from now, or months from now—one of these people will come upon me, and say: "Don't you remember? It was in Eugene..."

18

Home! This machine. The window. A feeling in the world. Only the absence of my children is increasingly painful. Central America. An uncertainty, still, about dates and leaves. But not about eyes. There is a difference in focusing on eyes, bringing my

Mother and daughter in San Pedro Norte, Nicaragua—a small village on the Honduran border. This image was the first in a series of photos of mothers and daughters.

own around and over, saying inside myself: "look," and then
looking. The slow relief, the joy which speads through me, allows
my own eyes to move through the surface of those others. I walk
in. Deep. And I find, on the other side, the world I have been
looking for. Or, at least, its threshold.

19

Flight from San Diego to Albuquerque. On the Phoenix-
Albuquerque lap I sat between two middle-aged women. To my
right, an Hispanic woman, who had visited her son in California.
She lives in Omaha. Spent the entire flight working out "find the
word" puzzles from a magazine which specializes in only those.
To my left: a heavy woman, reddish face but smooth, thin, dyed-
red hair. She seemed grumpy at the beginning of the flight. In any
case, I was in no mood to strike up a conversation. Then, about
halfway along, she suddenly began to say—out loud and to no
one in particular or everyone in general—"It's cheaper and so
much more fun!" I couldn't help but ask, finally, what it was that
was cheaper and so much more fun. "Flying this way," she said.
"Why I used to fly non-stop just about everywhere. But lately I've
taken to making as many stops as I can! It saves money, and it's so
much fun! You get to see all these airports, and the cities from the
air! I'd never seen Albuquerque from the air, you know" (we were
then beginning our descent), "and it's beautiful! Albuquerque is
beautiful, and Phoenix...why I never knew Phoenix was so
large! And Los Angeles...well, Los Angeles is just the biggest
thing I've ever seen, from the air! And the airports. I have an hour
to kill in Albuquerque, and I think the Albuquerque airport is
very very nice. I really do!" I told her I thought that was just
wonderful.

20

The poem stops before the end. Sometimes it stops right up there
in the title, and no matter what I do, how many times I rework
and tear up, there is nothing to be done. The music seems not to
be in my verse these days but in my thought, which is beginning

140

to flow once more. There is an excitement in that, of course. Almost like a child when she begins to pry the world open, make something of its swirls and crevices, bring it towards the hand and eye.

If the eye is blind, the hand feels more. If the hand does not work, the eye encompasses everything. If the ear is deaf or the mouth does not/cannot form words, the eyes and hands have it. Too often all one's faculties are dulled by constantly having to go beyond and beyond, beyond the endurance point. I wonder what it would have been like to have gone too far. For of course I did not. I held steady, somehow, always on the line, until slowly I came back. And so I have the experience of almost, but not the experience of the total going.

I am living in an intense renewal of my body. For most of the past three or four years, perhaps longer, from that last year with Antonio, when things went badly, my body was not alive to me. It is alienation, the alienation of oneself from one's own skin, muscle, shape, all sensory stimulation. In a large sense, at least physically, I did not exist for myself. In fact, there was a kind of warped satisfaction ("make the best of it, always!") in walking always outside the possibility of giving, receiving, feeling. Except for very brief moments, the exploration was about my own life: history, reality, future. But the physical was removed, like a huge hole cut from a piece of cloth. Now, at exactly the time when it seems that I am beginning to go through menopause, I begin to feel everything once more: chafing skin till I get to tissue and tendon, stretching muscle, touching bone—and fire.

21

Memorial Sunday this year has an amazing Unknown Soldier ceremony with Reagan quoting Longfellow and people "coming to terms" with the Vietnam experience. Papers are full of stories of the "bush vets," men who, in order to continue living, must submerge themselves in the wilderness of northern Washington state, who freak at the sound of a car backfiring, and sleep (some of them, at least) on the floor in the corner of a room, surrounded by newspapers, and with a hunting knife beside them.

"I'll know if someone's approaching," one of them told the

perennial reporter, "because I'll hear him treading the paper."
These are the ones who were sent off to do what their country
asked of them, and then came home to a nation divided about
whether they'd done right or wrong. They "did their duty" but
they were not heroes. (The heroes were in Canada, with their own
problems.)

May 28, 1984

A woman comes off a mountain
walking slowly.
She carries a child in one arm
looks out at valleys
and close at the texture
of bark and rock.
Her cloak is green,
a rich dark green, almost black.
Wearing the same cloth, the same heat
another woman walks before her.
She too walks slowly. Her face
is a map, forests and small clearings.
The first woman's eyes hold music, the second
has moss on her fingers.
All the doors to all the world's houses open
one by one.
In each there is another mountain,
another path winding down
another moment in time
when air becomes liquid
and the calling pipes answer those others
calling them forward
until time itself is light.
And all the velvet is green, black,
green moss, startled.

The fact of love
leaps as it inhabits everyone.
I used to believe it unique.
Now I know it possessed by all peoples,
in all places, growing

22

My kids. After a silence, I finally had long letters from Gregory and Anna. Gregory his usual extraordinary self, concerned about the family, putting time and energy into a discussion of problems, people. Anna blooming, in spite of difficulties (which she seems to be channeling, and getting solved). She is exuberant but steady, rejoicing in finding herself, a process of which she is highly conscious. Her class advisor at school called her in and showed her the letter received from her teachers. At the end of this term she will be promoted from the third to the seventh level. She has done that well, and learned English in the process!

June

1

A body-wrenching experience last night. Floyce had been wanting to show me a Kubrick film, *The Shining*, and I had more or less wanted to see it, or at least I had been curious about it. So last night we put the tape on the VHR. I don't like horror films, but I was not predisposed to hating this one. It was described to me as the story of a family caught in the Colorado Rockies over the winter. The husband and father is a writer, he goes crazy, and eventually tries to kill his wife and son.

The initial scenes are beautiful, as the camera pans in from the air and follows a tiny Volkswagen winding up the mountain road through majestic snow-capped peaks. Immediately I was involved. I lay comfortably on the couch, my bare legs stretched out before me. As I watched this film the fear inhabiting my body seemed to open my vulnerability to everything. I knew it was an irrational fear, and yet I couldn't control it. I remember, about three-quarters of the way through, I looked down at my out-stretched feet, crossed and shoeless, and saw them as the feet of someone who was dead. The skin was ivory yellow, the skin of a dead person, with the texture of wax. I remember thinking then: my feet are those of a dead person, and it was as if they projected out of some strange cocoon, projected into the death state, from the rest of my body which was somehow only a proving ground, a preparation.

The film's central male figure, the white middle-class writer who has not however written anything worth mentioning, evoked in me the whole predicament of white male America: the bravado-filled human being trying to mask his impotence. Were I to choose a single word to convey what I felt the film was about, I would choose that word: impotence—a nation's ultimate impotence in the face of international rape, a society's impotence and the resulting impotence of its patriarchal norms, the bottom line of which is woman- and child-abuse.

The storyline has this man take his wife and young son to a great luxury hotel during its impenetrable winter months—when it is closed to the public. He has given up a teaching job, he wants to write, and this is the ideal setting. The job interview and decision are all his, of course. One sees a flashback—or, more accurately, a simultaneous switch—to the mother and son waiting in their apartment, and knows they do not really want to go. The mother is submissive to her husband's decisions, and puts on a good face for the kid. The child, however, is possessed of "shining," a supernatural power which enables him, although only partly at this point in his life, to see into the past, other parts of the present, and the future. He's scared.

Although the husband has sought and taken on the job, when the family gets to the hotel it is the wife who—in spite of her vacuous amazement at the size and grandeur of the place—takes on the various tasks required of him. While she checks the boiler, prepares their meals, operates the telephone switchboard and radio set, he sits at a table in the great hall pecking away at an old typewriter. He will not be disturbed, and one of his first fits of irrational rage appears in response to his wife interrupting to ask if he's hungry. Towards the end it is the wife who, horrified, flips through the box of neat pages he has written and finds, line after line, page after page, in differing graphic arrangements, the same phrase: "Work and no play make Jack a dull boy."

The initial scene sets the tone. The family is driving up the mountain to the hotel and their first day of work. The father is at the wheel, the mother sitting beside him. Both are tired, beginning to yawn. The air is rarefied. The mother comments on it. The father answers briefly. Then the son asks when they are going to arrive. "I'm hungry," he says. The father shows a bit of irritation, controlled irritation, and he responds: "Well, you should have eaten your breakfast." The mother speaks out of a simple and natural desire to respond to the son's needs: "We'll get you something to eat as soon as we get to the hotel." An allusion is made to the Donner family from covered-wagon days, who tried to cross a similar pass, and the father says they had to resort to cannabalism "in order to survive." The image is a strange one: cannibalism = survival. The mother chides the father for speaking of such things in front of the child, but the child says: "It's o.k. I know all about cannibalism. I saw it on TV." Then the father, in a voice which for the first time can be heard as slightly off, turns to his wife and says: "See. It's o.k. He saw it on the TV!"

The woman, a vapid sort of wife at first, starts out with a skin-deep smile that gives way, through the unravelling of the story, to almost constant terror. Her comments at the beginning are always sweet, light, everything will be o.k. She follows. She cares for her son. And in one of the early scenes, after the boy has become unconscious while experiencing one of his visions, she tells the doctor who has come to look at him: "No, he didn't adjust too well to nursery school. He had an accident, and then we didn't send him anymore." What kind of accident? Well, his father came home late one night and found his papers scattered around the room. He'd been drinking and he got angry. It could have happened to anyone. He grabbed the boy and must have exerted just a little too much pressure. It could have happened to anyone. He dislocated his shoulder. "But it turned out for the best," the mother added. "He promised me then he'd never touch another drop. And it's been five months now, and he hasn't." We look at the boy, whose age clearly places him several years beyond nursery school, and we know the effort of the mother to see the promise fulfilled by her husband. For this, too, is what the film is about: battering. The battering of the weak—women, children—in a patriarchal society.

Through the film's plot, the wife changes. She becomes strong, out of sheer need to survive. As her husband shows himself to be a madman, she becomes competent and fearless, cunning and resourceful. And she ends up saving her son's life and her own, her crazy husband running after them with an axe. (Earlier he had killed the Black cook, the only other person in the film possessed of the power of shining, who had returned to the hotel because he feared for the situation there.)

The woman and child escape down the mountain in the snow-mobile brought up by the cook. The Black man has provided the escape, and paid for it with his life. An interesting bit of information came out in a lecture given recently at UNM by a woman involved in the making of *The Shining*. When asked why the Black cook lives in Stephen King's novel but dies in Kubrick's film version, she said: "Well, someone had to die...!" Interesting they should have chosen to kill off the only Black.

For the film is also about those other components of capitalist society: racism and culture rape. We are told the hotel was build on the site of Indian burial mounds, and that the builders had to fight off two attacks during construction. The Indians used this land. The Black man shines. Yet the hotel was built, and rages, at their expense. "This place was visited by the jet set before there was a jet set," one of the managers tells the new caretaker as he shows him around. "Four presidents slept here...and royalty... all the best people." Race, class, and gender come together, then, in a complex statement about the ultimate reaches of a commodity-oriented world.

For I saw the film as an allegory of crazed evil, the evil born of impotence, the impotence born of social distortion. White, middle-class America—aspiring to inhabit the "hotel that was built for the best people." Our hero impotent in his jobless existence (where job equals activity, fulfillment), impotent when confronted by the growth of women (his wife), impotent when confronting his inability to create (write), impotent, even, before his own offspring and when faced with his particular weakness (drink). He even fails at this "task" of murdering his family, fails several times, and after the first failure is forced to promise his imaginary interlocutor—the figure of a past caretaker who had hacked his wife and small daughters to pieces—that he wants nothing more than to consummate that act, and will!

The relationship between the white male American and his wife, child, job, possible strengths, certain weaknesses, is also the relationship between classes, ethnic groups, and nations. The working class (increasingly jobless) oppressed by the bosses. The Blacks and Native Americans oppressed by the whites. Small countries oppressed by big ones. And I came out of the film aching all over, and tears welling up and spilling over. And amazed, hurt, at my own physical reaction. My body ached. My head ached. The nausea got worse. But the fear left me the instant the end credits came on the screen. I was no longer afraid at all, and in fact I couldn't even remember the fear, except as a physical echo. I looked at my feet and the skin seemed once again faintly pink. Living flesh. The fear was something of the past, but the anger, resentment, sadness were still present.

Why make such a film? For whom was it made? I wonder. People, ordinary people, the only ones ultimately capable of doing something real about their predicament, will not, I fear, understand the allegory. To them, or to most of them, it will remain a horror film. The ruling class might understand. It strikes awfully close to home for them. But they are delighted with the status quo and have so much—their lives—invested in it that it would be absurd to imagine they might want to do anything about it. The film seems to be made for an elite which enjoys titillating itself with a destructive reality that it might understand, but also delights in. And so I somehow hated this film. Afterwards, I felt alienated—from my body, from my intellect, and very sad. The sadness continued into sleep. And that, finally, seemed the real allegory: being made immobile. To bring about total alienation. The kind from which you cannot, will not, move. (And how good horror films are at that, in general!)

2

Dream: two nights before the primary elections here, I had a dream about Judy Pratt. It was twenty years into the future, and she had been elected President of the United States. Our first woman president. I had come to visit her at the White House, and we had just finished lunch. Judy looked much as she does now: small, wiry, quick—only her ash blond hair was grey, and she was a bit heavier. We were speaking about poetry. In fact, we were speaking *in* poetry. The president of the future, and the language of the future (for when I imagine speaking in poetry, I am imagining speaking in the very essence of language, from its core meaning, its throat).

3

Yesterday at 2:30 in the afternoon I had my first interview with an Immigration official here in Albuquerque. I had filed papers for permanent resident status—first step towards trying to retrieve my American citizenship—before I left on the trip east. My interview was set for June 7, and between the two reading tours I had the physical, chest x-ray, and so forth. I had everything in order. And—in spite of knowing better—had hoped this would be a routine interview, and I would then have my green card, the end of the first phase in my legal re-entry. Of course it wasn't to be that easy.

Mr. Brown was nice this time around. He wasted no time in telling me that he is an open, straightforward person, and informed me right off that I wouldn't be getting my card that afternoon. "We're concerned about your having lived so long in Cuba," he said, "logically, there will have to be an investigation." Then he asked me ("just for my own interest," he said) "what is it like to live in a place like Cuba?" Under oath he asked the specific questions which related to reasons one may be kept out of the country—had I ever belonged to a Communist party or did I now belong to one? Had I ever or did I now advocate overthrow of the U.S. government through violent means? I had no trouble answering all the questions no.

What Mr. Brown said, in effect, was that one of these days my doorbell would ring and a couple of FBI agents would flash their badges at me (these were his well-chosen words), and that I'd be "asked a few questions." When they complete the investigation, they will either give me residency or not. It seemed to be Cuba they were most concerned about. Mr. Brown even said that the investigation of my time in Nicaragua had already come back and that "everything is fine." "We want to know why you lived for such a long time in Cuba," he reiterated. "And then Nicaragua . . . there's a great deal of Cuban influence there, as well."

I found myself with an intense contained restlessness. A desire to disconnect, see a movie, walk. Floyce and I ended up going bowling, and I did badly every game. I just kept rolling the ball, making a different mistake each time. Ended up with a 97 average in six games. But it wasn't the fact that I was missing the pins that got to me. It was the deadness, the emptiness, and the anger that they could make me feel this way, that I could *allow* them to make me feel this way. As if that in and of itself constitutes a kind of defeat. I wanted to get a grip on the anger. But it kept slipping away from me. I wanted to grab it, hold on to it, use it to knock myself back into shape. But nothing has happened. Nothing has really happened. I may well receive my residency after this investigation. And if I don't, there's a long road of appeal, to fight the thing, which I will not hesitate to travel. I'm tired, but I would travel it. It means too much to me. I'm home.

And if I had it to do all over again, if I had the choice to begin my life again, I would do it all essentially the same. Oh, I wouldn't give up my citizenship. That was a mistake. But I would live where I lived and experience what I experienced, and commit myself to the things to which I have been committed. It is all valuable in my life, and I treasure it deeply. To think of it having been different is like thinking of having a different body, different eyes, different hands.

4

Toys. Up at my parents' the other night, Johnny and Shanti were also there, and Shanti was playing with a new electronic water pistol. Water pistols seem to be the thing here now, among his friends, and he had just bought this one with the help of some money I'd given him for helping to put up flyers for the course I'll be teaching at UNM.

Toys, toys are different from books, playing with them is different from engaging in recreational activities, riding your bike or hiking or some sport or other ways of spending time which seem more ageless somehow. I've long identified toys with kids who are a lot younger than Shanti—I guess because of my Latin American background with my own kids. I remember them being involved with toys, mightily, until the age of eight or nine; then they lost interest.

In Cuba, during the worst years of blockade and shortage, each child was entitled to buy one toy worth more than $3 and two toys worth less—each year. At first these were distributed just before Christmas. Then, when Christmas became a purely religious holiday, observed only by those for whom it had that kind of significance, the same toys could be had in early June, preceding International Children's Day. The distribution was made to all children twelve or under, but I remember my own kids and most others with whom I had contact, lost interest in the whole event before they had reached that age.

And Nicaragua? Mexico? I wonder if this is essentially a class thing, a cultural thing, or what? I know that the whole culture of toys has become very much a part of the total consumer society in this country. The child's electronic water pistol, or a doll that cries, drinks and wets is gradually replaced by the electronic can-opener or the automobile dashboard that receives music tapes, video tapes, and dials your home phone for you. What else can we buy?

I sense that at least in the parts of the Third World in which I have lived, children are fully children to a certain point, and then they are adults. The length of each stage very much depends on class, and also on the particular socio-political situation: is there a war going on? Here the lines seem less radically drawn.

Get Going

for you, Floyce

Splice the smile, get
going
under the arch of time
where memory rips pictures
(felt-backed figures
on a board)
and something as yet unknown
rips memory. Holds it. Rips it.

Salvation lies in anger.
Sorrow leads only
to fear. The tight-fitting shirt
has no place across this breast

151

fighting to breathe. To be
open.

No performance at sundown.
This is the gift, the greatest glory
of it. No performance
but a man
opening and touching. Letting me in.
Giving
his memory of future.

I will take time
in both hands now, knead it
and roll it out.
Gather and bring it in
once more.
I will part the bread as I see fit,
put some away for yesterday, make today
as long and full as I want.

No, not as I want. As I need.
As long and full as I need.

5

In a dream last night I was sitting on the edge of a loading dock, my legs dangling over the side. On my right: my father, in a pale yellow, lightly meshed sport shirt. On my left: Bauchi Van Schowen.* His face was particularly clear to me, his eyes luminous. I quickly looked at his body for signs of torture. Nothing. I remembered—as I did again upon waking—his words in Chile's hell holes in 1974 and '75: "You don't know why you are torturing me, but I know why I am dying." And the photo smuggled by a nurse out of a Valparaiso hospital close to a year later, Bauchi's unseeing eyes, his vegetable body, lying on a prison hospital bed, as if asleep. That photo became a poster, going

*Bautista Van Schowen was a medical doctor, member of the Central Committee of the Chilean MIR. He "disappeared" in early 1974. The Pinochet government has never admitted his detainment.

around the world. I would never put it on my wall. "We're coming back..." seems to be what the voice from the dream affirms as I wake. How many have already forgotten? I want to ask. How many never knew? We mustn't let them forget.

We left Albuquerque late yesterday afternoon. Drove to Flagstaff last night and have just now stopped in San Simeon, a group of middling to elegant motels on Highway #1, the California coastline.

The most amazing thing about the country is how it changes: first the rawness of New Mexico, the immensity of mesas and bluffs, red and orange, fading into blue as far as one can see. The space, which never ceases to rejoice me, the hugeness of it all. We must have hit the northern Arizona pine-tree country after dark, for we discovered it there in the early morning, on the road once more. At one point an altitude marker said "5,000 feet." And in no time—or so it seemed—we were down to 2,000, and then 1,000, and then the sea.

The heat of the desert is intense, even with the car window open and the heavy wind, which once threatened to blow us off the road. From the map, it looks as though the desert will have ended by Barstow; but then it's worse between Barstow and Bakersfield, and even after Bakersfield it doesn't let up. On those stretches I always go back to the times of the earliest inhabitants, trying to imagine how they lived, how they dealt with these elements, what this meant in their lives. And the gulf between those images and the convenience of a modern automobile is beyond my grasp.

In the tiny towns, sometimes a huddle of shacks, a couple of gas stations, two trees—I wondered what I would have been like, had I been born and raised there. What kind of poetry would I have written? None, perhaps. Or rock and roll, was Floyce's suggestion. Suddenly, the land looks like the velveteen seat upholstery of a 1941 car; you can almost smell the hills, resting beneath their tan coating. Then the rolling upholstery becomes the hide of cows, and spots of deep green foliage appear in absolutely delineated spaces where trees cling to the sides of the hills. There are orchards, and there are vineyards, and there are oil wells among the grapes. At one point, the oil fields are like giant lots, and each bears a small sign taking its claim: Gulf, Shell, Exxon, Chevron, 76, Texaco, Conoco.

153

Along the road to Acoma.

Along U.S. Interstate 40, heading for Arizona.

6

The sea is as only the sea can be: endless to watch, wonderful, changing. We sat last night on the beach, for a long while. Behind us, on the bluffs, two brightly colored kites made strange acrobatics in unison, side by side. When one dipped, the other did the same. How is that possible, I asked?

Dream: We are in some strange place. Northern Africa? Tangiers? Perhaps. We are on a beach. Floyce and a woman named Lucile (the Lucile who was married to Philip Lamantia back in the early '60s when I knew them) go off across the sand. I ask someone where they are going. They have gone off to play the game, I am told. What game? The game of standing on the beach, facing the incoming tide, and masturbating. He or she who masturbates farthest, wins. That's not fair, I say. A woman cannot masturbate *farthest*. A man must have made the rules for *that* game! Looking out I can see their two tiny black figures: they are moving back and forth, perhaps five or six feet from one another. The sea is beyond them. Above them, two tiny kites rise and dip together.

7

Today Ximena is twenty years old. In Mexico City. Naturally I remember the day of her birth. I always do, with every birthday of each of my children. Relive it, as I make my way through the details, every year. Four times a year. Ximena was always the "happy baby." The one who needed nothing. The one who never let us know how much she really did need.

8

Sometimes it seems as if life itself must climb awkwardly over its own gropings, in order to speak. I have felt this most of today—and most of yesterday as well. A dim nervousness, a closed ache. Like the distinct stench of frustrated wax and flame when a candle is snuffed out. I don't want to hold my hands to my sides. I want to spread them, hold them out, way out—and touch what I will

155

dream of tonight, or tomorrow. The dreams are always there, but the pieces flee as my eyes open. It's a rare morning when those pieces stay in place, fixed on my eyes, and I can open my mouth and speak them out.

9

It's our fourth day on the road. I am not *here* entirely. There is a screen across which beautiful moments move, sometimes slowly, sometimes whizzing by. We are absorbing the scenery; it is intense

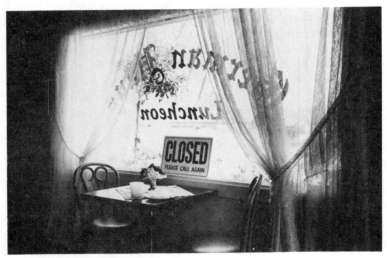

A cafe in Half-Moon Bay, California.

and radiant like an enormous sun. Or cool and shadowy, moving. We stop to see our friends, embrace them, listen to their lives ticking away at this particular moment we have touched, are touching. It's more vivid, more alive than letters. And this is good, travelling to cities where dear friends live. But I am plagued by the uncertainty of my life, harbored by it, it moves in my gut and eats away down there at the center of my existence.

A wonderful day. The sense-shatterers, the shadows and downers, didn't creep into the folds at all. In San Francisco it was parking the car, and walking. Up towards North Beach, City

The American Dream. The mail always makes it through... California Coast.

The fog moves through the branches of the California coastline.

Lights. Larry Ferlinghetti came into his bookstore while we were there, and that was a good re-encounter. As well as Ron Kovic, whom I had never met, but certainly read, after his tragic return from Vietnam. Ron is the author of *Born on the Fourth of July* and other books, one of them coming soon—and Larry, too, has a new book (about Nicaragua) coming in the next couple of months. Ron used to live with my old friend Joan Anderssen, so that was a connection as well. The encounters gave me energy, especially with Ron, who says "I have earned my right to take action in this country!" And he speaks of spending some time now figuring out how best to do that: run for Congress, maybe, or take a more active role in the anti-intervention movement. He seems so alive in his wheelchair; more than many who are "whole."

A street in San Francisco. From the "Human Architecture" series.

Then we went over to the Mission to spend an hour or two with Adam and Marlene, who have galleys of my new book, *Risking a Somersault in the Air*. Nearby is Balmy Alley, where Miranda, Jane and others are painting murals on people's garage doors—those who are willing, for there are a couple who have not been. Miranda says the guy whose garage door she is painting is a Sioux who is basically somewhat reactionary, but a very nice guy. He gives of his conversation—about twenty minutes of cliched

Inside a boutique, Sausalito.

but meaningful phrases each time she goes down to paint—and of his friendship. Both she and Jane have used some of my photos of Nicaraguan people—women mostly—for faces in the murals.

I got off on a large woman sitting in a Managua market. She had looked right at my camera's eye, and laughed. Later the picture I made of her provided a cover for *Ventana*—my fat market woman became a "cover girl." Now she is carrying a tiny picture of a disappeared son, representing a Salvadorean mother in Miranda's mural. And she is learning to read in Jane's. Her face will reflect itself in the eyes of those who walk down Balmy Alley. And they in turn will feel something, say something, perhaps do something, and that act will again reflect itself in the response of some other human being. And so the woman's face, and my image of it, will repeat itself endlessly out in time, from fighting Nicaragua to receptive San Francisco—and out into the world. I love that.

Dorothy Jones is a large, elderly woman, pale but sturdy. She sits behind a card table, on the sidewalk in front of Cody's (Berkeley's incredible kingdom of books—the best book selection I have seen in years). Dorothy makes belts. She slowly presses a quite ordinary motif repeatedly onto a leather strip, using a metal dowel and a wooden mallet. A large white dog sits beside

My friend Jane Norling in front of her portion of the Balmy Alley mural. The woman on the left is from my image of a market woman in Managua.

My friend Miranda Bergman in front of her portion of the Balmy Alley mural, San Francisco.

her, then runs off, eventually returning. He is half German shepherd, half Siberian husky. I begin taking pictures of Dorothy and she asks me what they're for, so I tell her about the calendar. She thinks it's "an awfully nice idea."

She tells me she's just managed to get a disability pension, moved out to California from the east because it seems "easier to work in the street in a place like Berkeley." But when I ask her if she makes a living with her belts, she tells me, "no, not at all. Why last weekend was Father's Day, and I sold only one belt all weekend long. But it gives me something to do. I'd go crazy in the house, just sitting there all day long. This gives me something to do." Dorothy still supports her two daughters, "though they're grown by now," she says.

10

When one speaks of people, families, there are times when nothing one can say is ever enough. Not enough, even to *signal* the complexities, the magic, the vastness. I feel that way about Miranda and her family, as I felt it in Boston about Ruth and hers. A web. One sees it, looks up or down, then gets close enough to touch. But there is so little time. The touching is often too sudden. What one intuits at the moments of touching only really assents to self-evidence later on. Then perhaps it is too late.

I had wanted to follow Ruth's family with my eye, the camera's eye, the pen. Go back and forward at the same time, follow indiscriminately the different lives like lines in a hand, fully expecting it all to come together at some point. With Miranda it is the same. In Minneapolis I touch this presence, and in Berkeley. In Managua it was there when Miranda worked on the library mural. And my memories drift back to Havana, where I first knew Miranda's brother, Lincoln. Or Vietnam, where I travelled for a while with the woman who had once been her sister-in-law, Arlene. This thing is in her eyes, and the way she moves her hands. In the way her hair fluffs out just about her shoulders, which she holds in a certain way. In her particular way of pronouncing words that end in *ing*: stopping in her voice's tracks for an instant at the end of the first syllable, and then sailing into the suffix.

At some point yesterday or last night, Miranda said, "You ought to take some pictures of women lifting weights." We had been talking about the calendar. "Great," I said, "where are they?" And that led to a couple of calls and Miranda finding a good women's gym in Berkeley, not far from the house. This morning she woke me early—she had spoken to the manager and we could go shoot before the 8:30 aerobics class began.

When we got there, three or four women were working out. I began to feel like I had walked into a dream. In a mirror-sided space, women physically very different from one another were working with different sized weights. There was a small, wiry black woman, close-cropped hair, and muscular body. A blond woman, slim and with great wild curly hair. An Asiatic woman, strong, with long straight black hair. An older black woman. And another Jewish and intellectual in her facial characteristics.

Weight lifters, women's gym, Berkeley.

Miranda went to each one of them, explaining who I was and what I was doing. When I heard her talk about "the Margaret Randall who has written about Cuban and Nicaraguan women..." I thought, "Oh, my god, people are going to back off!" But no. This is a place where women learn to feel good about

162

their bodies, not to slim them or trim them, or "make themselves attractive" for a consumer society. So yes, Cuba and Nicaragua are assets, not liabilities. Miranda spoke to each woman with love

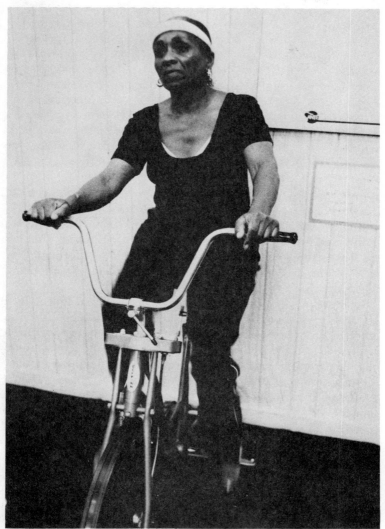

Weight lifters, women's gym, Berkeley.

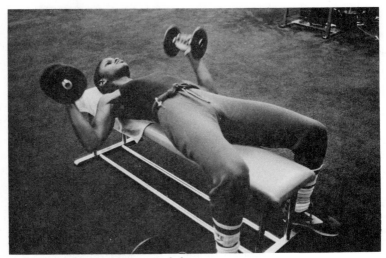

Weight lifters, women's gym, Berkeley.

and care, explained about the calendar, sought each woman's individual response and permission to be photographed. That left me free to simply shoot—and shoot I did, moving through four rolls of film, different lenses, really getting into the situation and its inhabitants.

Then we hit the highway towards Sebastopol and Jonah. At a truck stop where we had breakfast the woman cook was also gracious about being photographed, as she slapped strips of bacon and tossed raw eggs on the sizzling surface of a commercial stove. In a Chevron station it was the same thing: a young woman serving us was absolutely willing to be photographed, when I explained I was "making pictures of women doing different things." A man, working at the same station, was more suspicious. Even after I had the woman's happy consent, he asked me, "What are those pictures going to be used for?"

11

Off the freeway and into the parking lot of another ordinary truck stop/cafe. We needed breakfast, having left Sebastopol early with only a cup of coffee. As we neared the door, I noticed the sign: "Pantyhose crossroads of the world!" Pantyhose crossroads... I blinked. Is that what it said? But yes, and once inside it became clear. The waitresses wore crotch-short jumpers over ordinary pantyhose. That was the gig. The place was filled with travelers: truckers, families, people. Everyone cheerful.

On the walls: a series of plaques with sayings like "I'm o.k.—God doesn't make junk," or "What time did you say you needed it!??" (with a human figure, tied in knots of laughter). Buy them as gifts, they make great gifts! To our right, above the table where two middle-aged men were telling one of the waitresses they were sure they'd seen her somewhere before, was an arrangement of the real tour de force: brilliantly polished cross-sections of tree trunks made into clocks, each clock face superimposed on a brightly lacquered photo—there was Jesus Christ, Elvis Presley, an Indian maiden and Japanese gulls.

The coffee tasted like hot water and the waitresses wore hope pasted over their features like gloom. The America I've been circling all this time. The America shining along these highways. Filling up the empty spaces till the sun goes down.

Truck stop cook, Petaluma, California.

12

Granger, in the Yakima Valley of Washington State. This is where Floyce grew up, and his parents still live in the home that has emerged—over all these years, since 1946—from under the generous hands of his father, Manuel (they call him Alec). On the wall of the garage behind the house, where Alec fixed people's cars and trucks after leaving Arkansas and the mines, among outdated girlie calendars and signs telling the clients their business is sincerely appreciated, there is a slightly dusty eight-by-ten of a small windowless wooden shack. Standing before it are Alec and his wife Lorene, little Floyce with this arms very stiffly at this sides, and another man and his son: friends who had come with them from the south.

This was the shack they had found on this land which they homesteaded—Alec showed me, on the present house, where the front door had been, and where he put the first bathroom. This was where they lived when they put in seven acres of vineyards and began, bit by bit, inventing and building the home they have today. Alec is one of those real geniuses in overalls, a self-made man whose curiosity has never stopped and for whom pain and frustration center on "not being able to do it anymore."

Some years back they sold the grapes. This is Floyce's first time here without the fields, the fields he used to hoe. The house is a piece of magic, where mechanical wonder shares space with knick-knacks, prayers and family portraits, an American flag raised above it all. There are two garages out back—today they house a flamboyant camper, fully equipped (Alec bought it from a state trooper); two small Honda motorbikes and a larger Honda motorcycle, a covered pick-up with a winch he designed and made himself ("Never hooked this up to anything I couldn't pull out of trouble," he told us); and the family car. The garage doors open and shut with motor-driven paraphernalia, and Alec proudly showed us every last bit of the set-up.

But the most amazing part, to me, is the house itself. Alec made it all, occasionally helped with one part or another by friends who knew how to lay a floor, or set bricks. In the big downstairs bathroom—they told me—Floyce used to escape with his books, to study and read "and get away from the TV." One day Alec decided he wanted a fireplace, but where to put one? The only

Sue and Angela, mother and daughter, Granger, Yakima Valley, Washington.

possible place required taking out the stairs! So he put his elevator in, an elevator and a fireplace (the latter has since been renovated with a gas insert—"another mistake," Lorene says).

Well, you walk into a plywood box and step onto the elevator floor. Then you press UP and the thing begins to move. Slowly it brings us up to the second floor, which is much like it was when Floyce lived at home, so many years ago. (That was one of the things that most moved and also disturbed me: that people build their lives, cut them from sunup to sundown work, and the son's place is always there, always ready to receive him home. So is the daughter's, for Floyce's sister Sue has her room as well, similarly untouched, on the first floor.) The upstairs apartment, every inch built by Alec, has two ample bedrooms, a vestibule dividing them, a full bath, and a small porch. On the outside of the house one can go up or down a flight of stairs. But inside there is only the elevator. We installed ourselves in this top-floor apartment, among the nostalgia of Floyce's left-behind books, highschool and college diplomas, Goya prints tacked on the walls, pictures and poems.

When Lorene and Alec got home around seven, he began showing us everything, how each thing worked, and telling us its

167

particular story. The warmth I felt was immediate. Alec talks about making things, making them work, "figuring them all out." He used to play a fiddle and a guitar, but insists "I can't do that anymore." When he's been drinking he says he's stupid. He claims Floyce's first job was "cutting out paper dolls," meaning that his son never had an interest picking up his tools, learning the mechanics trade, carrying it on as he clearly would have wished. But one can also see that he's proud of what Floyce does.

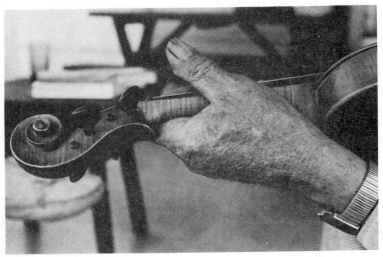

This is the hand of a miner become garage mechanic and harvestor of grapes. He still takes out his old fiddle and plays once in a while.

Lorene begins to talk. One thing leads to another. In less than an hour I have heard about some of her dreams and her hopes, the bad times of Floyce and his ex-wife, her daughter Sue's marriage and its breakup, her son-in-law's failure to support his kids, a couple of Floyce's job experiences, and her yearning to travel, to see, to know.

"Got your ears on?" The cracked voice comes over the local-listening Citizen Band radio set on the kitchen counter. People talking to one another. People chatting, mostly, passing the time of day, communicating in this place described by yesterday's young people (the two young women who were here when we arrived) as "a place where nothing at all happens...it's real slow!"

"Breaker one-four...ten-nine" (that's "repeat")...or double-seven (when someone's not coming through as clear as he/she should be)...ten-thirty-six ("what time is it?") or ten-seven (I'm signing off now"). But mostly it's just conversation, the conversations of people like these, who live their lives between family and work, church and local problems. "My daughter-in-law is here, you know, she and my son came in yesterday, we was over at some friends, had a kind of birthday or potluck..." and on it went.

13

Alec wants Floyce to try driving the camper. So we go out exploring this valley: gentle ups and downs, back roads, an occasional row of tall poplars that look like cedars of Lebanon from a distance. There are fields of hops—I've never seen them before—growing up along the lattice-work like taller, sparser vineyards, and fields of barley, orchards of cherries, apples, peaches and apricots, pears, plums, and occasionally vegetable gardens.

We stop at the Clem farm. Ginny is a woman in her late sixties, probably. She is hardy, works this land—oversees its working, really—every day. Her husband Everett was down on his tractor. She had just come up from looking at the workers (Mexicans, mostly; some women among them) who were thinning out her apples. We talk about things like Floyce's beard (an anomoly, in this place), the season, when the cherry-picking will start (ripening up for next Monday—and taking a chance on it not raining before then).

The racism here is inveterate and itinerant. The migrant pickers come and go. Many of the factory workers are Vietnamese, Mexican, Laotian. There's a strange mixture of heritage and consciousness when these people talk—it's apparent with Floyce's folks, and with others. The old stereotypes prevail, mostly, but there is a seeping through of decent human recognition as well. Some people's sons and/or daughters have married from among the other nationalities. That probably shocks, and then helps.

169

Lorene is proud of the fact that their local library has books in Spanish, for the Mexican population.

I got some good pictures in the apple orchard, women thinning the fruit on the trees. Mexican women. When I spoke to them in Spanish their whole way of looking at me changed instantly, like a picture suddenly come into focus. What was indifference became interest; what was tolerance, an opening for some communication.

In the afternoon Lorene and I went to a bait factory and I had a ball. Mostly women, some ninety-five percent I'd say, working at every phase of the confection. Lorene would occasionally recognize one of the women: "Aren't you one of the Rolleen's?" And talk would begin, about their families, their kids having gone to school together. "It *is* a family," Lorene says. "And all our kids have had the same problems: marriages breaking up, the job-hunt, financial stuff. . . maybe some illness. Makes it nice."

A great deal of the interfamily communication seems to take place on the CB (Citizen Band). They speak to each other in the mornings, mostly the women in their kitchens, as they fix breakfast or prepare their days. They have radio names ("handles"), like Diaper Rash, Wheels, Sagebrush, Buckets.

The historic break: leaving the land. Leaving what the older generation has made, with its hands, with its courage. With years of work and years of successes and failures. I can see it here, perhaps more clearly than ever before. Alec is a man of the land in an almost stereotyped way, a man from *within* the land (the coal mines of his younger years), a man who puts his hand in it and his mind to it and has made it work for him: seeing, touching, shaping, producing. Lorene as well. She speaks of the roses, the summer peas, and when she drove me past the old Catholic church today, which is being renovated for a town library, she told me one by one all the objects they'd placed in the building's cornerstone. With Alec it's the artesian well, the grapes ("going up and down those rows, thirty-five years"), the room added to the other rooms, the names of those near and familiar.

These people, like so many others, have seen their son and daughter grow up and move out, reject the idea of carrying on what they began and what they sustained with so much love and hard work. When Lorene and I came back from the bait plant this afternoon, Floyce and his father were sipping coffee on the back porch. "Well, we've done sold the place," Alec said, "packed up all the stuff and moved it out." A sad joke. "Take a big truck to move it all out," said Lorene. "Yeah...guess it'd take a semi to clear it all out," replied Alec. "No down payment, though. Not even a buyer yet..." Alec and Lorene take it better than many. There are jokes and there is the sadness. But there is an acceptance of the fact that Floyce has moved out beyond this kind of life, and could never come back.

Thinning apples in the orchards of the Yakima Valley, Washington. The thinners and pickers are mostly Mexican migrant workers.

14

Alec is seventy-two. For several days he has been making half-serious attempts at humorous cracks about his age, his inability to do what he used to. He works all day, from early morning till late at night; then he falls exhausted and in pain, and dwells on "losing it." Yesterday I saw him out in the adjacent field—not even his responsibility anymore, since he sold the grapes—on a tractor he'd borrowed to cut back the weeds. This morning, while we were eating breakfast, he went out to raise the flag. And when he

171

came in he said, "Put it halfway up is all." "You mean at half-mast?" Floyce asked. "Why did you do that?" "Well," he replied, "I guess I'm more dead than alive."

We'd been listening to the CB since six-thirty. People getting up and checking in, as it were: Swinging Sam, Leaking Bladder, Wheels, and a few others. Once in a while, when it was a particular friend, Alec would get on and let them know it was his birthday, and then there would be birthday wishes and a bit of conversation in and out of this house.

At one point, two guys got on and began talking about Jesse Jackson. One of them bitching about the fact that "he must have twenty-five or thirty bodyguards—and you know who foots the bill for that!" (Impossible, for them, to imagine or approve of a Black man being protected.) The other mentioned Jackson's recent trip to Cuba, and said, "I don't know what he brought them twenty-two dope peddlars back here for...coulda just stayed down there as far as I'm concerned!" And they got in some fifteen or twenty minutes of talk about Cuba, Fidel, "that commie island...we could sink it easier'n we could blink..."

The first voice made a case for politics without Jackson on the grounds of church and state separation. It was clear he was using that as a pale coverup for his racism. Moral Majority leader Rev. Jerry Falwell would hardly have brought a complaint from him, I'm sure. I asked Lorene, who was frying up some sausage and mixing pancake batter for our breakfast, if she thought the opinions being voiced by the men on the air more or less reflected the sentiments of people in the valley. "Yes," she said, "they do." And then she volunteered that "I think God makes people alike, but I don't think Blacks and whites should marry. For the children, more than anything else. Somewhere along the line they're gonna get hurt." I said I thought the advantages would outweigh any possible disadvantages, and she thought a moment and said, "Well, I guess the world is changing. If it's changing, I guess that's o.k."

15

Lorene graduated from highschool, married Alec and inserted herself in the life of a miner of share-cropping origins, then came with him and their young son (pregnant with their daughter) to the Yakima Valley. Here Alec opened his mechanic's shop and began working the land, as he built a family kingdom with his hands, his heart and hers. But Lorene could easily have been a school teacher, a small-town librarian or—why not?—an historian. It is the story, so often repeated and repeated, of a woman balanced between two worlds, two sets of possibilities, two ways of seeing herself.

Yesterday, back of the house, I was watching TV and she was thumbing through a manuscript of Floyce's newest poetry. Suddenly she looked up and said: "Margaret, I've been wanting to ask you something personal. If you don't want to answer, of course you don't have to..." My throat immediately got dry, I imagined it must be something about my—to her—strange lifestyle. "Of course," I said. "If I don't want to answer I won't."

"Well," she said slowly, "it's about Cuba. You hear so many things. And yet you have a daughter living there. What's it really like...?" And that was the beginning of a conversation that lasted at least an hour, in which I began as much at the beginning as I could and tried to answer her questions about the mysterious country. She had lots of questions—straight from the daily news, and very precise. And I made my answers as precise as I could, as well. It was a wonderful conversation. Her final comment: "They sure do fill you with a lot of propagation. A lot of propaganda, I mean!"

Lorene

What I'm trying to do, she says
is keep us from getting like my mother
(Altzheimer reveries
in an LA nursing home)
and she puts the margarine on the table.
But I want to please, she adds
and sets the butter beside it.

Driving country roads she talks to truckers and to trees
out loud.
Looking at stones—old Sunnyside graves—
she matches their names

to pickle factories and cherry orchards,
country roads and friends
growing old in this valley, as she is.

When she asks about Cuba
it's to set the propagation straight.
Or the propaganda. That's it. "Hard to know
what to think," she says
and she thinks centuries
as her blue eyes move
from hand to hand.

If she talks about the son
she adds details of marriages and deaths,
sales and the Library Club,
the vineyard that was sold
or the calls in the middle of the night
to go down and pull Singing Sam
out of the ditch. Her husband never said no.

Lorene tells us about the mail order marriage
down the road aways
and her soft laughter echoes
off the four walls of her mind.
"Stairway" is her handle on Citizen Band
because her husband put an elevator in.
The day her man said he was awfully tired
and hurting bad

she went out and brought his pistol
in from the shop.
"Hid it," she says, "and he still don't know
where it is.
Come, let me show you my nasturtiums."

16

Yesterday was Alec's party. All day (and for most of the previous
days) there had been talk of "what to do"—Floyce's sister Sue who

lives in Puyallup had wanted to do it right for her parents' fiftieth wedding anniversary, just past. It kind of fell into place to invite a few close friends of Alec's and Lorene's—a couple named Lloyd and Barbara, who are actually closer to Floyce's age, and Sue came over from Puyallup. Floyce and I went into Toppenish in the afternoon to buy some "fixins"—potato chips, dip, a roll of colored film. When we came back, Alec had moved his vehicles out of the main garage and was sweeping the floor for dancing.

Lloyd and Barbara called over on the CB for Alec to come over with his pickup and get their instruments and sound equipment. They both play electric guitars, with the whole range of amplification, mikes, etc. Soon they were setting up. I was interested in making some pictures of Barbara—had it in mind since San Francisco to try to find images of women musicians. But what a difference between this Yakima Valley Barbara and the women playing music across this country today! Those women play for themselves, and their own relationship to the music plays itself out in their bodies, on their faces. This woman plays "for her man"; Lloyd sang (chose the songs, moved right into them, did any and every vocal solo, led the whole thing) and she accompa-

Sonoma County, northern California. I look at the image and think of *Psycho*, the old Hitchcock film.

175

nied. It was hard, even, to get an expression on her face. Or some action in her moving fingers. They'd brought their own liquor, which they drank discreetly from orange plastic glasses which they set atop the amplifiers when they played.

It was a good evening in many ways. Good because Alec loved it and it was for him, after all. Good because they were friends who had come over and given their evening, their music, to make him happy. Good because the music itself wasn't half bad. But it was interesting for me to hear these songs and think a bit about how they sustain every rotten value this Valley typifies: "good natured women" putting up with "hard livin' men," love that moves with a consumer mentality, even a song specifically putting down (in the grossest terms) anyone with long hair, a beard, who smokes dope and/or isn't a Marine.

Floyce at the Grand Canyon.

17

The changing country again. The farmlands often like green and blue velvet, stretching out to mysterious highland country, spotted with snow. Both Idaho and Utah have superwhite, racist,

Navajo waitresses at a cafe near Gallup. I felt uneasy taking their pictures. I know Native Americans have their own sense of the camera. It felt different from what I was used to in Latin America.

and politically right-wing atmospheres. You can almost smell it as you drive. Tonight, in Provo, we ate at a very good restaurant, but you could tell it was the kind of place people go to so that they will not see anyone who looks different from themselves—including waitresses and busboys: not a Black, chicano, Native American, gay or lesbian to bother them while they eat.

18

Early this morning we got up to watch the sun filling the abyss with its lights and shadows. Mather Point was a moving place to be. We walked along the rim there, and stood motionless at different spots, taking it all in, taking it in again and again, to hold it and keep it with us.

I was quiet almost all the way home. Sometimes driving, sometimes sitting beside Floyce as he drove. Out of the highlands and forests of Arizona. Through dry arid vacant stubbly spaces. To Gallup where I shot pictures of a group of Native waitresses at a restaurant where we stopped for lunch; they were eating at the counter and waiting on each other. Through western New Mexico, finally the great rocks and mesas—the land that feels like home.

A power plant on the desert. Like Dante's Inferno in the twentieth century.

July

1

Anna came in on Friday. Around noon. I insisted on going early to the airport. Fidgeted while Floyce and my dad watched the Wimbledon tennis matches on the waitingroom TV. Anna came off the plane tall and thin, her hair cut very short, and with dark glasses. The first thing is always to bridge the space that has grown—and on my part that seems to mean cutting through the defenses she has surrounded herself with, touching her, showing her even with my body that I accept and love the Anna who is finding herself. For her part she asks for a greater demonstration of physical love than I can usually muster during that initial reappraisal period. She sizes me up. And tests me out. And then it's good. And then very good.

She and Floyce hit it off from the beginning. And Anna showed a strong desire to be with her grandparents, my mom and dad. She said more than once how joyous she felt at finally, after all these years, being able to communicate with them in a common language (her newly learned English). Since her arrival we have talked a lot, she has read Benedetti out loud to me and I bits and pieces of the calendar I'm working on out loud to her. She asks to read my books—almost a first. She particularly wanted *Women in Vietnam*, and I wanted to share *Carlota* with her. This business of communicating with one another in English is also new for us. For me, it means finally being able to share some of the deepest things I've written, with one of my own children. We speak English to one another, as well. Always when others who only speak that language are present. When we are alone we tend to revert to Spanish.

Sarah

2

My children who are, for the most part, no longer children. They fill my consciousness. There is some strong, some solid and often heavy way in which leaving one's children is so much a part of my existence these days. It is a process, of course, and it began several years back. I suppose it really began when I decided to leave Cuba and go to Nicaragua. I took only Anna (who was eleven). The others opted to stay behind. In some very important

Ximena at the Grand Canyon.

way, Sarah, Ximena and Gregory ceased being my children then, in the conventional relationship of daily responsibility.

But I very much continued to feel the responsibility—economic as well as emotional—to all four of them. I have always somehow been the core, the one steadfast adult figure in their lives. Their several fathers came and went. Their relationships with them, the communications (and certainly any solid financial support), were sporadic, to say the least. I was there. And that was important to them, and to me.

When I left Cuba, Gregory assumed more than ever the role of center. He had always had that, as my male counter-part, in the family. And taken it extraordinarily seriously. I began to see more clearly each of my kids, each man or woman, and his/her own being. Going in a unique direction. Ximena opted for coming to live with us in Nicaragua after about a year. It seemed to have as much to do with being with her mother again as it did with a change in place. My last two years in Nicaragua were spent with Ximena and Anna both.

Then the new home. My decision, which was a long time in coming, meant, for Ximena and Anna, the need to make personal decisions of their own about where they wanted to be. Ximena decided to move to Mexico, with her father. Anna decided to move to New York, with hers. So the four are scattered now: Paris, Havana, Mexico City, New York. And I, here in Albuquerque, am beginning to settle into what that means in my life. Free-

Gregory

dom in great part. Delight in seeing each of them move off, head for his or her particular star.

But the break, internally, is never clean, I guess. Neither of the girls' fathers seems really able to deal with financial support. They never were, and when the girls lived with me it was alternately a bitter struggle or simply a giving up. Now that they have their daughters with them, have been "forced" so to speak to take on the commitment, they have done it. But I must, and wish to, help them as well.

There is a lot of uncertainty in my own life, economically and in terms of my Immigration status. As yet I don't have a good job coming up, which means no real economic security. In a meeting

Anna in New York City.

the other night, with the architect who will be building the wonderful house my father is giving us, we realized we must cut down fairly radically on the number of rooms. There just isn't enough money. It's still a luxury house, for me, and the culmination of such a wonderful dream. But one of the rooms which had to go was Anna's. Now there's no reason why Anna— who doesn't even live with me—should have a room. And yet having that room for her meant, to me, that I could say to Anna: Here is your place. Even if you don't want or need it now, it's here for you. And it continues to be your center. *I* continue to be your center. But it won't be there, and I am not Anna's center, except perhaps in the way in which I love her. These are complex emotions. (When I told Anna that the house plans had had to be altered, and her room no longer exists, she understood; it was fine. No problem at all. The problem seems to be in me.)

Anna 1984

The woman grows tall in time
within the memory of the girl.
A new language swims to the surface
and her lips speak new words.
Freckles remain
telling the world she is the same
and different.
How does my own hand fit now
right now
on the curve of her shoulder?
Inhabiting separate cities
we discover a voice. Plain. Erector blocks
magnetized though complete in themselves.
She talks about her boyfriend
reading the old poems
out loud. She dances.
There is war in her dream.
She is straight in her crystal saddle
tapping her feet. Putting the two halves
together.
For years she will be putting together
the halves, matching,
smoothing the seams.
Showing hurt or delight.
I am her mother and we smile
as we move apart. Waving.

3

When I was in New York City this past April and May, on my eastern tour, I spent two long mornings with Bell Chevigny. We talked and taped. I think we both felt that it had been profitable, although, as always happens, the time limitations of the ongoing conversation began to raise as many new questions as there were answers to the old ones. In yesterday's mail, then, another letter. This one raising some of those new questions:

The experiences I have had with some of my books, Bell, at least with ones of and about women, I have never had with any of the others. For example, people (especially women) have written to me, or come to me, and told me how *Cuban Women Now* or *Sandino's Daughters* opened them to a whole new way of seeing the world, of feeling, of living. More than once, women have come up to me at readings, in public places, or even on the street and almost made me cry by telling me how much those books have meant in their lives. I knew they were speaking of the window that had been opened. I do not want to take the credit. It is Cuban and Nicaraguan women's voices they are hearing. What I did was take advantage of the good fortune of being in those particular places at a particular moment in time. Transmit those voices. Allow them to be heard. Women's voices have been silent for so long. Have been silenced. Forcibly silenced. To the extent that they very often didn't know they possessed a voice. The realization that this voice, these voices, *do* exist, the historic realization and also very much the sound of each woman, individually, is something that belongs to this century. To now.

I had another experience which I almost hesitate to mention, because it may seem self-serving, or overly concerned with whatever small contribution I may have been able to make. But I will mention it, because it belongs in an exploration of this question. When I spoke with the women of Nicaragua, with the fighters, leaders like Monica Baltodano and Dora Maria Tellez—when I interviewed them for *Sandino's Daughters*—when I asked them to describe their own struggle within the Sandinista National Liberation Front (FSLN) in the early days, their struggle to win a space for themselves, their struggle with the men in their organization, they inevitably mentioned a series of books: Simone de Beauvoir's *The Second Sex*, and *Cuban Women Now*.

Some of them also mentioned *Las Mujeres* (a small anthology of writings from the North American women's movement, which I selected and introduced with an essay of my own). Of course I know that when they mention *Cuban Women Now,* they are not speaking so much of anything I contributed as they are of the Cuban women themselves, their lives and struggles, their problems, the strength they got from their own history. Just as, when they speak of a book like *Las Mujeres,* they are speaking about the North American women's movement, to which I—at least at that time—was more a foreign observer than an active participant. But whatever role I may have had in bringing those realities to the lives of our Nicaraguan sisters, I'm grateful for it.

Much has been said, especially by the more superficial and scandalous chroniclers, of the negative effects which the women's movement of the industrialized world may have had on the lives of Latin American and other Third World women—separatist inclinations dividing political struggles, and so forth. On the other hand, there has been a lot of misunderstanding. American women coming to places like Cuba in the mid-seventies and showing concern because the Cuban women weren't interested in burning their bras or discussing abortion (to which they already had free and ample access).

Of course this kind of commentary comes more out of fear than anything else, and it comes, as well, from the inability to adequately analyze particular situations. Not enough has been said about the real and deep exchanges, how the lives and struggles of Latin American women have influenced our lives, and—yes—how our lives and struggles have also made a mark on those of our sisters in Latin America. I have long felt that this needs to be re-explored, and reinterpreted. I have long felt that socialism and feminism need each other.

I have seen, in my own experience, the mistakes made by orthodox Communist Party women who—in so many countries—ignore the substance of sexism and shy away from any kind of meaningful ideological struggle around women's oppression, because they think it's all "in the economics of the thing," and besides, they really don't want to struggle against their men. I have seen how that focus holds us back. And I have seen (during the same historic period) how little many feminists really understand, or ever care to understand, the economic forces that move society, and how, in what specific ways, their own oppression is forged and affected by those forces. They have bought the system's slogan that "women's lot is the same everywhere." They don't see that economics *is* the basis for liberation, although certainly not the whole process.

So there is a blindness on both sides, and I think I have contributed something, very modestly but something, to that clarification. Perhaps where I have most contributed is simply in listening to, and making available, the voices of those who have most deeply lived these problems, in their everyday experience.

You ask about Mexico in 1968. So much has been said about that terrible time. I think Elena Poniatowska said it well in her *La Noche de Tlatelolco*, as much because of her courage in doing that book when no one else was yet speaking of what had happened (since then, it has become much easier, even fashionable), as for the worth of the book itself, so moving, so total.

Well, the Mexican student movement was, I guess, part of a general world-wide rebellion among students in many places. Certainly, historically, it must be inscribed within the same movement that produced the Columbia University strike in New York City, or the Paris May. But it also had its own peculiarities, very much Mexico, very much Third World. More than a thousand people were brutally murdered and those murders were covered up at Tlatelolco. That fact alone, more eloquently perhaps than any other, gives one a sense of what happened there. And how.

The Institutional Revolutionary party (PRI) under Diaz Ordaz was particularly corrupt, treacherous, murderous. They stopped at nothing. They created a paramilitary force in the country which wasn't that much tamer (though certainly less publicized) than those which came later, in Chile, Uruguay, Argentina. And yet the Mexican Revolution *did* stand for something in that country's history, and there proved to be a series of channels for changing the course of that tragic history, later on. So it's complex. At the time, the imminence of the Olympics, held in the Mexican capital just days after the massacre, produced a crisis—a political and social, and of course economic, crisis—almost unequalled in Mexico's modern history. The massacre had to be hidden. The Olympics had to take place. At all costs. Extreme terror was the only answer.

In that context, *El Corno Emplumado* early on took the side of the students. When the magazine supported the Vietnamese against U.S. invasion, when it spoke about the racism in the American south, or poverty in Latin America, that was fine with the Mexican authorities, many of whom supported the magazine (Bellas Artes, the Ministry of Education, even the presidency). When we began to speak out about Mexico itself, that was another story. All the magazines worth their weight in dignity in those days sided with the students, and the Mexican government immediately stopped their grants, forcing them to close. *El Corno*, being bilingual, being international to some extent, didn't depend exclusively on the Mexican government for its livelihood. We had always had subscribers, we had always held benefits, asked for and received donations. So we campaigned for more of that, and we kept the publication going. We kept the protest going too. And that was unacceptable.

So that's one of the things we were doing, and certainly that played an important part in bringing the repression down on us. We were also involved on a more personal level, as everyone was at that time. Everyone with the smallest sense of justice. In my case I worked with students from UNAM's School of Medicine. I worked on translations of their communiques. I worked with the information brigades. I helped them get the news out internationally. After the October 2 massacre, I helped hide and feed people. That was the extent of my "subversive" activity. Looking back, I'm sure the government thought I was doing more.

Being a foreigner, and perhaps being a foreign woman, certainly must have called attention to myself. The outcome, as you know, was that the magazine was forced to stop publishing, and I had to go into hiding, be separated from my four children (the youngest was three months old at the time). I spent the next twelve years without documentation (passport) of any kind. Becoming, from a legal point of view, a non-person. Of course others went to prison and many didn't survive. I was lucky.

4

My work with Doris Tijerino, that testimony—to go on to another question of yours, Bell—it was International Women's Year (1975) and the Sandinistas were fighting hard in Nicaragua. Few, in other parts of the world, were aware of that, much less of the particular role of the FSLN. I guess a number of things came together for me in that project: the desire to go deep with a single woman, hear her voice, sift it, produce it, listen to it and tell it, bring that to life for people in other parts of the world. Produce a book about a woman, in International Women's Year, when it just *might* be noticed by someone. And also, say something about what was happening in Nicaragua, bring *that* to the attention of the people.

Doris Maria was chosen for several reasons. She was one of the oldest continuous members of the FSLN, a woman, alive—and available. Her story, in so many ways, paralleled the story of twenty years of Nicaraguan history.

Interesting note: I entered that book in the Casa de las Americas literary contest that year, in the testimony section. The 1976 prize in testimony was to be given to a book about women, in honor of the year. Eleven entries were submitted. And the prize was declared vacant. Why? Because two of the judges were members of conventional Central American Communist parties and didn't want to see a book about the FSLN win.

Seen from this distance, it seems almost ludicrous. It wasn't then. Those were the kinds of divisions that kept people's struggles back. Yes, I think the book has its faults. It was my first attempt to write a book directly in Spanish and my Spanish wasn't nearly as polished as it became later on. As it is now. That, of course, was the official reason, given by the jury. But it was clear to me then and it is now that any good style corrector, from any good publishing house—and certainly Casa is that—could have gone over the manuscript and polished it. Which, of course, is exactly what happened when Extemporaneos, in Mexico, accepted the book for publication about a year later. I do want to make it clear that the decision was not Cuba's; the judges who had objected to the book because it dealt with a non-CP revolutionary organization, and who had made "poor literary style" their excuse, were not Cubans, but Central Americans. In fact, the only Cuban judge was quite favorable to the book.

5

A wonderful phone conversation this morning with Ruth Hubbard, George Wald, Debbie Wald. George was recently in

Paris on a human rights tribunal concerning, I think, Armenia. And Perez Esquivel, the Argentine Nobel Peace Prize winner, was also there. After the event they had gone to speak with Francois Mitterand and Regis Debray. Esquivel discussed the situation in Argentina, and then George brought up Nicaragua.

Mitterand had offered mine-sweepers for Nicaraguan harbors back when the CIA admitted mining Corinto. But he had wanted other countries to come in with France on the project, and there were no takers at that time. The U.S. government could easily have seen such an act as provocation, invoking the Monroe Doctrine. George thought then, and continued to think, that a better idea would be for a cargo ship, filled with the cargo of peace, to travel to Nicaragua from a neutral country, and for France to send the mine-sweeping equipment along to insure a safe docking. Mitterand like the idea apparently—Debray especially liked it, George said—and Perez Esquivel, who went to Norway after France, mentioned it to Norwegian government officials.

The Norwegians took on the project as their own, and the Norwegian government immediately pledged two million crowns of cargo, as well as the ship. I believe the Norwegian prime minister is in fact co-ordinating the whole affair. Sweden then followed suit, pledging three million crowns of cargo. So, the ship will sail from Panama later this month, and George, Perez Esquivel, Linus Pauling, an Irish woman who won the Nobel Peace Prize, and other Nobel recipients will be aboard. They will dock at Corinto, in Nicaragua. The important and newsworthy thing about the whole event, is that it is governments who are involved. A first, I certainly hope they manage to break the news blockade so people can be aware of what they're doing.

6

News of the day is Mondale's choice of Geraldine Ferraro, forty-eight-year-old congresswoman of Italian Catholic descent, from Queens, New York, as his running mate on the Democratic ticket. The first time a major party has nominated a woman for that high an office in this country (in spite of the fact that in modern times women have held higher offices in England, India and elsewhere, though certainly not always to the glory of our sex). Yet it's such a big thing here.

190

I am glad the democrats were intelligent enough to take this step. Mondale is such a dreary opponent to Reagan, but the important thing will be to try to oust Reagan. It doesn't look good. Some analysts are saying that by choosing a woman as a running mate, Mondale has "catered to another special interest group," as if that's all women are! Many say he catered to pressure from NOW, and other women's groups. I hope he did. And I certainly hope those groups have the power to get women out to the polls in November. NOW in Albuquerque isn't much— not as strong as the Women's Political Caucus. If sufficient numbers of women really did understand our needs and our power (as well as our responsibility) in this country right now, the gender gap that very definitely does exist could be made to work for life, instead of death.

7

Sixty Minutes—as everyone reading this no doubt knows—is a Sunday night hour-long newsy human interest mish-mash that often has interesting items. Tonight's has left a grating echo in my ears. Depro-Provera is the name of the game. It is a once-a-month injection used as birth control by women which was banned in this country, but is still being pushed widely in Latin America and other Third World countries, and it is now being given to convicted rapists to "diminish their sex drive."   We were treated to bits and pieces of an interview with some doctor at Johns Hopkins Hospital—the prime mover of this new treatment, some supposedly sincere conversations with several convicted rapists (one serving eighteen consecutive life sentences for multiple rape) who are on the drug, a woman who was raped twice by a guy who came into her home naked and masked (one month between rapes; then a third he couldn't bring off), and this same guy's lawyer who argued for, and won, his client's right to treatment with the drug instead of prison.

In an interview this lawyer said, "As rapes go, this was a mild one." The Sixty Minutes interviewer mentioned the cancer risk of the drug. One of the imprisoned men answered him with something like: "Cancer? Cancer? I'd rather die of cancer any day, than have this uncontrollable urge...!" And that's what the good doctor seems to be saying: that rape is an "uncontrollable urge," a problem for many otherwise "good" men. You don't really want to rape. You don't really hate women. Oh no. You just can't help yourself. And a shot of Depro-Provera will fix everything. As though rape has no social causes, only biological ones.

At the end of the feature we were informed that those on this new drug program are not only men in prison. They are also convicted rapists who are being treated this way rather than go to prison. The clearest message, though, and I can still see the guy's crazed face as he put it across, came from the man serving the eighteen consecutive life sentences: he argued that we have to "stop all this going off on one blind alley after another, stop all this bullshit about trying to understand the rapist. Just understand the *urge*, that's all. And Depro-Provera will take care of the rest."

8

July 19. Carlos's dream. Jose Benito's dream. And so many others: Idania Fernandez, Arlen Siu, and those who survived as well—Dora Maria, Tomas, a nation. Their dream is five years old today, and in Managua, all over Nicaragua, people are ripe with pain and joy. I hold mine deep inside.

9

I got home from the darkroom to catch the last of the TV coverage of the nominating eve at the Democratic Convention. A first ballot victory for Mondale (now enhanced by Ferraro) was followed by some late news and a special feature on Truman's life—commemorating what would have been his 100th anniversary this year. I half sat, half lay there on the livingroom couch, almost mesmerized by what was being put across. Truman was being vindicated not in spite of his having ushered in the age of atomic death, not because of the stand he took against the McCarran-Walter Act, but because of the very thing that gives us the shivers: his dropping of the atomic bomb on Hiroshima and Nagasaki—described as "the ability to make courageous decisions." He was pitied out loud because Roosevelt didn't pay much attention to him and because he was kept out of the inner planning circles during the last eight months of the president's life. And much was made of his delicacy at not moving into the White House immediately—out of respect for Eleanor Roosevelt.

In fact the whole drift of the TV special was "small town boy...failure at most of the things he undertook...all thumbs...crude-talking 'Honest Abe' type, made good!" Interestingly, one sensed an analogy between the Truman years and the Reagan years, and towards the end of this program, which had me in a dull but smoldering stupor, I realized the analogy was clearly intentional. This is what we may expect from another Reagan term: the courage to launch another Hiroshima, perhaps this time taking most or all of the world along.

10

Working in a darkroom again, in spite of the inconveniences of not having it at home, not being able to move freely from negative to negative, in spite of only being able to use the room at nights and on weekends, I *am* happy again! Didn't even realize the extent of my need for this particular creative expression. Last night, driving home, all I could think of over and over again was how fortunate I am to have found people who would trust me to use their space, share it with me, and leave me alone! The Moon Tree people have been wonderful, helpful, respectful, and accommodating. It will be hard to repay their trust and kindness.

I am reading the new Grove Press edition of Judith Malina's diaries from 1947 to 1957. They are fascinating. These may be the first journals I've read by a woman whose concerns, at least in a general way, parallel my own. I have always been fascinated by Anais Nin's diaries, and have had periods of reading them avidly. And, in fact, I feel closer to Nin than to Malina in the purely formal aspect: the how of the writing. Nin is richer; Malina almost cryptic at times—her entries for an entire day or an entire idea can be a single sentence, or a short paragraph. I admire her precision and economy. But what I really get into with her, are the connections: moving with her as she grapples with things I've grappled with (and am still grappling with, in some cases). With Nin I find that her specific concerns are rarely my own. With her it is more the poetry, what she did with the words.

11

Working concurrently on a number of projects. Fighting the temporality of my life right now (my Immigration status still up in the air; not having a proper place to work, to order my papers and my life, to dedicate maximum creativity out of my beginnings) by reaching out as far as I can in every one of my directions, pushing my need to the limit with my eyes and hands and energy. It is a way of saying, with my whole body: no, you will not defeat me.

In the darkroom I am printing pictures for the calendar as well as beginning to work on my mother and daughter series, which I hope to show somewhere. I am also working, slowly, on a strangely architectural series, for which I seem to take an image every great once in a while. More than looking for these, they come looking for me.

There was a strange Sullivan building down on Houston Street, in New York City, and prancing high up on one corner of it was a gilt little fat-bellied top-hatted man blowing a bugle. Or was he holding a mirror? There is an interior of a small church in northern New Mexico. There are two shots made at a place called

When the ferry docked at Vashon Island, I was on the prow, looking down from an upper deck at the shadows of the people standing with me.

In a housing project called Alamar, on the sea near Havana, Cuba, 1979.

Masked children in the streets of Leon, Nicaragua, celebrating June 2oth, the anniversary of that city's liberation.

Half-Moon Bay, up on the California coast. One is a storefront with a large American flag and a sign warning Beware of Dog; the other was taken inside a small cafe where we stopped and had croissants: the lace curtains in the window and the particular curve of the straight-backed chair placed in just the way it was at a small table. And the sign saying "Closed. Please call again," facing into the cafe's interior. There is an abandoned old house in the Nicaraguan countryside; and two delapidated wicker chairs set out on a small bluff overlooking Puget Sound from the back-yard of a friend's house on Vashon Island—those chairs seem to be in deep conversation. There's a string of tennis shoes hanging beside the image of the Virgin in a Managua market; a little girl playing with a dozen plastic shoes in a housing project in Havana; a boy's face emerging mask-like among a delirium of real masks at a festival in Leon; a small girl hanging upside down from the strong criss-cross of a latticed quonset jungle-gym on a New York City playground. These are my architectural pictures; the archi-tecture of ideology, if you look close enough.

12

These months home from Latin America, among the many other much more interesting and/or relevant-to-the-world-at-large pieces of the jigsaw, have taught me a few small but painful and rather intimate bits of my make-up. One thing I realized recently is that I am almost unable to go into large stores. Consumerism does something to me which is hard to put into words. It's almost an allergy.

At first I thought I just didn't enjoy shopping. In New York, whenever I set aside some time for buying the few things I wanted to pick up—a bit of clothing for myself, some books for Floyce, a few gifts—I made sure I had a friend along: Susan, Rhoda. Before going off on that eastern tour I realized I needed boots for the snow and ice of Minnesota and Iowa, and I found myself asking my father to go with me to an Albuquerque shopping mall. Later I realized I couldn't have bought those boots without him. I told him so, but imagine he thought I was simply thanking him for coming with me. I'm sure he had no idea of how difficult it would have been for me, perhaps impossible, to do it alone.

Now I have to face this head on. I need underpants in the worst way. I am wearing shredded panties; there are times I don't know if I'm putting a leg through a hole or a rip. Yet I haven't been able to make myself go out and buy new ones. I want them. I need them. I hate wearing these cruddy ripped up panties. But I can't face going to the stores by myself. And almost everyone I know here has better things to do than to zap off to a shopping mall for panties.

13

Recognizing: the overwhelming intensity, and the danger, of emotional zones I had entered those last two years in Nicaragua. Reorganization of personal priorities. Realization of the need to move deeper in my creative work. The photography, and the writing. And recognition that sacrificing these to necessary activism was, in my case at least, synonymous with a fear of failure should I risk doing these things as I believed they needed to be done. And realizing that risking the doing of them now, will perhaps be of more value to the world than any amount of activism, in my particular life. Inhabiting, with a clearer intention, the dream space. Seeking solutions to problems, in dreams. Using that, without trying to understand how it works, by what means.

14

Anxiousness falling away. Especially, anxiousness about the work. If I have not written a poem in weeks—or months—does this mean I am no longer a poet? No, it does not. When I come to a specific moment in a project, one which threatens to give me anguish or despair, I try sitting back and attempting to understand the problem in a different way. This allows, I believe, the freeing up of a different area of consciousness. Nothing mystic here; scientific, probably, and explainable had I the concepts through which to do the explaining.

Example: the women's calendar. When I had collected all the texts, and out of seventy or more had chosen fifty-three I wanted to use, I knew I must devise a way of deciding the order they would take in the year, the progression, the place for each. I sat for a long time, reading and rereading them. Then, slowly but very surely, I began placing them in an order. An internal order that seemed to speak to me. And they began to move. Almost of

Half-Moon Bay, California.

199

their own free will. When I read over what I had done, it made perfect sense to me. And when, curious about how many were from each continent, I counted those from Latin America and those from the North, I realized, startled, that the proportions were the same.

Then began the task of matching the photographic images with the texts. The usual explicitness had to be rejected early on. I have testimony from women steel workers in Buffalo, but no photos of them; testimony from shipyard workers in Oregon, also without images; photos of migrant workers from the Yakima Valley but not texts to go with them; testimony from lesbians recalling the gay bar life in Buffalo in the '30s and '40s; poems from sophisticated poets; a song by Violeta Parra; photos of mothers and daughters; images of weight-lifters in a San Francisco gym—to name just a few.

So I spread the photographs out—thirty or forty more than I could use—and began flipping through the pages of the already ordered texts. The combinations came to me, powerfully, one after another. When I had them all matched up, I shivered at the relationships established. I made a few changes, but not many. And when I finally went through the whole thing, once more, to check for Latin and North American representation, I found that it had worked out perfectly: the images, like the texts, are equally divided between the two continents.

15

In *Another Way of Telling*, John Berger goes like an arrow to where I am standing, when he says: "In life meaning is not instantaneous. Meaning is discovered in what connects, and cannot exist without development. Without a story, without an unfolding, there is no meaning. Facts, information, do not in themselves constitute meaning. Facts can be fed into a computer and become factors in a calculation. No meaning, however, comes out of computers, for when we give meaning to an event, that *meaning is a response, not only to the known, but also to the unknown: meaning and mystery are inseparable, and neither can exist without the passing of time. Certainty may be instantaneous; doubt requires duration; meaning is born of the two.* An instant photographed can only acquire meaning insofar as the viewer can read into it a duration extending beyond itself. When we find a photograph meaningful, we are lending it a past and a future." (My emphasis.)

16

This is process. And process is much more than half the journey. Meaning and mystery. Adrienne Rich pinpoints this when she speaks of political art: "...it might persuade us emotionally of what we think we are rationally against; it might get to us on a level we have lost touch with, undermine the safety we have built for ourselves, remind us of what is better left forgotten."

At times in my life the religious faith of people I met or came into contact with seemed to me only bred of ignorance. When I got close to the people who made the Nicaraguan Revolution, and was forced to examine, without taboos, the *activity of their faith*, I was forced, as well, to understand that the mystery is not necessarily evasion, it can be relevant and meaningful. If it leads to an undeniable changing of reality.

Meaning and mystery are inseparable. It is so clear. Why, then, do we fear emotional persuasion to what we are rationally against? The fear of seeing the other half of the moon, or the sun.

17

The thirty-fifth anniversary of the beginning of the Cuban Revolution. How vilified that experiment is, for the most part, in this country. The reactionary extremes in the government here seem to hate (fear) Cuba more than any other single situation. Yet, even within establishment politics, there seem to be cracks in the facade. Jesse Jackson's recent trip to Havana was twisted every which way by most of this country's press, and the powers that be wouldn't even receive him to hear the message he brought back. But when Jackson spoke at the Democratic Convention, I looked at the faces of people who were looking at him, and even though the bigtime cameramen were trying to give the public the image *they* wanted us to have, one could clearly see that the expressions on those people's faces said loud and clear that they felt represented, I believe, *for the first time in our electoral history.*

The Twenty-third Olympic Games became the mainstay of TV with Saturday afternoon's inaugural events. It was a Hollywood show every step of the way—eighty-four grand pianos and patriotism to spare. News camerapeople did a lot of focusing in on people's faces, people waving American flags in the stands, movie stars who were spot-interviewed for their opinions. A lot of talk about "this could only happen in a free country," a lot of the "American first" aura which I've come to associate, over the past couple of months, with Reagan's re-election campaign. A re-election campaign which has seeped into all phases and levels of normal non-campaign advertising, making people feel that the economy has never been better, never have there been more people working, no, taxes will not be raised, and all the rest of it. It makes one wonder where all those who are *not* working, where all those—workers, minorities, youth, women—for whom the quality of life is decidedly worse, *are.*

I've been watching the actual sports events with real interest. I don't know why anyone would want to brave the LA traffic, parking and smog, when you can see every event up close, in normal and in slow motion, from straight above and every other angle, from the comfort of your own livingroom (or wherever it is you have your television set). The possibilities of TV coverage these days are almost beyond belief.

The gymnasts are particularily beautiful to watch. The male compulsories in that discipline were held yesterday, and China, the United States, and Japan did exceptionally well. The People's Republic of China, who hadn't come to these games in years, got six perfect scores—hard to do in a series of elementary exercises. The United States' athletes went through those same paces in the evening and also did very well, but got only a single perfect score—mostly they were around 9.90, 9.85, or 9.95. Those are great scores, but it was interesting to see how the announcers viewed them as "better than the Chinese..."

Politics is so much a part of these games, and that's only interesting because the U.S. sports announcers make such a point of denying that to listeners and viewers. One of the ABC announcers, in the main control booth, repeatedly mentions that the Soviets and East European countries have boycotted these games, but when they mention the absence of the U.S. and some of the western bloc countries from the 1980 Moscow games, the word "boycott" is curiously absent.

August

1

When I enter the darkroom, I take the two big rings off my left hand, and place them on the shelf that supports the enlarger. When I'm arranging everything, I stand a small tape recorder up against the wall, to the right of the enlarger, and a small stack of tapes—women's music, country and western, Bach, Vivaldi—directly in front of it. Next to the tapes I put my rings. Then the timer. And there's always a bit of room left over, in the space closest to where I stand, to put my antistatic cloth. Then I begin to work. It's a ritual I always follow.

When I leave the darkroom I get into my car and then I decide which way I will come home. Straight up Candelaria to University? Or onto the Freeway? I use the Freeway and Candelaria coming down, but going back I have begun to choose Edith for my crosstown trip. It comes off Candelaria at a light, and almost immediately it turns into Broadway. Mysteriously. I've never been able to figure out how that happens.

Last night I was driving and dreaming along Broadway, and I

decided to turn up Central instead of Coal, see what was happening on a Friday night, Albuquerque 1984. I was just turning onto Central when the time suddenly turned to 1907. Storefronts settled into their sharply angled space. People were riding horses, or walking. The pace slowed. A police car to my left in front of the old public library became a sheriff on a horse, and the library a large saloon.

The noise level changed, and I could begin to distinguish words here and there. Words from the same language, in a different time. Things became lighter, quicker. I marvelled that I could be driving a 1981 Toyota in 1907, and began to laugh. But it was a different laughter from last week's, when I found myself running so many errands one morning I'd begun to laugh and laugh to keep from screaming. This was a light laughter, even faintly musical. I thought: my father would be proud of me now, I can even carry a tune when I laugh!

When I'd gotten through the fabric of images, and 1907 began to recede, giving way to 1984 coming around Stadium and turning onto Buena Vista, I realized that Albuquerque does in fact have a good deal of the old frontier still spattered throughout its modern

Roadside stands where they sell strings of red chile peppers—they're called ristras.

Irrigation ditch, near Rio Grande River, Albuquerque.

facade. Yesterday there was a bank robbery in plain light of day and midtown. The gunman was a young Hispanic, and he asked one of the tellers for "all the hundreds you got." She said she had no hundred dollar bills, but handed over what she did have. And then he walked off—on foot. It that isn't 1907, I don't know what is.

Albuquerque is a place where automatic banking windows and instant computerization are along side Indians sitting under the portals of Old Town haciendas, selling the kinds of things they've made for a hundred years—along with the junk today's tourists are so anxious to buy. The businesses along Central Avenue in the downtown section of the city look tiny to me every time I drive by. They seem to grow from memories of my youth; then they were imposing and I was small. It is as if they stopped somewhere along the line, and remained the way they were then—forever. The fact that many are empty, unused and waiting for renewal, removal, replacement, adds to their aura of make-believe. It's like a toy city, or a movie set, surrounded by the *real* Albuquerque that has Los Angeles as its model and becomes more freeway-laced and functional every day. Yet, even in the real city, even in 1984, something will happen one day that sends you back to 1907, without batting an eye. You expect to see everyone riding horses. And if you look hard enough, you do.

Time of Our Lives

Hominids to homo sapiens, 10,000 generations
where almost nothing happened.
People living as their ancestors did, no
generation gap.
Nothing to talk about except the weather.

Then the Neanderthal buried their dead
and the Upper Paleolithic made art.
An explosion of art, cave walls
covered with great animals, running.
Reds, yellows, blacks.

Today we have breakfast in San Pedro Norte,
dinner in New York.
A bomb wipes out a city in minutes,
and our love is four months old
though I cannot remember a time
when the heat of your body
did not bring my memory to life.

Our children cling to us, flee from us,
come back and stand up.
They have their own memories growing fingers.
We move back to our mother, father,
look at childhood pictures, patch
the dark spots,
raise our eyes from the source of light.

The world is moving fast and faster, we are
slowing down to keep up.
I am looking at cave walls again, holding
a mirror in my hands.*

*The idea for this poem came partly from the book *The Creative Explosion, An Inquiry into the Origins of Art and Religion*, by John E. Pfeiffer, Harper and Row, New York, 1982. The book traces the emergence of creativity in human beings, and speculates on why people began making art. It is a fascinating story.

2

In the Olympics, women's basketball, women's and men's swimming and gymnastics, and of course track and field, are knocking me out. Upping my TV time considerably, keeping me on the livingroom couch. Yesterday Mary Lou Retton—the only woman on the U.S. women's gymnastic team who looks more like a nice Jewish girl from the Bronx than like a native of southern California—whipped her tiny four-foot-nine body around Pauley Gym and won the gold medal in women's gymnastics, after nights of exciting and very close bouts with the wonderful Rumanians. Nadia was in the stands.

Yesterday, as well, the Olympic Committee told ABC to tone down its terribly pro-U.S.A. coverage of the meets. Their bias is beyond even the usual "we're the biggest and the best," a complex which most people and institutions in this country are born with, and at their worst—which is less frequent, of course—ABC is downright racist regarding the other competitors. They revel in speaking of "pro-American audiences," as if there were the slightest possibility that Iran, Brazil, Nicaragua, Saudi Arabia, or even West Germany could possibly send crowds like the Americans, who naturally fill the stands in Los Angeles.

I've often wondered, as I watch the different events, whether it doesn't occur to the spectators themselves at times, that an unbroken chant of USA, USA, USA, USA, USA and the continual waving of American flags isn't just a bit out of keeping with the supposedly non-political and certainly international spirit of the games.

Yesterday I had a lovely shooting session with Anna, Farrell Brody's great aunt who is eighty-eight. She has come to live with them—just next door to our apartment—since Farrell's mother died in San Francisco in June. Anna was from Russia, came to this country and grew up in Pennsylvania, worked at the same cork factory from the age of thirteen to her retirement at sixty-five, never married, spent her life working and caring for her own parents ("they always liked to be with me," she says), was known for a very special omelette and for giving back rubs to her family and friends.

At yesterday's shooting session she was a bit stiff at first. She had dressed carefully in a lavender print dress and was sitting happily on the couch when I came in. Once in a while she rearranged the neckline of her dress, to make sure that the patch, which Farrell puts on her breast for her heart trouble, wasn't showing.

Slowly I got her to talk about her years in the cork factory. She was an inspector, yet she speaks of loving everyone, and of everyone loving her. How is that possible, I asked her. Inspectors aren't usually very well liked by the workers they're forced to inspect. And that got her talking. She spoke of the work, and she spoke of the time she had to leave, when she retired at sixty-five. "They gave me lots of presents," she said. "And I went from department to department. They even gave me a hundred dollar bill!"

Anna came to live with her great nephew, our neighbor Farrell Brodey. She told us about her life working in a cork factory, from the age of 13. She was enthusiastic about everything. Then she died. She was 88.

3

The intensification of anti-Soviet hysteria finds a perfect context in the Twenty-third Olympiad. As the games and the newscasting progress, the amount of time devoted to making pointed remarks about the Russians increases. Rarely, if ever, are we reminded that the United States boycotted the 1980 Olympics in Moscow. It would seem that this current Soviet boycott is a first, and the length of North Americans' memories being what they are, there's little questioning of these attitudes.

The war clearly going on behind the scenes of the monopoly ABC broadcasting is interesting in itself. The first few days we had such an emphasis on U.S. competition—almost to the exclusion of any rational mention of the other countries involved— that the Olympic Committee (hardly noted for pro-Sovietism) filed an official complaint. For a day or two the reporting seemed more balanced. But then it was reported that Pravda had picked up on the complaint against ABC. Obviously the Olympic Committee had their ears pulled. They must have been told that their remark had given the Soviets grist for their mill, so they ceremoniously, at an official press conference, withdrew their complaint. Suddenly, we were being told, again, that ABC coverage was "extraordinary, just what the American people wanted to hear!" After all, it was argued, other nations are receiving their own coverage (the implication being that they can and will applaud only their own players).

Once in a while you hear a reporter speak of a player or players from one of the Eastern European countries as having a definite edge in one of the sports. An East German swimmer, for example. Or a Rumanian gymnast. One day I heard one of the experts beginning to talk about Cuban boxing. I thought we might be hearing at least a mild round of applause for such all-time greats as Stevenson, or Horta. But no. The piece was designed to make us understand that the Cuban boxers had been good at one time, yes, but they are "has-beens" by now. "If the Cubans were here," it was argued, "you probably wouldn't see much difference from the American sweep you're seeing right now" (at that point the U.S. boxers had won every match they'd entered). The great Cuban boxers of the last decade might well be "has-beens" today, but of course it wasn't even intimated that the Cubans might also have replacements.

All this might not be so serious if one knew it began and ended with the Olympic games. But it is just one more chapter in an on-going and intensifying high-powered campaign to drum up as much fear and hatred as possible against the Soviet bloc. Simultaneously with all this, a new film is being advertised. It's called

Red Dawn, and the title is, without explanation, in Russian and English. The spot begins with the words: "In our time no foreign power has ever landed on our soil—until now!"

Of course the most frightening part of all this is that none of the bits and pieces are isolated. They're all part of a whole. We are seeing an active revival of the most reactionary values. Reagan is an excellent actor, and his ability to make people believe that the country has never been in better shape seems to go way beyond his speeches and other public appearances. Key journalists have picked up on it—the chorus gets stronger and stronger.

The figure of Truman was powerfully vindicated at the time of his 100th anniversary, and vindicated precisely on the basis of his greatest tragedies: Hiroshima and Nagasaki. Yesterday was the anniversary of Hiroshima, and while in Japan tens of thousands gathered to plead for no more nuclear weaponry, here the talks between the two powers are off—and needless to say it's the Soviets' fault. It's interesting that figures like Nixon are also coming back into their own. We're being asked to remember him in his "greatness," to "understand" him.

Nothing is too far-fetched to be used in this campaign. It's almost as if reporters were being paid something extra for getting in their digs. In the Olympic game reporting, for instance, the Rumanians aren't noteworthy because they have won so many medals; they're praiseworthy because they "defied the Soviet boycott." Last night, during a boxing match between an American and a Rumanian, with the crowd chanting an unbroken "USA, USA, USA, USA," the announcer suddenly droned "the Rumanians are very popular here, this is the team that defied the Soviet boycott, so this crowd is not as onesided as it may sound.

4

The blatant racism and sexism in the daily reporting of the games is no less aggressive. During the men's gymnastics and semi-finals, ABC's male announcer gave a play-by-play of Peter Vidmar on the pommel-horse: "He's all over that horse as if it were a naked lady . . . !" was one of his choicest remarks. "Now for a look at a really physical sport: boxing," was another comment, for which Jim McKay—the mainstay and a bit more sophisticated voice—

had to apologize a few minutes later. "We didn't really mean physical," McKay explained, "but violent..."

When describing one of the Chinese women divers, a (woman) announcer commented: "It's hard for those Chinese women to keep their feet together." "Oh yes," cracked a friend of mine when he heard that remark, "we've always known theirs is sideways!" Last night the guy doing the play-by-play for the women's volleyball finals—the U.S. was playing China, and China won the first three games, to take the gold—really got carried away. Every other comment was undisguised sexism, when referring to the Americans, and racism with regard to the Chinese. "That's a lot of woman," was one remark made about U.S. Flo Hyman, "that's a lot of woman to warm up!"

5

Thirty years ago this summer I and some five hundred others graduated from Highland High School, a new and waspish institution which at that time was one of the only two highschools in town. The other was Albuquerque High. It was the first, it was downtown, and with the opening of Highland, Albuquerque High was left to the downtown population—largely Hispanic, also Indian, some Blacks, and mostly poor. The Blacks were almost all sons and daughters of the redcaps and other workers on the Santa Fe railroad.

My Highland graduating class celebrated its twenty-fifth anniversary in 1979, and I remember sending a telegram from Cuba where I was living at the time. Mary Ann Shumann (she was "Puddin" Kimball, when I knew her back in school) called the other day to invite me to a luncheon to commemorate our thirtieth year. It was like being in a time warp, television talk show, dream and horror film—all at once.

Entering, I could already see the faces behind the faces. The features of faces approaching fifty fell away revealing jaws, eyes, cheekbones, freckles, hairlines, mouths, noses, eyebrows, and expressions I remembered. Some produced instant recognition; others had to introduce themselves. Some names I remembered; some I didn't. Everyone seemed to know who I was, and in fact I discovered that, for many of these women, I was a kind of celebrity. (There were some twenty-five or thirty women, and a single man.)

Histories unfolded. There was the perfectly groomed Jewish matron whose first son, now twenty-seven, was brain damaged. She puts her energies more and more into voluntary work with the retarded. There were two or three heavily made-up society women who, when asked what they do, replied—almost in unison—"Have fun!" There was the wife of an international basketball coach who is currently living in Somalia. Over chicken salad, we discussed the horrors of clitorectomies. There was the artist who teaches math; the plump freckle-faced kid we called Puddin, now a slender librarian and grandmother. There was a runner whose bad back had finally forced her off the track. And a pianist who described herself as suicidal since a series of operations on her right arm.

There was more than one army or air force wife, only a few women who had never married, and most of those married were still married to their highschool sweethearts. More than anything else, I found myself unhappy that we had so little time to find out about each other's lives.

Yet there is that other sense of it as well. The anger such a moment evokes in me, anger at the well-heeled mores of a society that creates so much pain out of so many potentials for creativity, a society that twists and destroys. I felt the anger intensely, when I looked at the tiny perky turned-up nose sitting somehow defiantly, somehow uncomfortably—still—in the middle of the face of the women who had it "fixed" so as to better fit this nation's concept of beauty. I could see the old nose, it loomed in my memory, completing this woman's real face now forever altered in a kind of quiet madness. I winced with anger when she explained that she couldn't eat the plate set before her because she is on an allergy-reduction diet; said of course she would pay for it anyway, and then turned to the rest of us at the table and confided how embarrassed she is, still, not to be just like everyone else.

I boiled with anger listening to another of my sisters describe a third's twenty-year struggle with multiple sclerosis. "Having those kids literally destroyed her body," the woman said (her face a mask I could not decipher). "But he (the sick woman's husband) wanted them. And you know Jimmy: a Marine to the end! She died soon after giving birth to the second..."

213

It came over me in waves listening to another who spoke, as if it were something to be ashamed of, about having had her daughter late in life. "I guess I was before women's liberation," she said. "I wanted to travel and make music, to do something with my life. I worked on Wall Street for a while, and thought I might want to be a broker's analyst. Until I realized my co-worker, a man, was making twice as much as I was and was half as able. So I decided to settle down . . ."

Scenes of our highschool were hitting me from all sides. The "high quality" education. The "opportunities." Yes, it was "the best highschool in town" then, the only alternative being the downtown school, full (to our young and impressionable minds) of rowdiness and danger. Interestingly, today that old downtown Albuquerque High is considered the best of the city's many high-schools; parents fight to get their kids into it.

Many of these women fluttered and hovered and chirped about me at one time or another during this luncheon. They were de-lighted to see me, they admired me more than I knew, they had followed my career with pride, they bubbled with the knowledge that I was one of them. What were they really thinking, these women who fought the same anguished battles with surroundings and social expectations, who necked in the backs of the same cars, often with the same boys, and never let them "go too far," who kept their skins and shells above everything, and who set out on a road which, for most of them, had no return; what were they real-ly thinking? What do they really think?

6

Last night the men's marathon was the last event of the Olympics, and everyone made their triumphant entrance into Los Angeles' Memorial Colosseum as a part of the final ceremonies. There was an interesting twist to the whole thing: the marathon winner was an "upset," a thirty-seven-year-old bank loan officer from Portugal named Carlos Lopes, slightly balding on top; the an-nouncers could neither speculate on his "U.S. favoritism" nor his "barefoot African liking of hot weather!" In fact, Lopes' victory, an easy and dignified one, put something of a hole in the terrible ageism so touted throughout the media in this country and of course so prevalent at Olympic Games at which it is perfectly natural to say "...by the time the 1988 games roll around, so-and-so will be too old to compete..."

Ageism, like racism and sexism, seems to be one of the mainstays of U.S. advertising. From the most obvious displays, like the various beauty contests and the rush on health spas and youth aids of one kind or another, to the more subtle jabs one encounters every day and in every way: simply being too old to fulfill the image of one's would-be employer, partner, friend or neighbor.

There is an interesting commercial currently on TV which I think sums up the philosophy better than most, *if* one can disconnect enough to read between the lines. It's an ad for a certain kind of shampoo. A man passes a woman going through a revolving door, and he comments to the audience (us): "Look at that hair! Wonder how old she is...?" Fast shot to the woman, by now getting ready to step into a taxi cab. The whole thing, of course, is couched in Fifth Avenue elegance. And she answers to us: "Over forty, *and proud of it!*" Great, But there's just one thing: she looks about twenty-five. So by *apparently* making a statement about "old being beautiful," the advertisers, TV station, and society as a whole are really telling us "old is beautiful—as long as you don't look it."

7

It seems to me that there's one way and one way alone to be able to continue to feel beautiful, useful and energized throughout your life, and that lies in somehow learning to know yourself, to feel good about what you can make and do. Develop a creative passion. Become deeply involved in a task you are convinced is important for the world. Live through creating, producing, being. I am fascinated by people like Meridel LeSueur, who at the age of eighty-four is still travelling by Greyhound to give readings, and to give of her grace. George Wald, who at seventy-seven just organized the only project in which governments are filling a ship with needed items for Nicaragua, and who will actually be on the ship himself as it sails into Nicaragua's Corinto harbor. Arnaldo Orfila, who is close to ninety, was a leader in the 1918 university reform at Cordoba, Argentina, and who continues today to actively espouse every important cause as director of Mexico's Siglo XXI Publishing House. The millions of unnamed grandmothers who, as the Ma Tine in Sugarcane Alley, sacrifice their whole lives to give the young ones the opportunities they themselves never had. My own parents, who at seventy-eight and seventy-four continue to make a transition in their lives as few I know are even interested in making. The list could go on and on. These people are models for me.

8

I see everything double. I see the TV program and what's beneath it, within it, the message being spoonfed to us as we watch. I hold a conversation, and not only hear the words being thrust at me but hear as well, entangled with those words, the words emanating from the brain, the memory, the gut. I walk down the street and someone says hello. Beneath the mask of her or his face, another set of features is squirming. Boiling.

Yesterday as I drove towards home, I suddenly saw a spot of snow on the ground, in the shadow of a parked pickup. It was at least ninety-two degrees. I thought to myself: "Hmmmmm... snow...funny there should be snow when it's so hot out..." Then I did a "bugs bunny" as I slammed on the brakes and the car behind me almost demolished the back of mine. Of course it wasn't snow at all, but a white diaper or cloth of some kind, lying crumpled by the truck.

The light is brighter than Havana's, brighter than Managua midday, brighter than a southern California beach. It illuminates everything, and everything is sharper, finer, blasting one's consciousness, hammering at one's eyes. I remember years ago Don Peterson saying he sees so much that he feels he will surely go mad. I empathize with Don now, and his painful supervision. I feel I cannot only see more of everything, but through things as well, to the other side. What is beneath an average day, an ordinary smile, a casual wave of the hand?

While the Republicans are busy making as much as possible of the fact that Geraldine Ferraro first said she would disclose her husband's income tax declarations for last year and then said he didn't want her to, the Democrats got a good one to chew on when Reagan—apparently testing a mike before his five-minute address to newsmen at his west coast ranch—said, "My fellow Americans: I am happy to inform you I've just signed a bill outlawing the Russians. We start bombing them in five minutes . . ."

One major network and Cable TV recorded the remark, and it soon became the talk of the day. White House officials, of course, brush it off as "an off-the-record remark," and this country's leading reactionaries claim that the justifiably outraged Soviets "don't have much of a sense of humor."

The saddest part of the whole thing, for me, is that it seems clear the remark won't do him any harm. Because of sexist attitudes, and the fact that it still seems so difficult for some in this country to accept that a woman is running for a major office, Ferraro's relatively meaningless problem with her husband's tax forms—which he is not required by any law to reveal—seems likely to do her much more damage.

9

It's early morning. A little after six. In my dream, of all those who would miss me and all those I thought I would miss—does one miss others, when one is no more?—there was a young girl. Nine or ten. Her large eyes reminded me of photographs of Anne Frank. A face most would not have stopped to retrieve, from the many in crowds or public places. A pale face, with brown hair, neither long nor short. Her body was eager, her shoulders ahead of the rest of her frame. "I'll miss you," I told her, "I'll miss you a lot." We were walking along an unknown city street, and it was beginning to rain. Lightly. "I'll miss you, too," she said, looking up at me, taking my hand. "I wish we could have spent more time together, gotten to know one another better . . ."

Perhaps the little girl is me.

10

Bisbee. A town of some 7,000 souls left over from the closing of the copper mine in 1971. Bisbee was a company town, the typical

Bisbee in the late afternoon, between the death of a mining town and the birth of a developer's dream: a simple town, being loved and lost by artists.

dependent community. Phelps-Dodge was the company, and the Wobblies had the union. In 1917 the company smashed the workers' struggle, taking the union men out onto the desert where they abandoned them to starve in the sun.

The endless spiral of tunnels gave way to an open pit at some point in this history, and approaching the town today you suddenly come upon it: a great gawking ruddy and amazing hole in the ground, where the maze of tunnels has become open circles of ridges along the banks. In the pit: the thick yellow water of still ore-rich earth.

We stopped for a moment to gaze at that hole, and a tall old man, large-boned and gentle, walked up to where Phillip Whalen and I stood. "I worked in the mines" was his opening remark, as he waved a sheaf of pale blue booklets in one hand. *Souvenir of Bisbee* was the title. By a Re-Cycled Miner, Ray Ewing. We heard him out, bought copies of his book at $2 each, and begged our retreat to make it on into town in time for a five o'clock press conference. "This is my open-air office," the unemployed miner had told us.

The Bisbee Poetry Festival, in its sixth year, already has a strong history. This year the roster included May Swenson, Phillip Whalen, David Antin, Gregory Corso, and myself. Kathy Acker, invited from London, was hospitalized at the last minute, and her replacement turned out to be the revelation of the festival for me: a thirty-two-year-old performance poet from Atlanta, Debbie Hiers.

Bisbee is the mining town with a dead mine. (Some thirty or forty men are still employed in a bleaching process; the rest are gone: many to work at a nearby high security army intelligence station, where it is rumored the check on Latin America takes place; or to occupy themselves with the few local services; or to putter with such occupations as rock collector, bartender, turquoise polisher, or mayor. Along the deep canyon roads, burro racing and arm wrestling were once competitive delights. The town is almost on the Mexican border, where people crossed over to gawk at one of Pancho Villa's battles in 1915.

This is the town where everyone has a post office box because they won't deliver the mail door to door—too many steep hills, they say. Where you can still buy a house for $8,000 or $10,000 or a miner's shack for $700. Where artists from San Francisco and New York love living because they don't have to lock their doors and their children can play anywhere in town, no crime at all. Where the developers, closely related to Phelps-Dodge and Company, want the poets out so they can build a brand new hotel, high-rise condos and turn the central parking space—now free—into a lucrative paid lot.

11

The festival format was loose, caring, yet intense. Sunday afternon at two Gregory Corso and I read. Gregory was drunk from the time he came until the time he left; he alternates between a posed five-year-old and a fifty-four-year-old in continual demand of reaffirmation of himself, white shirt-sleeves rolled up to expose a lifetime of tracks on his arms, and a thick white paste on his tongue in a totally toothless mouth. He speaks to himself as he speaks to those around him, endlessly questioning or admonishing "Gregory, that was a terrible line!" or "Gregory, what did you do that for?" He seems alternately tender and sheepish, angry and

The oldtimers in Bisbee rage before the intrusion of the developers.

The woman in the window. Bisbee, Arizona.

abusive. His relationship with women is a caricature. And yet there is that genius, that brilliance which cuts right through, touches you—as in "The Marriage Poem."

12

My reading was one of the experiences that made my time in Bisbee. Some 300 people crowded into the hall—all the events had been well-attended. People stood in the back and along the sides. People who were absolutely still. And who cried. I found myself rewriting the poems as I've rarely done before. I often change a word, a pause, perhaps leave out a couple of words or a line, during a reading; but this time it was many lines, whole structures and tenses, which I tried to remember afterwards because they were improvements. I felt connected with this audience as I rarely have in the past. And I began hearing voices asking for more.

13

The southern Arizona desert is different from the New Mexican. After a season of quick monsoons, the land was green. Much gentler than New Mexico. Limestone mountains. More ordinary, not so muted colors. The saguaro cactus seemed to me the image upon which modern break-dancing stakes its claim. In the very early morning hours, driving back to Tucson in the dark and watching the horizon lighten and pale with the hours, a thick mist settled over the road and ever more distant ridges of black mountains cut through an intensifying orange light.

Bisbee faded.

14

My first day of classes began to rise before my eyes. There were eleven women—a Palestinian who has lived in Saudi Arabia, two chicanas, a white woman who has lived four years in Israel, another who is going to work in Peru, women who work full time, two graduate students, majors from the schools of Business

Phil Whalen and I stopped to eat between Tucson and Bisbee. There was a smooth plastic, life-sized horse, hitched to a wagon in front of the restaurant. But the cactus was real.

Administration, Anthropology, Sociology, Liberal Arts, a woman doing her masters thesis in an area of Economics, two women with small children, and several who intimated—when I asked them what they hoped to get from the class—that they wanted to somehow deal with their own attitudes. (Racism?)

15

I'm beginning to feel like a teacher, see the possibility of something meaningful for me and for those who would study with me here, and beginning to hold the experience as being more than a job for survival and/or simply a stop-gap measure through which to give and learn. The second meeting of my Third World Women class had twice as many women—unfortunately, no men—as the first time we met. They are enthusiastic and they seem to represent a broad spectrum of experience and interests.

As we began looking at the experience of Rose McAlister, a poor working-class woman from Northern Ireland and one of the Armagh Prison inmates, the issues I'd hoped to get at through women's testimony came quickly to the surface: colonialism and racism, working women's struggle and feminism, confinement as an example of oppression (the prison of prison, the prison of conditioning, the prison of silence).

One woman said something to the effect that "...reading this kind of testimony we might have the tendency to say to ourselves: my god, look what this woman has done! And what have I ever done that's comparable?" She said it would be important *not* to fall into that kind of trap, but rather to bring the thing home, and use the new knowledge of another kind of life and struggle to empower ourselves in our own lives.

Jasmine, a Palestinian woman who has lived for some time in Saudi Arabia, made the observation that "marriage and then divorce seem to be a kind of stepping stone to awakening among Third World women" in her experience. "We are expected to get married," she said, "and because our marriages are based in distorted conditioning and values, we get divorced. Divorce is still a big step for us. It's the beginning of bringing the personal into the political arena..."

During the criticism space, which we did manage to get into at the end of the class period, a graduate student named Leslie said she wished I had provided a bibliography with the packet of selected readings which had been xeroxed. "Many of us might want to look up the books and pamphlets from which these readings were selected," she said. I conceded that she was right, and committed myself to providing them with such a bibliography soon. The students seem to take easily to the idea that this is my first teaching job, and, in fact, that university itself is new to me.

September

1

Age. Ageism. In a society rooted in a virtual cult to youth, the nature and circumstance of youth are often grossly distorted. But the nature of age is invisible.

On the instructions for filling out a particular grant application, I note that "applicants should be between the ages of twenty-seven and forty-five, although the Board is empowered to select some applicants below and above that range." On many grant applications I have seen, twenty-seven is the cut-off age.

In my class on Third World Women, we deal with the idea of confinement. Most of the women in the class link confinement to imprisonment, poverty, gender oppression, marriage, childrearing, sickness, isolation, physical disability. But one woman, who is forty-five, speaks of age as the confinement she most fears. When we speak about it, it doesn't seem to be age itself so much as an uncertainty as to *where* her body and her mind stand, where they are going, a contradiction felt between her feelings and the image she has (created in her by a web of social and cultural

225

stimuli) of her physical state. She speaks of retaining an "inner sense" of herself at eighteen or twenty-eight or thirty-five, continuing to dress and act and plan as if she were still one of those ages—and then suddenly looking in the mirror and feeling off-center (at best) or betrayed (at worst) by an image that does not coincide with the conditioned expectation.

We come upon our age, as members of a highly industrialized consumer-oriented society, and as women within that society, in different ways. Physically, we slow down. Or forget. Fewer options seem open to us than before. Our emotional relationships change. As lovers we look for a different kind of fulfillment than we once did. As daughters we want to care for our parents rather than expect care from them, and our relationships with our own children—if we have any—is also different: no less loving, but certainly more distant, less immediate, dependent upon a different kind of space. We no longer control them. And we miss them! The dislocation created out of the contradictions between how we feel and look and what we know, and how society perceives us— physically, socially, economically, emotionally—is a very real part of every day.

For a woman, menopause seems much less adequately dealt with than the onset of menstruation. It's true the onset of menstruation is still often sadly shrouded in a lack of basic knowledge, in shame and mystification, especially away from the big urban areas. But increasingly there is a literature which speaks not only of the biological process but of the psychic and emotional processes as well. This literature is not nearly so broadly available as it should be. But in time it will be.

Menopause, even for the more conscious woman, still seems a mystery. Something is written of it in its physiological aspect; little seems written of it in other, equally important spheres. I am going through it now, and have found little, if anything, that satisfies me. Everything seems unexpected. One makes room for one event, and it does not materialize. Or materializes in bits and pieces. Then something else, equally strange and unexpected, comes along, calling out, demanding. One may fight annoyance, or even depression, with some degree of success. But I, for one, am left with a question about the positive changes, the unknown glory. Only last night, while visiting a good friend from San Diego, and hearing her say her hot flashes were preceded by little waves of nausea, did I realize *my* little waves of nausea might be "normal" rather than some sign of illness I was trying, not too successfully, to ignore.

2

Ann and I went to the New Mexico State Fair, took her son Lucas and his friend Anali. We walked through those streets and past those booths I frequented every year between 1948 and 1957, take a few, give a few. I remember getting drunk at a New Mexico State Fair—I must have been seventeen or eighteen—and throwing up on some vast grassy space, filled with couples and radios and color. Now the radios are silver and the size of consoles. Kids carry them on their shoulders as signs of status: the bigger and louder, the higher the status. Wristlets of black leather, studded with metal, and belts that come together in fake handcuffs instead of buckles: all part of the current punk culture.

The State Fair seemed immediately cleaner and friendlier and more inviting than my memory had it. The Indian Village and the Spanish Village are places to go. Their culture has *not* become plastic, not yet. There are still those expanses of grassy green, and couples and families and woman and men and children cluster in groups, rest, eat pizza or Indian fry bread, talk and enjoy the sights and smells. Farther in are the animals, where young people show and sell pigs or goats they have raised and nurtured for a year—since the last State Fair. And there's the race track which is, somehow, like the youthful dream become bigtime and nightmare America. There are the rides, at the State Fair they are bigger and better than anywhere else.

At the Democratic information booth Judy Pratt's supporters were working hard this year—as they are in parking lots and shopping malls, in supermarkets and city parks. At the Republican counterpart, where an oversized color photo of Reagan and blaring patriotic music were backdrop to demagoguery of all kinds, I overheard the single phrase in a conversation: "we'll drown 'em out!" And there was the Choice booth (womaned by some 100 supporters, each for a three-hour stretch). Resting at one point, and seated in a bit of shade, I was approached by a sickly young man who asked me if I'd like to sign a petition against

The status is in the size and shine of the radio/recorder. New Mexico State Fair, September, 1984.

One of the dancers caught my eye. She seemed to move differently from the others, slower, as if the drum-beat came from within her own body. New Mexico State Fair, September, 1984.

abortion. "Against abortion," I exclaimed. "No, I'm *for* abortion!" His small eyes seemed to move even closer together in his pimpled face. "You're for . . . ?" and his voice trailed off. Then he trailed off, hurriedly. I was sorry I had answered so brusquely. Would have preferred trying to engage him in some sort of dialogue.

3

September 11: the commemoration in blood and sorrow—eleven years since the Chilean coup wiped away so much of our communal dream, so much work, so much struggle, so many of our comrades, so much family. I think of Chile, and I force myself to think of the renewed resistance, of the fight that has *not* been defeated, of all that continues to live in the eyes and ears and arms and hearts of a new generation. Growing up today in every street and mountain of that long, thin, strip of pure suffering. The new culture being created, from shards and broken memory. The women, especially, as they have led—and lead—the marches, the re-emergence in the streets, the open defiance of a stronghold that it seemed no one could defy. Eleven years. By what measure is it a tiny chip of time? By what measure is it forever?

4

Yesterday, in one of Ann Nihlen's classes, she showed a film called *Killing Us Slowly—U.S. media use and abuse of women.* Beyond the standard—subtle and blatant—examples of objectification of all kinds, the dismembered breasts and thighs and fingernails, the six-year-old made into a glamor girl, the men looking tough and the women looking at the men, there was one angle which, while not new, was nonetheless of specific interest to me. We were shown an advertisement depicting two women, one totally naked in a leafy underbrush, the other wearing the bra for which the ad was making its pitch. The text? "Such and such a bra *gives you back the natural you!*" The natural you is braless, but you must buy a bra to have it! A perfect example of taking the natural you away, packaging it, putting a price tag on it, and selling it back to you so you will look "natural."

I was struck by a similarity between society's manipulation of women and the imperialist relationship between nations: the highly industrialized capitalist countries take what belongs to the developing nations, refine and package it, and then sell it back to the peoples of those nations with their respective price tags. Again, I was hard hit by the links, the way it is all simply part of a single giant hype.

5

At least 30 million workers suffered unemployment from 1981 through 1983. Needy persons losing all food stamp aid: 1 million. Number of working poor and others losing *some* food stamp aid: 4 million. Increase in the number of Americans living in poverty: 6 million, from 1981 to '82 alone. The rate of poverty is now at its highest in seventeen years: fifteen percent of all Americans. Cuts in the program to aid families with dependent children (AFDC) $4.8 billion, or thirteen percent, 725,000 families affected, 1.5 million children (interestingly the same figure constantly mentioned by the Bishop of Boston when he speaks of children "murdered" through abortion). Cuts in child nutrition programs: twenty-eight percent. Cutbacks in higher education loan programs: twenty-seven percent.

This report, which is compiled from the AFL-CIO Department of Economic Research, the Congressional Budget Office, the Children's Defense Fund and various U.S. government agencies, states that "as a result of Reaganism, two out of three adults in poverty are women. Seventy-five percent of poor people are women and children. The number of female-headed households increased by ninety-seven percent between 1970 and 1980. In 1981 these homes had a poverty rate of sixty-eight percent for Blacks, sixty-seven percent for Hispanics, and forty-three percent for whites. There are 44 million women in the paid labor force, but eighty percent of them are restricted to just twenty of the 420 occupational categories (retail sales, services, clerical, factory or plant work). Women who work outside the home earn, on the average, fifty-nine cents to every dollar earned by a man: Black women earn fifty-five cents, Hispanic women, fifty cents. Fully employed women highschool graduates have less income on the average than fully employed men who have not completed elementary school. Three-fourths of the elderly poor are women, and one half of all widows and single women live in poverty."

6

Bathed in a great white light, we are making love on a parking lot—the small familiar lot in back of my brother's bookstore. I admit that, once a parked car, I have become an egg. But only for a moment. I immensely enjoy loving, but am at the same time aware that I mustn't remain an egg forever. My "owners" will emerge from wherever they have gone to buy whatever it is they are buying, and they will be surprised—perhaps even shocked— to discover their car has been replaced by an egg. As our lovemaking becomes more intense, however, I realize I have no "owner," that I am indeed my own owner, and that I may remain an egg for as long as I wish, having earned the right of passage, the entrance into a new or subsequent state of being. Giving birth to myself in the act of loving is somehow, in my sense of it, linked to the fact of menopause—a joyous passage into another stage of life, where understanding that this time, finally, I am the one giving birth to my own sense of myself, frees me for that last "giving birth" which is death. It is not a sense of death, however, but of life. And peace. I am conscious of the intense warmth of the light. Everything around me is bathed in it, warmed by it, fed by it.

7

Speaking with Susan Sherman on the phone the other night, speaking about this whole question of women and creativity in the United States, she offered the year 1950 as one in which the whole thing "took off." So my mind conjures up 1950, political repression intensifying into the McCarthy period, the public appearance of the women's movement still fifteen years into the future (at least), names of great women creatives in this country still very few and far between, vastly overshadowed in every field by men.

True, Emily Dickenson had lived and died. So had Gertrude

Stein. The Taos group had lived out its day. Georgia O'Keeffe was perhaps at her peak, but who noticed? Alice Neale, Elaine de Kooning, Lee Krasner—they were still young, and greatly in the shadow of their men. Meridel LeSueur and Tillie Olsen had long been artists and activists, but who knew that in 1950? Adrienne Rich was, almost unnoticed, beginning to find her road.

Today's powerful Black, Native American and chicana women writers, poets, painters and musicians were still largely unborn, or an enigma, even to themselves. How could they have been otherwise, given the racist oblivion in which they were forced to grow? And most of the important white women creatives were soon-to-be groupies around a movement that freed a vision and placed it outside academia and into the streets—but the Beat movement also objectified women and, in the case of most of its important names (Kerouac, Ginsberg, Corso, Lamantia, McClure, Bremser), treated us either as something to be taken along, propped in a corner, fucked, used in service roles, or simply to be scenery. And yet 1950 *does* seem like a pivotal year.

8

Perhaps, for women, the road from academia to the streets and highways of America was more important than it would at first seem. With the people (as opposed to some complex institution) making the rules, there comes also an opportunity to know people, their lives, struggles. Academia had played its role. Almost without exception, women writers coming to prominence, even in their greatly unequal proportion to men, were college women. Women who had had the opportunity of a university education. They had read and researched. They must have begun to notice how under-represented they were, in all fields. And begun to ask why. Tillie Olsen, in her extraordinary *Silences*, makes her/our way painfully through the statistics (one out of twelve textbooks in freshmen English literature was written by a woman, according to a 1972 survey).

In the streets of America, women who did not, for one reason or another, defy the "natural" role of women: marriage, motherhood nurturing "till death do us part," had no time for creativity. Then, during the Second World War, which had everything to do with advanced monopoly capitalism and nothing at all to do with women's liberation, women were out of the homes and into the factories. When the war ended they were herded back to the home. But not without that taste of freedom.

Pioneering birth control, the concept—however, incipient—of the single parent, day care (more an ideal than a reality then), and the increase in the availability of some household appliances, must have made a difference. Still, Olsen, points out, in this century as in the last, until very recently, "almost all distinguished achievement has come from childless women: Willa Cather, Ellen Glasgow, Gertrude Stein, Edith Wharton, Virginia Woolf, Elizabeth Bowen, Katherine Mansfield, Isak Dinesen, Katherine Anne Porter, Dorothy Richardson, Henry Handel Richardson, Susan Glaspell, Dorothy Parker, Lillian Hellman, Eudora Welty, Djuna Barnes, Anais Nin, Ivy Compton-Burnett, Zora Neale Hurston, Elizabeth Madox Roberts, Christina Stead, Carson McCullers, Flannery O'Conner, Jean Stafford, May Sarton, Josephine Herbst, Jessamyn West, Janet Frame, Lillian Smith, Iris Murdoch, Joyce Carol Oates, Hannah Green, Lorraine Hansberry."

The women's movement was reborn within the context of movements for Black, Native American, and chicano liberation, even though the familiar patterns of sexist oppression were being continued in these movements. Its early years produced a variety of hypotheses and theses, gradually sifting out into two broadly defined and often antagonistic directions: that which, taking off from a rather rote overview of the Marxist classics, pronounced class as the only barrier to freedom and therefore class struggle as primary. Women would eventually achieve complete equality, it was argued, once their economic equality was assured. Ideological struggle against sexism, indeed an understanding that sexism is defeating not only to women but to the human race as a whole, was seen as extraneous, or as something to be dealt with "after the war was won." Many women felt safe with this thesis, and many men did too—for obvious reasons.

The other direction was seen, by many, as "radical." It saw women as a class, and men not as victims—the system's vehicle in sexual oppression—but as the enemy. Separatism was, of course, the logical conclusion to this line of thought. And a lot of the separatism, *in practice*, was important. As wrong as it may have been in theory, practically speaking it gave women a space in which to act fully, know themselves, develop, stumble with their ideas, grow. Recognize and nurture our own creative voices, minds.

The distance between the largely partisan political women, whose organizations and parties saw any deviation from class struggle as revisionist, and the "radical" feminists who saw party politics, hierarchical organizations in general, and any male input at all as suspect or irrelevant, grew for a while.

Many women struggling in life-and-death battles outside and within the United States (Vietnam, Cuba, the Black movement in the '60s in this country) accused their more feminist sisters of dividing the ranks of more important struggles and of being involved in what they saw as superficial or even crazy issues: the fight for a dignified self-image, control over their bodies, the burning of bras, and the disruption of "Miss America" contests.

The separatists pointed to women in struggle within the mixed movements as being—still and forever—subservient to men, minimally represented in decision-making roles, perpetuating relationships which, after whatever victory was won, would surely continue. They went further. They doubted that a meaningful change could take place for women in a struggle that did not recognize and deal with their oppression *in its making*.

Cultural imperialism played a great role here: Cuban women resented their North American sisters coming to tell them how oppressive their carefully tended fingernails were beneath the canecutter's glove. Vietnamese women spoke of control of their own bodies while their bodies—female and male—were being genetically malformed, napalmed, and murdered by our government.

But issues were confused in other complex ways: some lesbians in Cuba, for example, had come to a point in their lives where, in their recognition of themselves as women-identified women, they might have envisioned more space or freedom for themselves in a place like the United States—where the illusion of freedom-for-all depends, in great part, on the margin provided by a higher level of production. In Cuba, traditional homophobia and misled zeal, within a situation of real people's power, made for a temporary— but nonetheless real—oppression. But some of these women understood that a more equitable situation for all people—gay or straight—could be fought for under socialism. But for many the personal oppression became too heavy to bear.

234

I believe the lesbian movement in this country has been central in providing a lasting space for unfettered creativity by women—all women. It questions, once and for all—and finally in a massive and visible way, in spite of the neo-conservatives and right-to-lifers—*all* the traditional roles into which women have been cast, in secondary, subservient, and nurturing, rather than visionary and central, positions. It questions relationships among human beings, relationships between parents and children.

And we have only to look to the concrete product this creative explosion has already produced: Sweet Honey in the Rock, Chris Williamson, Holly Near, Casselberry and Dupree, Adrienne Rich, Audre Lorde, Blanche Cook, Susan Sherman, Harmony Hammond, Joy Harjo, Judy Chicago, Kate Millett, Michelle Cliff, Ntozake Shange, and so many of the great new performance poets, dancers, musicians, artists of all kinds.

I look at what I have written so far. It's many hours later. I am having to go at this by bits and pieces, as I must do everything in my life these days: school cutting into the writing, committee meetings cutting into thought, politicking cutting into class preparation. And everything cutting into darkroom work.

9

In one of my classes the other day, a young woman who is bright and active, vice-president of the UNM Students Association, a classical musician and a very interested student, confessed that she had never heard of Gandhi until she recently saw a movie about his life—for a class! I had to rethink my concept of student knowledge after that.

This came up because, coming out of an elevator in the Humanities building an hour or so before, I had crossed paths with two young women going in. One said to the other: "Did you understand what he said today?" The other replied: "I never understand anything he says!" And the elevator doors closed between us. It was clear they were speaking about a professor and a class, and my first reaction was a self-satisfied: "I'm glad *my* students understand what goes on in *my* classes!" Then I did a slow double-take. Do they really? All of them?

So I posed the question to my class an hour later. An older chicana student raised her hand and said no, she doesn't always understand, and followed her confession with an explanation about "having raised my children while you all were doing more important things...studying...etc." I tried, first of all, to address myself to why or if studying should necessarily be considered more or less important than raising children. Then, together, we devised ways in which we might alert each other when something threatened to pass by not understood. By the time we finished the discussion, it appeared several members of that class do not understand all or much of what is discussed.

10

Back to women and creativity. The great women's magazines were born: *Chrysallis, Heresies, Calyx, Ikon*. The myriad of newspapers first: *Off Our Backs, Sojourner*, and others. Then the magazines of literature and thought. Serious women's archives. Publishing houses like Feminist Press, Crossing, Persephone, Sinister Wisdom, Spinsters Ink. Women Studies followed the different ethnic studies programs begun at many universities. Slowly ground began to be gained (it's still a struggle) in the seemingly endless effort to reveal history's woman's face. Give validity to a way of seeing, knowing, making, which has always been seen as secondary, supportive, less important.

Now the connections seem particularly important.

Creative women are finding a voice that is different from the traditional male voice. It is no longer a question of "writing like a man," "painting like a man." The woman's voice sometimes complements the male voice, but it is its own. Its relationship to a public is different. Its critics judge it, finally, by a different value system. A tremendous and empowering creativity is being unleashed. One which is beginning, even, to have its effect on the still very much male-dominated and male-oriented world of letters, world of theater, world of music, of painting, dance, photography, philosophy.

Women who are artists are making significant statements. And they are also saying that it's o.k. to be a woman and an artist. We can express our love for the world by writing a symphony as well as, if not much better than, by mending a sock. Our love. Our wisdom. Our anger. It seems important to me that, in a collective sense, women's art is different. Not simply personally different. Collectively different. For it comes out of a different set of assumptions about the world. And about ourselves.

And this is another door opened by the lesbian movement: the idea that the nuclear family, and women's place within it, is not the *only* solution to human relations. A woman who remains single, who chooses to live alone—and perhaps dedicates herself to one or another form of creative expression—is no longer a failure at life's traditional female role, she is no longer a spinster or an old maid. She can be a woman, as independent and creative as a man. Sharing her life with her work, her aloneness, a man, or another woman. (Of course she still must work six times as hard to win the approval, security, or renown a man will have for the same degree of accomplishment.)

The door has been opened. There's no way it will ever be closed again.

11

Meeting Meridel LeSueur for the first time in our twenty years of knowing of one another's existence, of occasionally writing, of reading one another's work—and of course the sustenance I have gotten from her is enormous. She came down to Albuquerque from Santa Fe, where she is currently "boiling away the sugar," as she puts it, on the trilogy she has written, but has not yet finished polishing. "I just need three more years," she said, soon after we'd sat down to talk, "to finish it up. That's all I need." Meridel is eighty-four but she looks and acts ageless. She breathes strength. And connections.

I asked Meridel where she had gone when the House Unamerican Activities Committee served her a subpoena, and she simply never showed up for the hearing. "The Indians hid me," she confided. "They hid me here, in New Mexico, in the north. In a place called Nambe." And she began to speak of the Indians, and we had been talking about the women's movement before that, the different stages it has gone through in recent years, and Meridel linked it all to the Indians in this country, and began to speak of a balance.

"It's not sexual," she said, "but it has to do with woman and

Meridel LeSueur. She signed her books. . .

with man. It's not antagonistic; it's not a battle. Today young people make love and they have to fight each other. It's a contest. And they have something called orgasm. Today they have to work to have an orgasm! But I'm talking about something else. You could see it at the trials after Wounded Knee. The Iroquois Council women practiced it, and so did their men. It is less like female and male, more like ying and yang. There are feminine and masculine roles, but they are not necessarily played out by women and by men. But by both and either. The Indians are very dialectical," she said.

Meridel looked straight at me, at one point and asked, "Well, how does it feel to have come back to the United States right in the middle of the eighteenth century?"

12

A cliff, over a valley I cannot even see, it is so far below me. But I know it is there. Myself, sitting in a rocker, carefully sewing seams in a great garment. I am sewing by hand, and the seams seem strong as I push my needle through one side and out the other. But as I let the garment slip to my lap, the fabric pulls apart again, before my eyes. I seem helpless to prevent this from happening. What is the garment? And for whom is it being made? Unanswered questions.

Meridel's face, and her voice, telling me about the blood. Telling me that the Iroquois women believed that men lacked some specific skill or talent for living, because they didn't bleed. Telling me I, myself, will find renewed energies (or perhaps energies which are new altogether) because I do not bleed anymore. Meridel, telling me again and again, that creativity increases with age. Good, I say, good. We will move forward. We will go as far as we can.

13

Meridel was already sitting around talking with a few people by the time I came—a good twenty minutes before the reading was scheduled to start. She signed books and let those lucid bits of wisdom, which she so easily imparts, fall where they might.

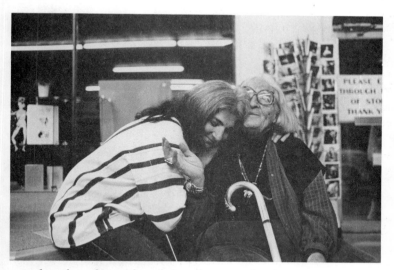

...and we brought our knowledge of one another into a more personal sphere.

239

Without chairs, but with a nice new carpet, people sat on the bookstore floor, filling the place up—there must have been 100, 120 people there.

Meridel stood tall and straight in her eighty-four years, and talked and read and read and talked: about her roots, about the Wobblies, about the great cultural-political movements of the '30s, about Minnesota and breadlines and freight cars and the stories of women, grandmothers, the voiceless. She spoke of Indians and the depression and of the repression under McCarthy. She said the government gives grants to writers as if it's dung, and the writers then have to traipse around behind the horse.

When she'd read an hour, she asked what time it was, and when I said eight o'clock she just smiled, asked if we had a problem with time around here, and kept on reading. Then she invited questions, telling people "it's not often you get to ask questions of a hag as old as I am" (quickly following that with a retrieval of the word "hag" which, she says, was used in the matriarchal societies to refer to the old wise women, the astrologers and seers).

October

1

I write the date, and I'm amazed. October 2. Has it been only sixteen years since that terrible night in the Plaza of the Three Cultures, Mexico City? When the official death statistic was twenty-
six, and more than a thousand had been murdered. What happens
to statistics when they mean human lives? Or dates when they are
co-opted?

Entered the bank this morning and saw a sign on the door:
"Closed For Business October 8—Columbus Day. And I thought
to myself, my god, I didn't know October 8 was Columbus Day. I
always thought it was the day Che Guevara was killed in Bolivia!
And then some almost incoherent things went through my mind,
fast, as I moved over to take my place in the line formed before
the row of cashiers' windows. We will commemorate Columbus
Day. But I will commemorate Che's sacrifice, as I do every year,
year after year, silently, in some small way: a thought, a dream.

2

My life seems disembodied now. Or perhaps bodied would be more accurate. I am menstruating again (first period in several months) *and* having hot flashes all day and some parts of the night—a double whammy, unfair to say the least.

And I received my first paycheck for the classes I am teaching at the university, a check that comes to the grand sum of $382! Which has me in a not-too-silent rage. For I have placed so many of my energies, so much of my time, so much of my total enthusiasm and caring and concern into these classes—the actual classroom experiences (which are four times a week, once for three hours and three times for fifty minutes each), the preparation time, the office hours(another four hours a week, and the committee meetings (I'm currently on two).

This is the major focus in my life right now. And apart from my present classes, I am devoting a lot of time to my "university future": preparing the colloquium for American Studies (through which I hope to nail the title of adjunct assistant professor); I am applying to compete for the course on Women and Creativity for Women Studies during the spring semester; and god knows what else I am doing. And suddenly none of it seems worth it.

I make $1,000 giving a single reading or lecture. So why am I investing so much of my time and effort in this constant and always to be renewed work, for so little? I ask myself the question, and I don't have an answer. Just frustration.

This afternoon I had a vision of teaching a class which has nothing at all to do with the university. Students, women, would simply come and we would study together, once a week perhaps. I would have the class at my home. We would learn together. It would be a simpler way of sharing what I think I have to give—for I do believe I have something to teach, to give—and I would not feel subjected to the indignity of this humiliating system. But of course, who would take the class? Not being accredited, it would probably be considered worthless.

3

Meridel LeSueur spoke of the Wobblies and their attitude towards culture. The great poetry fests and song fests, the publishing and the way books were circulated in far greater numbers than any commercial house, the best commercial house, was capable of circulating them. "Each of us felt a commitment to sell those books," she said, "each of us carried them with us wherever we went, and we travelled the country, and we distributed them hand to hand!" It was a people's culture, and it was a culture of solidarity.

Several days earlier, Meridel had mentioned something interesting that Jerome Rothenberg had said during a meeting of people gathered to open an art program in Santa Fe. Meridel had been present at some of the sessions. She quoted Jerry as saying that one thing that differentiates a people's culture from bourgeois culture is solidarity. Solidarity cannot be part of bourgeois culture.

I thought of this when, at the reading, she spoke of the Wobblies. Of their concept of solidarity: "When someone was in trouble," she said, "when someone was in trouble in Seattle, hundreds would hop freight trains and go to where that person was. They would fill the jails to be with him, to show their solidarity. It's not like that anymore." And yet, when someone in the audience asked Meridel why she was so optimistic, with the state of the nation as it is, she immediately responded with an appraisal of how far we've come—not a short-sighted view of the current administration or the immediate future, but a long-sighted, humanist, historic view, of our lives as part of a continuum of progress and future.

Lately, I have remembered again how difficult it always is to explain to people who have not seen or felt it, the solidarity that is generated by people's revolutions in action. What internationalism is, in a word. What it means for the Cubans to be sending teachers to Nicaragua, when they themselves have no teachers to spare. (Reagan says they are not teachers, but ideological infiltrators.)

But I *remember* Anna's fifth grade teacher, leaving to go to Nicaragua. And how Anna's class had to regroup with another fifth-grade class at the same school, and how all that year there was never another teacher to step in, and how the class consisted of fifty-four kids, in a country that had fought with all it had to reduce its average classroom size to thirty.

And I remember well the confidence that young teacher had as she went off to Nicaragua, and the confidence the teacher who stayed behind had as she urged us, the parents, to help her get

243

through the year. And the confidence we all had, because in some way we were contributing to children in Nicaragua being able to study, perhaps for the first time, in a country wracked by war, with so many dead.

I got to know many of those teachers when I finally went to Nicaragua myself to live. They worked in the most difficult areas. They risked everything. They earned almost nothing. And they took great pains never to impose their ideology (Marxism, and perhaps in most cases the absence of a belief in God) on their Nicaraguan charges. They were specifically instructed to stay clear of subjects involving religiosity, so important to the Nicaraguan sensibility. For they were not there to indoctrinate as Reagan would have us believe, but to work, to show solidarity, to help out. Perhaps, if one has never experienced solidarity, this is difficult to grasp. They were there to share what they, as a people, had struggled so hard for.

4

I once said, in a poem, something to the effect that coming from the middle class, I had no ideology; or that I had no ideology as a child. Certainly I learned a great deal from my parents, and even from certain professors and other role models: honesty, a work-ethic which served me well, at least a disposition against racism and classism and sexism.

But I do believe that the middle class lacks an ideology that is strong and stands up, either on one side of the struggle or the other. There is no ideology like that of the working class, born of gut struggle, of need, or being exploited for your labor power. And there is no ruling-class ideology, though there seem to be lifetimes of aspiring to that. There is, in fact, a great deal of contradiction, a great deal of wavering between the spoken stance and the power to live by that stance, completely. And that is confusing to a young person trained to take things seriously, as she grows up.

I remember my parents very strong on equality. Negroes, as Blacks were called then, were to be considered equals. The color of their skin "didn't matter." Yet when I once asked my parents to rent their spare room to a Black man, a college friend of mine

244

from the Ivory Coast who was having problems finding a room to rent in the Albuquerque, New Mexico of 1954, they resisted "because of what the neighbors would think."

It is clear that the neighbors would have thought a great deal. They probably would have made life miserable for my parents, and for my brother—still a youngster. My mother and father were unable to take a real life stand behind the anti-racist line they had put forth all our childhood lives. To their credit, I should say that they reconsidered when I reacted with sweeping dramatism, marching out of the room and threatening never to speak to them again. Childishly, I refused their come-around offer: I didn't *want* my friend staying with them, I told them then!

That my parents are unusually good and caring people is not in question. Neither is the fact that, at that time, I was unable to deal with such a problem in a dispassionate way. What the incident continues to say to me is that a consistent ideology is hard to come by in middle-class America. People like my father and mother were too dependent, then, on "what people would think," the maintaining of property values, the opinions of neighbors, and of the school supervisor for whom my father worked so hard to earn a meager wage as a string teacher in the public system.

My parents have changed a great deal over the years. They have broken with dozens of rules and regulations of their class. They have grown as few I know have. And they have become examples, not only to others in their social milieu, but to their children too.

5

When I was in San Francisco last November, and speaking with the people at Solidarity Publications about my projected book on Nicaraguan writers, I learned that they would be publishing a collection of Roque Dalton's *Clandestine Poems*, the last poems he wrote. They showed me the translated texts, which I remember thinking at the time were pretty rough. I suggested they be reworked. But I was excited about the book. It has taken so long for Roque's work to come into our English language, to be made available to North American readers. Adam Kufeld, of the Press, asked if I wanted to write something for the volume. I was delighted, and then and there sat down and batted out a few pages—personal recollections of Roque, what his work means to many in Latin America, something about his life and struggle.

Last month the book was published. I received a copy. Solidarity did some struggling around the translations apparently, and the San Francisco Roque Dalton Brigade revised them. They are not perfect, but they are a good deal better than what I saw last November. The publishers used my piece as a kind of introduction to the book. I felt good about that.

Then I received a letter from the powerful San Francisco poet Jack Hirschman. He's angry. He had written an introduction, he says, which for whatever reason was not included. He is angry at me, as well, because in my introduction I said that Roque, like all humans, had problems. And that sexism was one of those problems. And that this poet and revolutionary, towards the end of his life was dealing with his sexism. And that the "Vilma Flores" poems are a tribute to that.

Vilma Flores is one of five invented poets, who Roque imagined and developed to "write" his poetry when he was underground. He could hardly write under his own name in his small country then. And Vilma Flores, as a woman, dealt with sexism a great deal in her poems. Just as the other invented poets, four of them and all men, dealt with other areas in their work.

I had had many discussions with Roque about feminism, and I always saw those final Vilma Flores poems as Roque's grappling with that in his own life experience. But Hirschman said I was "beclowning the memory of a great revolutionary." There are people who still think you can't talk about revolutionaries as if they are human beings, with problems, human struggles, faults. It's the religious attitude towards revolution, and I hate it.

And Hirschman was angry, too, about something else in this book. On pages 116 and 117 are the facing bilingual texts of Roque's poem "La jauria" ("The Pack of Hounds"). The poem uses the word "homosexual" in a derogatory, and decadent, way. It appears in a list along with words like "cuckolds," "sadomasochists," "bad breaths," "hustlers." Well, this is a poem written by a Central American male back in 1973 or '74. Roque had no consciousness about gayness then, if in fact he ever did before his death in 1975. He subscribed to the stereotypes, the macho, sexist stereotypes, in which gay men, particularly, were likened to weaklings, informers, good-for-nothings. Should he have known better? Yes. But I think we must also try to understand his time and place, his culture, and the task he had at hand—helping to win his country's people's war. It was a big enough task, and he gave himself to it fully; we can appreciate that without expecting perfection in his every quality.

Solidarity solved the problem of this poem by publishing it exactly as the poet had written it, and adding a footnote at the bottom of the page in which they stated the following: "Solidarity Publications strongly disagrees with the anti-gay attitude expressed in this poem. We have included the poem because it is a part of the whole work. However we believe that the vision of a world free of oppression that Roque Dalton lived, fought and died for must include the liberation of gay people."

And Hirschman strongly objects to this footnote. He says, in his letter, that Solidarity has "no sense of humor." He really goes out on a contrived limb when he says that "the publication of this kind of footnote will allow the establishment presses to get away with anti-Soviet footnotes" (as if the establishment presses have ever been influenced by what a press like Solidarity does or does not publish), and he cried "Stalinism!" at their position.

I, personally, feel the footnote was the only possible solution. And rather than a lack of respect for the poet, it shows respect not only for his work—in printing the poem in full—but for his process; it assumes his capacity for change, had he lived and considered this other area of struggle. Solidarity Publications is a movement press. They're not in publishing to make money but because they believe in what they're doing. And believing in something means being able to stand behind it. To have refused to print the poem would have been "Stalinist" I think. To have printed it without any qualifying commentary at all, irresponsible. Irresponsible to Roque's memory, to Roque's work as process (rather than some dry, static, ahistoric continuum of words), and certainly irresponsible to the gay community.

But the incident brings up the larger issue of censorship, and especially as concerns the left, women, human dignity. The right-to-lifers and other extreme rightwing groups are promoting a frightening series of state bills, whose surface intent seems to be "against pornography." Good, many women are saying; it's time they stop using and abusing our image! But closer reading of the texts of all these bills shows clearly that they will be launched against us as they pass in state legislature after state legislature. Books like *Our Bodies Ourselves*, serious gay literature, even poetry by some of our finest writers will be the target of these bills; not the offensive and revolting skin mags, not the real hard porn. It's too necessary, both to the economics of our society and to the value system that supports it.

Within the women's movement itself there is a polemic around this issue which has divided women who might otherwise be on the same side. Several writers have drawn up a statement on pornography, demanding restriction of certain abuses and *giving the government power to enforce those restrictions.* Others in the movement are violently against such a law. I stand with the latter, in that it seems clear to me that no matter how specific one is in this type of statement, there is always room for interpretation. Who would be making the interpretation? Those who rule us. I cannot see how anyone in her sane mind could contemplate giving more power than they already have to those who rule us! And putting power in their hands to be used *for* us is almost an open mandate that it be used *against* us. For that reason alone, I would prefer other types of public direct action projects around incidents of pornography, abuse of women in print, etc.

6

The summer has gone. It is cooler in the days, and seems hotter at night when the air is condensed and artificial inside this apartment, and one is dependent on dials, cooler, heater, not one's own needs but some central prefab decision, determined by faceless people who have judged when the air-conditioning will go on in the daytime, when it will go off at night, when it is cold enough to warrant heat all the time.

Yesterday Nina McConnell—a woman from California who wanted to do an interview with me—and I worked up at my parents' house in the mountains. The time is growing close, I hope, when we will begin to build there, close to them, among that yellow-flowering sage, up against the huge boulders which become Sandia Crest.

When we arrived yesterday morning I saw an earth-mover. It

stopped directly across the street from the place where our house promises to be, and some men got out. I had an instant dream that it had come to begin digging the foundation, or preparing the land. Then I knew better: we do not yet even have the permission from the flood-control people, which means we don't yet have the building permit to start. It must be for someone else's house, I thought.

But later, this evening, speaking to David Harrison, the builder, I found out they had in fact come up to look over our land, and that we should hear, this week, that we can go ahead. This is surely the greatest of the many gifts my father has given me: the chance to be with him and my mother in their later years, the chance to be supportive of them at close range, as they always were of me as I grew up, the chance to live out my own years in search of a way to write, make pictures, and, I hope, support myself better than UNM can help me do. All the desert shrubbery blooms and glows this time of year. And the light and shadow on the mountains vibrate on my skin.

7

After months of apparent inaction (apparent because of course an investigation was proceeding, but I wasn't yet hearing anything about it), I finally received a summons to a taped interview with the caseworker who has my file down at Immigration and Naturalization. My lawyer received the same notification and got in touch with the caseworker to ask some preliminary questions. He wants to talk to me about my time in Cuba and Nicaragua, of course, and he told the lawyer "I've been reading her books all morning." "Do you anticipate any problems?" the lawyer asked. "Quite frankly, yes," was the man's reply.

8

So, that's one line of tension: my books, my life, laid open to examination and appraisal by Immigration authorities who have it in their power to make the next years extremely difficult for me and those who love me—the whole issue of ideological exclusion such a matter of interpretation here. Another line of tension is the one holding forth inside my body. I'm going through the constant hot flashes and discomfort of menopause, trying to grasp onto the sustenance of the life change which can, I know, give me strength—but which more often than not gives me an aching annoyance.

At Albuquerque's annual hot-air balloon fiesta, the field yawns and begins to wake as the sun rises.

9

Just for counterpoint, Albuquerque's annual hot air balloon festival opened this past Sunday, and I managed to go up in one. Nina McConnell, who had been here for a week interviewing me and visiting Albuquerque, got the idea of trying to get us press passes for the event. So early, very early, Saturday morning, we drove out to the field, where 453 giant hot air balloons were being readied by participants from as far away as Scandinavia, South Africa, Hungary and of course many points across the United States.

It was cold, and people ran around dressed in heavy jackets and tough gloves. As the sun emerged from behind the Sandias, the trucks unloaded their wicker gondolas—each weighing about 450 pounds when their four propane tanks were full, and each with room for perhaps two others besides the pilot, in a fairly close squeeze—and their small motorized fans, and their bulky canvas sacks from which the brightly colored balloons appeared.

People ran around helping each other, each pilot seemed to have a ground crew consisting of a few friends or family—although in some cases they were professionals. The activity seems to attract a certain kind of person: very American in the best sense of that term, friendly, adventurous, the twentieth-century variety of mom and apple pie. People exchanged stories about their balloons, and about other events, about floating the skies of Seattle, Arizona, and elsewhere. Nina and I went over to the press trailer, and almost immediately we were able to go up with a pilot named Richard Glass, from Tucson.

I might well have been the only human being among 500,000 (newspaper estimate) who was photographing in black and white instead of color. Many ran around with polaroid cameras, producing instant snapshots of the marathon of color. I was fascinat-

There were a number of women among the 450 pilots. This is Kathy as she begins her ascent.

ed by the shapes, the great balloons being laboriously righted and inflated, first with the action of the fans, then with the ground-level work of the live propane: a bright yellow-to-blue flame shot into the great silken cavities.

When the balloon was attached to the gondola and stood ready to rise, the take-off seemed immediate. People helped one another. We climbed into Richard's gondola and in a matter of seconds were off the ground. The ascent is close to vertical, and quite wonderful. I hadn't expected it to be so gentle.

The sky filled with balloons—beneath us, beside us, above us—and of course it was of primary concern to Glass not to get in the way of others. He maneuvered skillfully, interspersing his burning and venting (opening or closing the propane flow) with snatches of conversation in which he answered some of our questions about his life in the sport, experiences at other events, and balloons in general.

We flew for some twenty or thirty minutes, over the largely barren southeastern section of the city, and then came down in a cow pasture and had to stay inside the gondola until Glass's search crew finally showed up to help us officially land and dismantle the balloon.

The air above the city fills with balloons, 453 of them on the first morning of the fiesta. I thought: "I am the only one photographing in black and white," as I positioned myself inside the gondola in order to shoot out and down.

10

Peculiar this sense of "not fitting in." Do I want to fit in? Well, no—not in any all-American sense. But there is the isolation I feel, at times even with those I love, at times with friends, at unexpected times and often with an intensity that far outweighs either moment or context.

11

In my Third World Women class today, the session began with only seven women present (of a possible twenty-four). In a few minutes three or four more appeared, and that was it. What happened? Well, today was the day people's midterms had to be in. Many apparently didn't have theirs done, and rather than come to class without them they chose not to come to class. I was amazed.

I told the group that I'm now really unclear about people's priorities in this country. How can one imagine that a test, a lousy test, could be more important than coming to class and sharing the kinds of experiences which have been so vital to all of us, from the beginning of the semester? I realized as I spoke that I was espousing values few, if any, agreed with. Or even understood. If it is indeed a "lousy test," then why give it? Well, basically because I know I am expected to. And again, the sense of not fitting in.

12

Yesterday's class: Agnes, from Isleta Pueblo, was giving her presentation of women in the Pueblo tribes. She spoke mainly of her own experience, slowly and almost hesitatingly at times. Often she said "I want to correct the impression given by . . ." and she would name a white anthropologist like Oliver LaFarge—the great misrepresentation of the Indian ways.

Then Catherine Baca asked a question. She said her best friend at medical school had been a Pueblo Indian woman, from Acoma. And that she particularly remembered that woman's difficulty in their pathology and anatomy classes, because her belief system prohibited her from touching the dead. That visibly moved

Agnes. She talked about her own decision to become an anthropologist in spite of her father's initial objection, "because I felt it was time Indians ourselves really understood and could combat all those theories the white anthropologists have put on us." And in light of that decision, Agnes spoke of the first time she had to examine boxes of potshards in a class.

"We believe that we must not touch the dead," she said, "and that extends as well to the things the dead used, their utensils, their belongings. It is especially problematic with shards, pieces of things which once were dishes or pots, because we have no way of knowing whether they were ceremonial pots, utilitarian objects, or belonged to the dead. And suddenly there I was, seated around a huge table, as my classmates passed around pot shards and I knew I would have to touch them or leave the room."

She told us she felt fortunate to have had an understanding professor, who told her that she didn't have to touch them if she didn't want to. But she made her decision, to go ahead and touch them, based on her commitment to them and to herself, not to show disrespect.

13

The dream: Something enormous and conclusive is going on in the sky. Great patches are turning black, a bluish, reddish black. In the distance I can see some of those patches tearing off from the vastness of the atmosphere and careening to earth as monstrous flakes of dry paint, peeling off and shattering against the earth. I look out in several directions. In one I see billows of black smoke—the universe is on fire! In the direction of the Sandia Mountains, where my parents live, there is a veritable storm of immense pieces of sky, churning and falling. Quickly I got to a telephone, and in some sort of computer code a scratchy voice repeats and repeats that my parents have been "heroic. They will be rewarded...they will be rewarded..." the voice cracks over and over again, into my anguished ear. As I roam the streets then, unearthing people hiding under mutilated fragments of buildings, others walking aimlessly, some muttering inaudible or meaning-less bits of phrases or sentences, I realize this is it: the end of the world.

Something tells me not to breathe in the dense air all around me. I take a deep breath. It is a sort of defiance. A last defiance. The colors—dark red-browns, blacks, smoldering bluish purples— keep changing in some gigantic slow-motion kaleidoscope of ultimate extermination. A naked leg gleams white in the strange light. It protrudes from under rubble so mangled and confused I will never know what it once was. I decide to try to concentrate on an immediate, short-term project: to find the children, my parents, Floyce. I wander and wander, but can find no one.

14

I spoke on the phone with Karen in Managua. Her voice tells me of the anguish of the situation there, the tremendous tensions, the toll the war is taking (an average of five deaths a day now). Her voice tells me people's morale is being affected, though still strong. Her voice tells me what constant military and political and economic pressure can do to a nation struggling for survival. All this as TV gives us the evaluation of Grenada on the anniversary of that travesty-called-success. And the campaign rolls on—with brute fumbling passing easily for charm and ignorance passing for intelligence.

15

It was 1960. I was living in New York City and I was pregnant with my first child, Gregory. I must have been six or seven months pregnant at that point, for I remember a large, tent-like pinkish dress, the way the particular fabric felt against my belly. A friend invited me to an uptown theater, a first-run film: *Psycho*. I can still recall the vague sense of glitter associated with the Broadway and Forty-second Street area, the idea of paying $5—or someone else paying $5—to see a movie! We settled into the elegance of well-manicured seats; there was a plushness in the air. About-to-be-single-mother or not, bulging belly or not, this was very much a date. That consciousness is also a part of it all.

The film began and the storyline proceeded with all the expected engagement. I remember it was a black and white film (color was much less prevalent then) and I can still conjure some of the scenes: a conversation in an insurance office, something about a lot of money, a flight in a car—was it Kim Novak? Grace Kelly? The perfect blonde in any case. And mounting expectancy as she entered the world of that strange old house, and the strange young man who lived there. But anything about the rest of the film is dwarfed by what happened to me, in that theater, when finally confronted with the central and culminating scene. The woman taking a shower, her perfect body powerfully suggested behind the plastic curtain. And suddenly everything going wrong.

A man has entered the bathroom, that vulnerable but inviolate space. I cannot now remember if we see his shadow or his hand, perhaps some dismembered part of his body, maybe the arm raised with the murder knife. I hate terror films and always avoid them. As long as I can remember. In that uptown theater, almost a quarter of a century ago, my open palms springing to cover my face as they always do in situations of contrived violence and packaged fear, through the slits between my fingers I continued my contact with what was happening on the screen. That double bind of rejecting what you're being fed, but not being willing to remove yourself entirely.

And, as the bloodied whirlpool of draining water and the single staring eye of the terrified woman, now dead, merged somehow upon the screen, I was suddenly aware of something else taking place inside my body. It was more than the tense excitement of the horrifying scene. It was different from anything I had experienced. My belly was becoming totally hard, taut as steel, invulnerable. Inviolate. Not painful, but painfully present. I took a deep breath. I tried to relax. I couldn't feel the baby, whose frequent movements had been such a source of delight and comfort.

When we left the theater, I tried to broach the subject with my friend. He laughed. That night in bed I gingerly rolled over to where the position and the pregnancy should have vied for privilege at least. Was it my imagination that I might well have balanced my body, face down, on that unyeilding belly of mine? The next day I went to see good old Doctor Zimmer, the aging and good-natured family physician who was seeing me through the nine months and the delivery. By that time I was anxious. I couldn't feel my baby kick. And I wanted to be done with *Psycho*.

Dr. Zimmer probed my belly and listened with his cold metal

horn. He smiled and patted me once again on the head, as he explained that "these things sometimes happen. A series of muscles protect the womb and go into action when they receive a signal of any kind, a threat to the child developing there. Yes, it would be all right. Yes, it had just been my body's way of responding to intense and sudden fear. Yes, it would surely go away in a day or two. Relax."

Indeed the rigid wall of steel did soften and disappear. I felt my baby's movements again, and several months later gave birth to a healthy boy. But when I contemplate what they are doing to us today, remaking us in an ongoing image of the system's needs through every commercial, subliminal ad, feature, news release, fashion, snatch of music or slice of life, I sometimes think back to the power in their hands, even then, to mold responses and slap our very bodies into shape.

16

Awoke yesterday—as did the rest of the world—to the news Indira Gandhi is dead. Shot to death by two of her personal security guards, Sikhs, who presumably are taking revenge for the Indian Army's entrance into the Sikh's Golden Temple in an attempt to dislodge a separationist movement there. The news hit me between the eyes. I felt a kind of emptiness in my body, and tears kept welling up in my eyes all morning. I felt vulnerable and lonely, and at the same time I couldn't really understand the nature of my feelings.

I admired many things about Indira Gandhi, abhorred others. Her death was a shock but it seemed to me that my reaction was overblown. As the morning unravelled, though, I began to understand it more. It was the fact that death had come from her own security guard, that more than anything else, seemed to cut into me, turning up layers of skin, turning them inside out and exposing them to the air.

On TV we had the usual: the "impartial" news reports, focuses they're called, in which these sometimes-prodding sometimes-ignorant anchor men (or women) interview one or two "on each side" of a question. Yesterday we had the Indian ambassador to the United States, subdued and grieving, articulate and occasionally riling against the extreme racism of the reporter. And we had a leader of the Sikhs in the United States, announcing to the world the total "normalcy" of the act, without flinching or any visible embarrassment. Terrorism dressed in a suit and tie. And the reporter asking him questions, as if he were Shirley Temple, or some Yale professor.

Reagan of course used a concerned face (it was Halloween) and spoke of how well Indira Gandhi and he had always gotten on. Margaret Thatcher became "soft and gentle"—for the first time I've seen her that way in the media—and spoke of the "special understanding" the two had had. One wondered how Indira's soul might writhe at such expressions.

The phrase "largest democracy in the world" was used over and over again in the news reports, but rarely was much attention paid to Gandhi's role in the Nonaligned Nations Movement, or to her success at having at least somewhat fruitful relations with both the United States and the Soviet Union, her refusal to be pushed into the so-called East-West struggle.

November

1

My eyes keep going back to an amazing discovery (of mine, for it has long been discovered by others) last Saturday when Ruth Hubbard and I made the rounds of museums and local curio shops. The Pueblo Indians here make a sculpture, a seated woman whose arms and even shoulders, whose lap and breast, are virtually covered with a myriad of smaller figures, children who are listening to her tell a story. These sculptures vary in size, and also of course, in magic. Some are quickly turned out for the tourist trade; others depict on the woman's face all the wonder of the storyteller tradition, and all the beauty of its history—the meaning in that. Trisha had spoken to me about the storyteller, but I guess I hadn't realized she was an actual figure, immortalized in a piece of traditional art.

Things like the storyteller raise me from the morass one feels around events like the Indira Gandhi murder, or—much more—the impending elections. I find myself physically *using* the figure to remind me that the world, as I know and love it, is still somehow in place.

The Pueblo Indian storyteller, in the statues of her, at least, reminds me of the extraordinary series of lifesized images at that small museum near Jalapa (Veracruz, Mexico) where the great Venta heads are on display. Along with those enormous heads is this series of lifesized images of women, modelled in clay, and called Women Dead in Childbirth. I remember now how they mesmerized me, held me for hours, as I looked first at one face and then another.

All the women seem to have died in anguish, the anguish of death and the anguish of leaving that moment of dual life, the child's life as well as her own. And yet there is something so intensely profound in those faces, something recognizable even when one has not faced more than the fear of that moment. They have always lived in me. They have never left me. And, strangely, I find myself going to them for sustenance, from time to time.

These days there is nothing on my mind more than how to face next Tuesday. How to deal, within myself as well as responsibly to others (and as a teacher very much to one's students), with the reality that will engulf us when what we fear becomes reality: Reagan is elected to another four years in office. Most people I know speak of this in a fairly routine way. They show their fear and even revulsion, but speak little if at all about how that will affect their lives. Perhaps none of us really understands it. Only vague imaginings.

Those who are old enough to remember the '50s, or have heard enough about them from others, perhaps have the closest sense. Younger people—because of the way history is chopped up in this country, and continuity is lost—have no sense at all. What will this mean in terms of bread and butter? In spiritual terms? In our everyday lives? Will we even make it through? Undoubtedly, many will not.

It's so important to see the daily, individual struggle, and to see its relationship to history. To keep a historical perspective. And to understand the dialectic between the two. This suddenly came clear again to me yesterday afternoon while seeing a film called "The Pink Triangle." This is a short documentary about homophobia and the repression of homosexual men and lesbian women in this country. Trisha showed it in her Heterosexism class, and I had suggested to my classes that they come see it as well.

The documentary is quite wonderful. It begins with a series of absolutely straight on-the-street spot interviews with men, women, kids. Most of the responses to the question "What do you think of homosexuals?" ranged from "they're disgusting," "revolting," "it's unnatural" to "it's against God's will." Only one little kid, when asked "What would you think if you found out your brother is gay?" answered with a big grin "He is!"

But the film goes back and laboriously retrieves the symbol of the pink triangle, telling many who don't remember or never knew that while Jews were forced to wear yellow Stars of David in Germany during the Holocaust, homosexuals in the same place and at the same time were forced to wear small pink triangles. They were picked up and sent to the same concentration camps, forced into the same slave labor, abused by the same mad medical experimentation, burned in the same ovens, and then those few who survived, when the allies came to liberate the camps, were often considered (by those same allies) "criminal elements" and were therefore returned to confinement. The pink triangle is revealed.

One part of the film moved me almost to tears. It is the story, told in his own words, of a young highschool kid who, as he says, always knew he was gay. He speaks of his struggle at school, to make friends, to go on in spite of the constant sneers and jibes. And he says: "I always knew I was gay. I couldn't lie to myself. I had to try to make friends on those terms."

He said it so simply, I found myself thinking: my god, here's this kid saying he had to be honest with himself! That—although many seem to have forgotten it—represents the purest strain of our tradition. What's cleanest and most beautiful in human beings. Why aren't our leaders chosen from among people like that? Why aren't we even permitted to choose our leaders from among that kind of people?

At the end of this kid's testimony, he looks straight at the camera and says: "My graduation was interesting. I wore a cap and gown, like everyone else, but it had a small pink triangle on it. I felt like I was redeeming my brothers and sisters from Nazi Germany on, who suffered because they were gay. When I went up to receive my diploma, a whole section of the public booed. These were parents, teachers, family. But a whole other section cheered. Those were the students. And I turned and bowed to them."

When the lights went on, and Trisha's Heterosexism class was expected to begin discussing what they had just seen, the room was quiet. It was clearly hard for these young people, most of them gay, to rise from the funk the film had sent them into, and discuss it. Then, of course, some began to do just that. And I noticed that their responses were mostly based in personal experience, events, problems.

Trisha put forth the idea of linking struggles, and asked people if they believed the struggle for gay rights could and should be linked with the class and race struggles. People seemed to want to say yes, but—again out of their own experience—brought up examples of having been sold out in past attempts. I suddenly saw the whole discussion as analogous to the experiences I have with my own students, often about other issues. And analogous, too, to next Tuesday, when we are going to need a perspective that will carry us through. Which will not sell anyone out.

I found myself making an impassioned argument in Trisha's class: trying to get the students to see that their own experience is important, that it must be the basis for understanding issues rather than the rhetorical formulae so often laid down by different theoretical groupings, but that also they must see life as a part of history, struggle themselves with the knowledge that *they* are a part of history, and not lose sight of that broader historical perspective.

Most of them do not have this historical perspective, because it is systematically sliced to pieces, strangled really, by our media and by the way history is generally dealt with here. But a real understanding of life and struggle comes only from a dialectical vision of the small, individual struggle, and the historical perspective into which it can be and must be placed. We are oppressed as women, as workers, as gays, as Blacks or Hispanics or Native Americans. But we have come light years from the Nazi Germany of the '40s, or even the United States of the '50s.

Ten or fifteen years ago, I told Trisha's class, there couldn't have been a subject called Heterosexism. So many of the things we've struggled for and won did not exist earlier in our own lifetimes. We are moving into a new McCarthy period, it's true, and the consequences are unimaginable to most, but it is still part of an ongoing move towards life and not a reversal to death.

Meridel LeSueur's vision of the world is so important here!

Perhaps one must live eighty-four years to really understand how much we've gained. Only by really incorporating an understanding of this into our particular and individual lives, will we be able to escape the anguish and resignation next Tuesday's events will otherwise put on us.

2

I had been preparing for this colloquium in American Studies for more than a month. Contrary to my usual feelings about reading or speaking in public, I was extremely nervous about this event. It was planned expressly so that the professors and graduate students in the American Studies department could vote on whether to offer me an adjunct assistant professorship.

I began writing a paper that sometimes seemed like it was aimed at future students, occasionally seemed like it was aimed at the colloquium audience (much more sophisticated), and more often seemed aimed at outer space. But I kept working on it, and getting more and more uptight. Yesterday when only a few hours separated me from the task, I felt miserable. But I went and taught my noontime Third World Women class, and then went over to my office to sit and stare at the walls for a while.

I had bought a new book of Alice Walker's poems, *Horses Make A Landscape Look More Beautiful*, and was reading some of them. Suddenly I knew exactly what I was going to do. I quickly went through the paper, typed in its final version, that I'd been carrying around for days. I crossed out exactly those parts I thought I should leave out, knew as soon as I re-scanned it that it worked better without them, decided to end with one of Alice Walker's poems,* and walked over to the small theatre in the Humanities Building where the colloquium would take place.

There were about twenty people there, or maybe twenty-five— among them personal friends who were very supportive, and the professors at American Studies who were judging me. Janet Caputi introduced me, and I got up to speak. It only took me two minutes to know I was doing what I had to do. Making no

*"Each One, Pull One," from *Horses Make a Landscape Look More Beautiful* by Alice Walker, Harcourt Brace Jovanovich, New York, 1984, p.50.

concessions, making a strong political and feminist statement about women and creativity, doing my best but not hiding who I am—and if they want me, fine; if they don't, that's o.k., too. I felt good about the presentation, and I think it went well. There were very few questions at the end—which either means everyone agreed or everyone disagreed. Since I know everyone didn't disagree, I guess it's safe to assume it was fine.

3

Perhaps the most painful thing I'm discovering in the teaching itself—and I say the teaching itself, because I am not speaking of the institutional structure with its mediocre politics, which so often seems to encourage conformism over real scholarship or creative space—is the absolute lack of historical context the students seem to have. It is not as simple as saying: the history is taught wrong, it is taught to nourish a vision of the past which is supportive of a distorted present (and future). No, it is much more complicated, and worse.

For what the students lack is a sense of where *they* fit into their own recent past history of struggle. Since the context itself has been erased from their consciousness—or was never allowed to grow there—they have no understanding of the process of even their own individual participation. What I am saying is that young chicanos don't seem to have a sense of what it was like for their mothers and fathers, for their grandfathers; young Blacks on this campus know nothing about the Black women who travelled this state founding Black Women's Clubs back when the only Blacks in New Mexico were working the Atchison, Topeka and Santa Fe Railroad line; gays get discouraged because there is gay oppression.

Someone circulates a piece of outrageous political propaganda accusing a local and very good person running for State representative of "supporting a bill for sodomy!" Rage against the propaganda is high, but there seems so little placement of that rage into a perspective of ongoing struggle. It's the sense of process that's missing.

I speak to a young student about her midterm. She has written nothing but a statement about her inability to write. As a statement it's interesting. As a midterm it hardly qualifies. We talk.

She is depressed, floundering, wants to drop out of school—and the world. She has no sense that there is nowhere in the world which constitutes a place to drop out to. She is struggling with problems grappled with—and to some extent, solved—a generation ago, greatly—I'm convinced—because she has no sense of that other grappling. She has not bothered to read the books.

This young woman cannot build on the struggle of mothers and grandmothers, or even of older sisters, because she is totally unaware of their struggle. Students know nothing of the '60s, even on their own campuses. Any sense of continuity they may have had has been riddled by the surefire of a media image, plastic and disembodied. Their identities have suffered so much as a result.

With Tuesday's election coming up, I have felt the need to speak to my students about this. Not to pacify them into believing it will be all right. I have told them that what's coming will be terrible in ways none of us can possibly imagine. I have spoken to them of the '50s. I have read them testimony by those who survived that decade, and by those who were crippled for life—or death. But I have also felt the need to tell them that the struggle moves forward. But it doesn't always move forward in a straight lines, that it has its terrifying downs as well as its empowering ups, and that they must begin to know their own history, so they can rationally struggle within it. Be depressed if need be, but *in* context, not out.

4

Today are the elections in Nicaragua. The right (the U.S. government and its supporters) set the Nicaraguans up for elections which could not be, and should not have been, priority spending and effort in a wartime economy. The major Nicaraguan conservative parties staged big-press walkouts in an effort to show that no democratic electoral process could take place in their country because the conditions weren't there. Then, of course, the U.S. began promoting the line that, since only the left was running, the elections were a fraud. (My friend Frances Romero, up from Nicaragua for a couple of weeks recently, told me she felt that Arturo Cruz had pulled out primarily so as not to be embarrassed by his very minute social base.)

Today's major newscasts focused in on the elections without

any show at all of on-site coverage. The major description centers on a U.S. State Department booklet "guiding journalists to avoid presenting a valid electoral process." Much more detailed on-the-spot coverage is given the Sikhs and Hindus doing each other in on the streets of India, up to and throughout the funeral ceremonies for Indira Gandhi. We are shown blood and burning without end around that incident, but we are not shown ordinary Nicaraguans going to the polls—god knows we should be permitted to compare their democratic process with our own, ask ourselves questions about the vital differences between our own candidates, compare notes about the relationship of funding to freedom. (The quarter page ad, "Artists, Writers, and Musicians for Judy Pratt" was run in today's Albuquerque *Journal*, hidden in the deepest recesses of the travel section. A moral majority full-pager occupied our attention with giant headlines on the back of one of the more popular sections.)

5

Well, it's over with, this intense preparation and almost unbelievable deadening of people's senses and ability to judge our future: beginning with the summer Olympics; going into high gear with the Republican Convention in Dallas; ending with the night of the 6th, election eve.

It became more and more difficult to distinguish Ronald Reagan's media image hype from a Marlborough ad—the same lone figure, tall in the same saddle. And an edgy patriotism began to squirm in people, prodded daily by our Olympic figures carrying off the wins (even with half the world not there), moving on through those same figures touring the nation and ending up in their red, white and blue jackets in Dallas on the eve of the Republican's day.

The symphony of TV features, soaps, newscasts, commercials, "impartial" interviews and the rest became more and more frenetic and the pieces meshed together less and less as separate input. We had *Call to Glory* and *Red Dawn*, we have "Dallas" and "Paper Dolls," we had the McDonald's ad in which any old man, woman or child *became* an Olympic star before our eyes. We had the Indian and the Bear in the Woods (one of the more sinister, and surely most effective ads the Republicans ran). We had the

266

Helms/Hunt campaign, with one ad alone—run by Helms and then re-run almost endlessly on all the major network analysis shows—in which successive Las Vegas-type gambling machines sprang Carter's, Mondale's and Jesse Jackson's distorted faces (this latter looking more like a primate than a man) so that racism and bad memories would also be able to do their part. Helms' campaign alone is said to have cost the people $20 million.

We had the situation comedies, when women, Blacks, gays and other important issues continued to entrench themselves in our consciousness—always from an establishment point of view, independent of subtle differences. We had issues in the campaign itself (raising taxes, Geraldine Ferraro's husband's tax returns, Mondale as boring vs. Reagan as endearing, Reagan's supposed strength and leadership qualities, Ferraro as woman when it could be clearly seen that the gender gap had gone totally awry, a tough defense, and so forth) pounded into our senses—compounding a fractured reality.

We had big business's input: like the computer ad for floppy discs, in which the image of a herd of elephants trumping their way through the Wall street canyons is one that doesn't easily leave the unconscious eye. Elephants = the Republican Party. It was interesting how much big business advertising during the campaign used the elephant image. And, finally, just to deal with the changeover vote the Republicans needed to nail their case, we had the commercial with father and son, in which the son—a man in his early twenties—walks down a country lane with his dad. He turns to him and says: "Dad, do we have to vote Democrat? I don't want things to go back the way they were. Things are better now, there's work . . ." And then, in a slow and dramatic gesture, the father answers: "When you pull that curtain shut, no one has to know how you vote!" The son smiles and says, "Thanks, Dad!"

So, on Tuesday night, we had what the media now call a *landslide* for the Republicans. Right across the board. Reagan with almost every state in the Union, in electoral college votes. Jesse Helms almost certainly to be the next chairman of the Senate Foreign Relations Committee. In the State of New Mexico, Judy Pratt barely getting twenty-six percent of the vote against Pete Domenici. And the only women winning respective offices being conservative Republicans, often winning over men who would have been considerably better for the job.

What this election wasn't however, was a landslide. Mondale, doomed to begin with, lacking charisma and lacking office, dragging the Carter image and seeming almost to have been nominated in order to lose, nevertheless won forty percent of the nation's popular vote. That's what can happen in this electoral system of ours. And no one can tell me that was really a forty percent vote for Mondale. It was a forty percent vote against Reagan. Meaningless in the most immediate sense, but certainly not a landslide for Reagan.

The insistent use of that word is a continuation of the media hype. That forty percent of the popular vote is a pretty good base from which organizing can be done, once a real, effective, intelligent strategy can be worked out. When the Reagan lies begin to fall apart in people's lives, when the economy begins to show deeper and more apparent signs of problems, when war seems more imminent or is in fact launched, when social services are cut back even more greatly than they have been, I'm willing to bet others will join that forty percent.

The only social base that really stuck by the Democrats was the Blacks. Real evidence of Jackson's work. Ninety percent of the Black vote went to Mondale. In the other minority sectors, and among women, it was disastrous. In order for the women's vote and minority votes to have really made a difference, those sectors would have had to have supported the Democrats like the Blacks did, right down the line and in high percentages. They didn't.

The women's vote interests me. So much was said about the gender gap. And it does exist. But what happened? Putting Ferraro on the ticket seems in fact to have worked more effectively against the Democrats than for them. She was pushed into a corner, her extraordinary strength and speaking talents permitted to emerge only occasionally, and she was constantly being put to tests which she managed better than anyone in recent U.S. politics, yet the media—once again—aided and abetted in the way that people viewed those tests.

During Ferraro's debate with Bush, she was clearly advised to tone it down, to be calm, cool, and collected, so she could never be accused of being "an hysterical female." The result: she came off grey. And Bush, who was entirely hysterical much of the time, was considered "forceful." The most explicit show of sexism in American politics I've seen in a long time. In fact, it seemed constantly amazing that we were daily treated to a show of how backward this country is in matters relating to women's rights. Even with conservative nations like England and Israel having had women leaders for years now, the very idea of a woman even in second place on a major political ticket just seemed to be too much for the American public to handle. And certainly women did *not* turn out in droves to support the Democratic ticket.

People now ask what happened to the equation that was almost taken for granted during the campaign, that if there could be a record turnout, the Democrats could win. There was a large turnout, but the Democrats would have had to have carried all the minorities, women, the poor, working people, youth. Hispanics failed them. Native Americans failed them. Women failed them. And youth failed them massively (clearly because they have no collective memory, and are so legitimately frightened of not having a job when they get through school that all they can latch onto is not wanting things to be the way they were in the '60s—"all messed up").

But of course it was not women, Hispanics, Indians, and youth who failed the Democrats; it was the Democrats who failed themselves. And very much, I believe, Mondale's absolute fear of recognizing and working with Jackson's historic contribution. People felt betrayed. And they were.

6

The night of November 7 I couldn't sleep. I had rattling dreams. I got up and cleaned house—rare for me, especially at 3 a.m. When the morning paper came, the first thing I noticed was that my friend Enrique Schmidt had been killed in the fighting in the northern part of Nicaragua. That was shock number one. I remember Enrique well, his gentleness, his humanity and political maturity. What does it mean when a nation has to send one of its cabinet members (Schmidt was minister of communications) to the front lines to fight?

Looking at it another way, the Sandinistas share in the terrible responsibility of giving their lives. Leadership rotates regularly, in three-month stints in the Omar Torrijos Brigade—a battalion in which high-level Sandinistas fight alongside their brothers and sisters so they will never slip into the criminal practice of using their people as cannon fodder, while they themselves sit behind desks or stand at podiums. Still, Schmidt is a terrible loss for Nicaragua. I wanted to cry, and couldn't.

By the time the polls had closed, and the election returns began coming in across the country, people's emotions were twisted, crunched, hardened, worn out. People take their sadness and rage out in different ways. My friend Trisha wanted to wear black yesterday. She wanted to make a statement of mourning. I felt more like making a statement of rage and, yes, strangely, obstinately, also of hope. Refusing to accept the word "landslide" seemed a beginning. And trying to get people to see the importance of a social base of forty percent.

In my Third World Women class at noon, the discussion was interesting. One of my students, an economist, told us that in the office where she works, there are thirteen economists, none of them on the left. Only three had voted for Reagan. "Across the country," she said, "I'd be willing to bet that the percentage of Reagan voters among economists is fairly low. Because we know what's going to happen with the economy. He couldn't fool us so easily . . ."

In that class, twenty-two of the twenty-four students had voted for Mondale. The other two had voted for Reagan. One of those is a young woman with an army job. The other is a middle-aged chicana woman who frequently claims "not to know enough."

Walking on campus yesterday morning, there were dozens of young and middle-aged men, with cardboard boxes. They were giving away small green New Testaments to all who would take them.

7

On the local scene, there was Judy Pratt, who had won in a landslide—yes, then it *was* a landslide—in the primaries against the ex-head of the State Democratic party. She is an extraordinary woman, a real people's person; in her case it is not simply the fact of her womanhood, but very much the fact of her overall political stance. She literally walked the backroads and villages of this state during her campaign, running against Pete Domenici, one of the strongest and most conservative senators in the country.

Over the past few months Domenici's threat politics became evident, in this state where the patron system still works, even people we know were approached after coming out publicly for Judy, and told to "get back in line!" But the most interesting, and frightening, thing about Judy's loss, is the lack of support from her own party. Was it because they, too, were intimidated by Domenici's people? Or was it that they simply can't stand someone like Judy, her politics, the fact that she is a woman? I would imagine more the latter.

The night of the election, down at the hotel where the local Democratic Party had gathered, after Judy's concession speech, Fred Mondragon (current head of the Democratic Party in the state) said publicly, on TV, something to the effect that "...I guess this finishes Judy Pratt off in state politics...she won't be running for anything anymore!" Pratt supporters apparently challenged him on his remark, and I've heard conflicting accounts of what happened next—running from a fist fight, to Mondragon's comment that he's getting out of office, and including a public apology (which I did see, last night, on TV).

But the important thing is what all this says about what must have gone on behind the scenes. My brother told me that on Sunday he was campaigning for Judy in Belen, a community just south of Albuquerque. It was two days before the elections. He knocked on over 100 doors, and found only one person even willing to listen. More telling: he says the Belen Democratic Party had just issued a flyer which was distributed to all cars, houses, local businesses. It had a list of Democrats to vote for, from the national candidates down to the lowest local official. Every name was on that flyer, except Judy's! When I think of the shit she must have struggled against, it's painful.

To be a woman in this country, to be Black, to be Hispanic, to be Native American, to be gay—when you're not invisible, you're so often despised.

8

A wonderful day searching for the storyteller, that seated figure with closed eyes (because she is thinking) and open mouth (because she is chanting or telling) and with children on her lap, on her shoulders, sometimes even clinging to her back or feet. The children may have toys in their hands (the more modern, mass-produced figures seem to go this route) or they may stand out for their individual expressions of wonder, contentment, surprise, joy, interest. Some are asleep, some are smiling, others crying. Some are being comforted by another child. Some of the artists are known for turning their children into see-no-evil, hear-no-evil, speak-no-evil figures, and their hands cover eyes, ears or mouth.

The expression on the face of the storyteller herself differs greatly from artist to artist. Trisha, Floyce and I drove to Santa Fe, and began in the shops, going from one to another to get a feel for the different figures brought in by artists from Cochiti, Jemez, Acoma and elsewhere. It didn't take long to be able to tell a variety of specific styles, common to Helen Cordero (the mother of the art form, who began making these figures at Cochiti in the mid-'60s when she was already past forty), Vangie Suina (whose figures are extremely polished and symmetrical, much more decorative than the others, and on which she uses commercial colors and what seems to be a slicker firing process), Toya or Trujillo, Lou Lucero, Louise Suina, Martin or Ortiz. In one of the stores, there were a few figures by Snowflake Flower, who anglo name is Stephanie Rhoads. One of them spoke to me immediately. It was a small figure, compared to so many intricate and larger ones, and it only had two children on its lap: a girl and a boy. The girl had both palms raised to her eyes; the boy one hand raised to his temple and the other extended. I loved the storyteller's boots and, most of all, the expression on her face.

We drove to Cochiti then, to hunt for the woman who made this doll. The pueblo seemed strangely empty, a few people working on their cars, most in their homes. A lone elderly man on a tractor stopped to answer our question about where one of the artists lived. At first it seemed he didn't understand me when I asked about the storytellers. Then he smiled and said, "Oh, yes. The tellerstories!" He directed us to a house down the road and a man who had been working by his oven came over to the car. When we asked him if someone who makes storytellers lived there, he said his wife was inside, and that she was working. He invited us into their home.

Ada Suina was sitting at the kitchen table, painting the figures of a nativity scene which she took one by one from her gas range

This is the storyteller doll I bought, and which now sits on my desk as I write. It was made by Stephanie Rhodes, who signs her work Snowflake Flower. She's from Cochiti Pueblo, and she made the doll in 1983.

oven ("where we place them to keep them warm," she explained). Little by little she spoke of the process: the clay dug somewhere not too far from the pueblo, then mixed with sand "because it's too sticky." The clay preparation dependent, as is so much, on the weather—rain making the mixture too damp. The work done almost exclusively with the hands and figures, modelling in the purest sense of that word ("...see, all she has is a toothpick, maybe to make the hole for the mouth," she explained, indicating a doll one of her daughters, Charlotte, was working on at the diningroom table). The colors—red, white and black—coming from their traditional sources: a smoothly powdered white rock, a smoothly powdered red rock, and the black of a deep purple flower whose petals are dried to a paste which improves with age. Then the firing process. They bake these dolls over an open grid. The figures are covered without actually being touched by an armature, a crude frame of crumpled wire, strong enough to hold the large flat pieces of cow dung which must also be collected and serve to hold in the heat. In those conditions the baking takes place.

Ada proudly shows us a wonderful large storyteller, a great and very special figure with a magic gesture and many many children on her lap, legs, shoulders and back. "I am trying to save this for my children," she explained, but consented to moving it into the diningroom where the light was better and allowed me to photograph her with it.

Storytelling is an old tradition of the Indian peoples, dating back centuries in their folklore and experience. Values, a morality, a code of identity are passed on through stories told by the elders to their children. It is interesting that, although the tradition is so old, the dolls only came into prominence around 1964.

Helen Cordero had been making pots at Cochiti, and according to a magazine interview I read, she said "they never really seemed right." It was a neighbor of hers who urged her to make figures, and the first storyteller emerged. A collector in Santa Fe apparently bought all the dolls she wanted to sell, and her success spurred her to make more, as well as motivated other women and some men to experiment with the form.

Now, as I said before, there are a number of people, at several of the pueblos, who produce their individualized versions of the storyteller. Those who are famous for this particular figure usually make nativity scenes too, drummers, and certain animals—turtles and owls. The storytellers and nativity scenes are the most popular of course, but for me there is nothing like the storyteller.

Ada Suina, with the doll she is saving for her children.

9

The situation in Nicaragua continues to be very serious. Contradictory statements emanate from the State Department, the White House, and the press. Different spokesmen seem now to agree that the Soviet ship did not in fact have MIGs on it, but other Soviet ships are approaching Nicaragua, and there is a constant background patter about how they carry weaponry of one kind or another. Helicopters, small arms, whatever it is, for the U.S. it's too much.

The line seems to be: "Nicaragua is endangering the military balance in the area," totally ignoring that the U.S. has made Honduras into one huge military base trained on Nicaragua. The arrogance in the statements is beyond belief. U.S. spy planes fly over Nicaragua every single day (and this is not my label for them, but the term used regularly by the establishment media on the scene, in line with the whole warscare psychology being pushed by the administration).

A press conference between Daniel Ortega and a large number of journalists was, in fact, loudly rent by the sound of one of these planes, which rattled windows all over the capital. The Nicaraguans are making desperate preparations for their own self-defense, students who were going to pick coffee in the north are being retained in the capital to defend the city, and all the while most U.S. news reports describe this process as paranoia on Nicaragua's part. Each day feels like one more day without war.

10

I've had somewhat good news from the American Studies professors. The meeting at which they voted me into the department ("into" with some qualifications, of course) was this past Friday. What it amounts to is American Studies being willing, on the basis of my showing at the colloquium, to make viable the university's offer of extending me an equivalent of a Ph.D. for my books and life experience. I will now be listed as an adjunct assistant professor with American Studies. What that means in black and white is that I will be able to design and teach courses through that department, with a salary at the level of an assistant professor's (though not, of course, of tenure track, nor with anything like that kind of security). My appointment will be open to renewal each year. And there is no money actually in American Studies that would provide me with an ongoing salary. That will have to come from the university's administration and/or from the salaries of different American Studies professors who may be on leaves without pay. But that does happen, and for the moment this is a big step up from working as an instructor.

Again, a giant bird has lifted me out of this southwest—which I am just beginning to know once more in its richness—and set me down again somewhere else, the midwest, Iowa, farm country, and people who are different.

Another college town, Ames is a country urb of some 50,000. Twenty-six thousand of them are students at the school, another

5,000 professors, and the rest either staff, people whose work has some relation to the college, and a few who are occupied in the local businesses: a few stores, post office, bank, movie theater.

The State University of Iowa is basically for students in the sciences and technology. Many are engaged in one of the engineering fields or an area of agriculture pertinent to the modernization and production of the Iowa farms. Lisa Crabill, my student host for the time I was there, is the oldest daughter of an Iowa farming family. She is in her junior year of agro-biochemistry, is already working on a research project, and hopes to do her graduate work in some other part of the country. I heard something of what it's like to grow up in a community of 500 people—Bonaparte, Iowa—on a farm, and with the particular viewpoint that sort of place provides. A viewpoint now in transition for her, as she opens to a world not in any way confined by Iowa State. For she, like others I met, is connected to the Institute on World Affairs at this campus.

Two thousand of the Iowa State students are from other countries, half from Latin America. For twenty years the Institute of World Affairs has been doing this week of activities, choosing either a region or a theme for its unifying factor. This year the region is Central America. They brought in the ex-U.S. ambassador to El Salvador, Robert White; Dick Bancroft; Sister Mary Hartman; Walter LeFeber; Edward Fischer, who works with Guatamalan refugees; Ray Bonner, a State Department official; David Kunzle; Manuel Rodriguez Orellana; Holly Burkhalter of Americas Watch; James Petras; and myself.

I was amazed to find such strong support and obvious interest in this week of activities in a place like Iowa. The Institute's budget for the week was $80,000, and the activities drew good crowds from the community as well as from the school. Close to 500 people must have been at my lecture, and my hosts told me there had been more for Robert White and Mary Hartman. Questions were knowledgeable and positive, and at least at my events, there were no hecklers (in spite of the fact that there is a large community of Cuban exiles at this school).

So it was a usual day of planes, lectures, quick but good meals, a reception to finish it off, contact with more people than I could handle in terms of real conversation, and finally curling up on my bed at the school's Memorial Union—to read, hopefully sleep, and wait to be awakened early the following morning and make it back to Albuquerque in time for my noontime Third World Women class.

The most interesting part of the experience, as always for me, was the glimpse, of another part of this country. Lisa, driving me back to Des Moines the following morning, spoke about her family; her father, her uncle, and grandfather (on her mother's side) run a medium-sized farm. They have corn and beans, some thirty head of cattle, and their main enterprise which is swine and feed. They have 500 acres outside the small town of Bonaparte, not far from the Missouri border.

The town is mostly Protestant, Lisa says, and there is an increasing influx of born-again Christianity. There is a single Black family in the town, but in recent years there have been also Koreans, Vietnamese, and peoples from other Asian countries. There are even a few Latin Americans. Racism against these people is strongest among the old people, Lisa says; the young people have found it much easier to accept them into the community. The sense, among the town's inhabitants, is that a persevering honesty and forthrightness reign supreme. There is communal amazement when a car is stolen, or—very rarely—a home is broken into. "We only began locking our front door about five years ago," she said, "when we began seeing unsavory characters out on the highway, and a couple of them came to our place."

This is Reagan country, as indeed most of the nation has shown itself to be, and in spite of the fact that the farmers have been having trouble, promises of economic improvement have been swallowed, here as in so many parts of America.

11

On the plane between Des Moines and Denver, I was already in my non-smoking aisle seat when a middle-aged couple slid past me to occupy the two seats to my right. They were pleasant enough, and began talking intermittently to one another about such things as a new technique in inner ear surgery, one of the current sitcoms, and the weather in Phoenix, where they were headed—for the husband's business I later found out.

The woman took a bottle of deep red nail polish from her purse and immediately began covering one nail which was apparently damaged before boarding. I continued to read *Nun* by Mary Gilligan Wong, a personal account of a woman who was a Sister of Blessing for eleven years and then left the convent. The book eventually sparked the interest of the woman. She began to ask me if I read many books like that, confiding that she loved biographies, rarely read fiction, but was currently enchanted with a book about the life of Princess Grace.

"I always cry," she said, "I just love reading about other women's lives." I wondered for a moment if I might recommend a few: Domitila, Rigoberta Menchu, even *Sandino's Daughters*. I decided against it. When the woman again interrupted and asked me if I'd read *Silkwood*, I told her I hadn't, but I'd seen the film. And I looked up to see what her reaction would be. "Yes," she said, "I saw the film too. But the book is better than the film. In the book you *know* what happened, no doubt about it! The CIA killed Karen Silkwood, no matter what they want us to believe!"

12

Gilligan says, in *Nun*: "Early in life I learned the joy of silence and solitude, learned to leave the whirlwind of activity all around me and find again the silence...I learned to open myself to the experience of God within, learned the contentment of living in harmony with nature, its rhythms and seasons...I learned the incredible nurturance of friendships with women, the incredible and largely unleashed power of women...I learned a deep compassion for the plight of fellow human beings less fortunate than I; I forged a life commitment to do my part toward a better world...By going away from the world for a while and then coming back, I learned a child's wide-eyed appreciation of the world's smallest pleasures."

I am still searching, sometimes desperately, for the joy of silence and solitude, for the silence. But clearly, the knowledge of this need of mine is something rather recently and strongly acquired. Opening myself to the "experience of God within," would perhaps be quite different for me than for someone like Gilligan, but again, the need is recent and strong. The "incredible nurturance of friendships with women..." is something central to many of us who have matured over these past ten or fifteen years. For Gilligan it was a convent; for me it is the women's movement. How could I live without the strength I get from my community of women? I do not know.

If by "world" one means the culture and society of one's roots, then Gilligan "left" hers by entering a convent and I left mine by going away for twenty-three years. I identified deeply with the way in which a type of removal produces compassion, an awareness of detail, an ever-new eye always outside the range of that march of simple acceptance, a critical perspective, a refusal to take on prevalent value and conventions simply because "that's the way things are."

13

In the current media muddle around Baby Fae and her baboon heart, abortion choice and the right-to-lifers, the moral majority's impact on national thought (via the Reagan administration, Jerry Falwell, born-again Christians, et al), and some of the more newsworthy individual dramas, a TV program addressing the issue of increased teenage suicide across this country caught my attention.

After the usual interviews with the "experts"—a psychiatrist at some respected center of higher learning, a student who had just earned three credit hours by taking a "suicide prevention course," and a few others—the commentator produced a bit of his own wisdom to the effect that there was a moral issue involved here, too. No, I'm wrong. It wasn't the commentator, but one of the psychologists or psychiatrists. It was suggested that if one were concerned about a friend it would be appropriate to ask not if he or she was contemplating suicide, but if he or she *believed* in suicide. The point, ostensibly, was that the person who did not believe in taking a human life, even his or her own, was basically o.k. That person would not commit suicide.

I spent a while trying to grasp why that brief TV commentary had so unnerved me. It was surely not simply the good doctor's total lack of social vision, for that is the common denominator of ninety-nine percent of what is fed us on TV. It was not his refusal to see suicide as a product of society's failings, or his insistence on speaking of it in "moral" terms. It was the absurd and dangerous moral majority aura to the statement itself.

If we do not have a right to *all* decisions regarding our own bodies, our own lives, then where are we? It seems to me that somehow in this society we are daily conditioned *not* to take responsibility for our lives. We can kill ourselves slowly by drinking, dope, smoking, pigging out with food (or refusing food altogether). There is always a club for alcoholics, the club for addicts, the club for smokers, the spas and weight-watchers and anorexia-anonymous.

There are counsellors to replace our sense of self-knowledge—and charge us for it, there are doctors of all kinds, psychologists and psychiatrists and therapists of every variety, style, and price. Revered religious leaders make us feel more concerned with the 1.5 million unborn souls yearly denied "life" than with the vastly superior number of women who suffer or die each year from illegal abortions.

No, the man on the screen was telling us, it's not enough to be against killing others. You must be against killing yourself as well. Oh, but you don't have to be too much against killing others—we still have the electric chairs, gas chambers, and lethal injections for those who get a thrill out of the idea. Or we can spend newscast after newscast telling you about a lone sniper in a Eugene, Oregon football stadium: his history, his first steps, even his previous suicide attempts.

Lately we have been treated, as well, to another TV special: the starving children (and adults) of Ethiopia and twenty-seven other African countries. In some of the camps four or five people die each hour. The scenes are repeated and repeated. They are horrible, and each is thoughtfully preceded by a blurb stating "the report you are about to see contains blunt and explicit language." Presumably this is necessary so that our children, who are encouraged to devour all variety of contrived violence and gore, can be kept from seeing what happens in real life if their parents wish.

The famine in Ethiopia and elsewhere in Africa has been adroitly made a part of the great puzzle the press serves us daily. During the last few days of the electoral campaign we were treated to scenes of the U.S. government flying food into a Marxist country, with never an opportunity lost to insinuate that the country's government "fed only those in the cities," or that its policies were somehow responsible for this almost unbelievable disaster. Here we were, feeding African children. Perhaps this would make people forget what we are doing to children in Central America. In Nicaragua, for instance, a country that has been struggling to better the quality of its life for five years now—while forced to confront every sort of pressure from the United States: economic, diplomatic, military, and paramilitary.

For days the single topic in all news reports on Nicaragua was their "paranoiac" alert vs. the Reagan administration's absolute assurance that no invasion is planned. But this approach didn't seem to spark the provocation the U.S. is clearly looking for. So now the new message is that Nicaragua is not simply on defensive alert, she's preparing an invasion of her neighbors: Honduras, Costa Rica, El Salvador. Undoubtedly we'll be hearing a lot more of that line for a while. When the U.S. attempt to convince people that Soviet MIGs were docking in Corinto dissolved in the proof that that wasn't so, shipments of Russian helicopters and even normal civilian cargo from that country to Nicaragua began to be spoken of with allusions to the Cuban Missile Crisis of 1962.

Today one commentator admitted that Nicaragua might have the right to defend herself against the contras, *except* that they are really "freedom fighters, supported by the United States. And we can't allow that, can we. . . ?" One way or another, the administration seems intent on justifying an invasion. One way or another Nicaragua's normal and necessary steps towards self-defense—and even her efforts to feed herself—are being portrayed as attacks upon the United States.

And all this against a background of food being airlifted by our good-hearted citizens into the famine-struck areas of Africa. We see U.S. schoolrooms on TV, in which cute little American children are collecting their pennies to feed the starving children of Africa, and meanwhile are being taught that the evil commie Nicaraguans are planning to do us in.

14

This morning, from just aften ten to just about noon, I participated in a session at the University of New Mexico which, for the first time, made me feel that the university is indeed a part of the real world, that real events can be discussed in a meaningful way, that risks can be taken among human beings there. And I do not refer to my classes, or even to some of the better meetings we have had in one or another committee or seminar in the Women Studies Program. For all these gatherings were also somehow "outside" the traditional university life. With my students, in the best of times, I might as well have been sitting in a circle in some grassy field. Our human and intellectual contact at times transcends the university institution which, true enough, had facilitated our coming together, but whose confines so often have to be stretched in order for real communication to take place.

The participants were faculty, almost entirely women (there were three men present, and perhaps 100 women). The event was a colloquium given by Annette Kolodny. She addressed the difficulties women face in the academic system, and she came to the subject through her own dramatic (and dramatically inspiring) experience.

In 1975, Annette walked into her office at the University of New Hampshire, opened her mail, and found that she had been denied promotion to full professorship and tenure. She taught English Literature at that school, and her credentials were impeccable: the best schools, the best degrees, more than acceptable publications. Her scholarship was beyond reproach. Her students loved her. What, then, had been her failings? In her opinion, the school had ousted her because she was a feminist and a Jew. And so she decided to take the risk, to devote the next few years to heartache, aloneness, psychological and physical stress, the possibility of being black-balled from teaching anywhere in the country—but a chance, too, at her own inner integrity. She decided to sue the University of New Hampshire for discrimination on the basis of sexism and anti-Semitism. She got a lawyer, networked, went into debt $50,000 over a five-year period, and finally forced the university to settle out of court for a very large amount of money.

It all sounds fairly clean and easy in black and white, of course. But one can well imagine what it must have cost her. The university paid its witnesses $1,000 a day plus expenses; she had to convince people to pay their own way and testify for her without recompense. She said that even after she won her case, some people told her: "Annette, if only you'd lost!" because few schools were willing to offer her a job after the kind of publicity she'd accrued. Effectively, she *was* black-balled for several years.

She spoke of the tremendous support she received from her students, from women all over, from her lawyer. But she also spoke of the pain when her female colleagues felt they could not stand by her for fear of what it might do to their own careers. She spoke of how she felt when her best friend from those years

Annette Kolodny, at UNM.

actually came and told her she didn't feel she should be seen with her on campus, "because it will make it harder for me to speak out in committee meetings. . . ."

Annette extrapolated from her experience: those for whom the system works have no problems with the system. Women and minorities have a hard time even making it through the gates. The system, per se, is corrupt. But it's hard for people to say the system is corrupt, because everyone wants to say I got my promotion (or tenure, or grant, or raise) because I deserved it. The implication, of course, is that those who don't get it don't deserve it. The institution functions on the basis of the myth of individual merit.

Annette referred to the fact that academia is filled with people who don't take risks, who are by nature conservative, who have learned to be conservative in their struggle to make it inside. Merit, then, becomes not something you earn, but something that is given to you by the system when and if it is willing to let you in. And the institution masks its own history as a necessary measure to keep the status quo in place. I see this around me all the time and at all levels.

15

Perhaps it was listening to Annette Kolodny talking about her experience, and the importance of recognizing how much we owe each other. Perhaps it was her story of her "best friend" who could not bring herself to walk with her or talk with her during her days of worst trial. Perhaps it has been my own anguish, the trials I have lived with and those I see before me. In the past few days I have thought almost incessantly of the support I have, and of those who offer it so freely.

16

Life moves because we push it.

So much of what we have done yesterday, so much of what cost us in bitter tears and in held breath a few years back, seems every-day now. What will it be like for our children, for our grand-children? Will they ("the third generation of Women Studies women," as Kolodny calls those who are coming up today) also forget the struggles that have cost us so much, as we too often tend to forget the generations that went before us? What generation am I? The first? The second?

And the university? It was always the place just slightly outside history, outside life. Then came the '60s, and another space was won. Classes were taught differently, students made demands that were met, and they made more demands, and those too were met. And the backlash came, and things swung back to—no, not the place they had been, but a kind of midway place, with the imprint of the '60s but dimmed by a faulty memory.

In twenty or thirty or forty years from now, will it be easy to become a part of a university if one has forty books published instead of a Ph.D.? Will matters of equivalency be easier? Will women be treated with more equality, and minorities, and gays and lesbians? Or will the dark fascistic Reagan era have put down roots so deep that our freedom struggles remain some kind of dim memory—recalled only by some?

The Gloves
—for Rhoda Waller

Yes we did march around somewhere and yes it was cold,
we shared our gloves because we had a pair between us
and a New York City cop also shared his big gloves
with me—strange,
he was there to keep our order
and he could do that
and I could take that
back then.
We were marching for the Santa Maria, Rhoda,
a Portuguese ship whose crew had mutinied,
they demanded asylum in Goulart's Brazil
and we marched in support of that demand,
in winter, in New York City,
back and forth before the Portuguese Consulate,
Rockefeller Center, 1961.
I gage the date by my first child
—Gregory was born in late 1960—as I gage
so many dates by the first, the second, the third, the fourth,
and I feel his body now, again, close to my breast,

286

held against cold to our strong steps of dignity.
That was my first public protest, Rhoda,
strange you should retrieve it now
in a letter out of this love of ours
alive these many years.
How many protests since that one, how many
marches and rallies
for greater causes, larger wars, deeper wounds
cleansed or untouched by our rage.
Today a cop would not unbuckle his gloves
and press them around my blue-red hands.
Today a baby held to breast
would be a child of my child, a generation removed.
The world is older and I in it
am older,
burning, slower, with the same passions.
The passions are older and so I am also younger
for knowing them more deeply and moving in them
pregnant with fear and fighting.
The gloves are still there, in the cold,
passing from hand to hand.

Rhoda Waller

287

My friend Ann Nihlen.

Whether things are better or worse forty years from now (and my optimism sees them naturally as better), I want people to know—if they think about me—that someone named Ann Nihlen, herself an untenured woman assistant professor, risked something to speak to the assistant provost at this university, and started me on a road toward fighting for a place in the sun here. I want people to know that Ann had a lot to lose, and that she did it anyway. Coming from a poor working family, virtually orphaned as a child because of poverty and desperation and paternal abandonment, Ann struggled for her own education in ways certainly unknown to most professors on campus. And she hasn't forgotten that struggle. Nor has she succumbed to amorality in order to "make" it.

I want people to know the names and risks of so many sisters and brothers who walked out to grab my hand, and grabbed it, often at the expense of their own comfort, stability, ease, peace of mind. I want to do each and every one of my friends the honor of recognition. At least that. I want people, years from now, if they think about me at all, to know how my children always stuck by me—even when it meant (as it usually did) having "a different kind of mother" (the kind no one in grade school or junior high or even highschool really wants). And how my parents stuck by me, through times when my attitudes and actions moved towards a space outside their ability to understand. How they supported me and were there for me and were even proud of me; and then, in their own lives, grew with my pioneering sense of things, incorporating some of it into their own vision and giving to mine through a dialectic I believe few have with their mother or father.

I want people to know about the network of women whose lives are part of mine in a powerful way, and about Floyce. I want people to know about the other men too, the bits and pieces of beauty as well as the long painful struggle. I want people to know about my students, and those many many (mostly) women who have come up to me at lectures or readings and told me that a book of mine, or a poem, or a picture, has made a difference in their lives.

17

Something else that feels like it holds a lot of promise is the home up in the Sandia foothills, the home I hope to someday inhabit.

The house plans lie on a pile of adobe blocks, as the walls of our house go up.

This will eventually be one corner of the livingroom.

At the beginning of the construction process.

Yesterday, after several weeks of waits, confusions and false starts, they finally poured the foundation. I drove up early in the morning, before the colloquium I had to attend at the university. From where you turn off Tramway Road I could already see the huge frame against the texture of mostly cloudy sky, and when I got closer I could see the whole operation: several red and yellow cement mixers lined up and alternately hooking up to a pump and high hose, spewing the mixture into the forms, and half a dozen men spreading and smoothing it. I was transfixed.

18

At times I overflow with a sense that I am moving closer to my particular image, my particular verb. At those times I glow, and the level of work energy mounts; the movements of my mind become more coherent. At Iowa State I was able to give my lecture without notes and without a single white spot. A sense of "getting better" warms me.

And yet, as if by some other, equally powerful magnet, I am pulled to the side of despair, not only by what is happening in Central America, but the direction of U.S. politics in general. The Eighty-second Airborne Battalion—the same that invaded Grenada—is said to be poised on the border of El Salvador. A battalion of Honduran troops is also said to be inside that country.

One of my students recently returned from a Witness for Peace trip to Nicaragua, and she invited people to brunch so she could share her experiences. Not much new for me, with one exception: she says that when her group visited the American Embassy in Managua someone asked the consul about the sonic booms they had been experiencing daily. The consul began: "Well, the alleged booms. . ." at which point the person who had asked the question interrupted by asking why he said "alleged." "Haven't you heard them?" she insisted. "Oh yes," replied the consul. "I've heard them. But this is the response the State Department suggests." And from then on, apparently many questions were answered by the consul with phrases like, "Well, do you want the official reply?" or "Would you like the State Department version?" This is certainly a new level of misinformation handling, at least in my experience.

19

In the December 1984 *Esquire*—that upper-crust *Playboy* one is forced, once in a while, to buy because it holds something you want to read—there is a series of articles about those the editors have dubbed "The Best of the New Generation." *Esquire* has subtitled the feather: "The men and women who are changing America," and one wonders how they deal with the fact that they—the magazine and those who make it—epitomize that which some of these men and women would hope to change.

One of the articles is about my friend Susan Meiselas. It's written by a wonderful writer, Gloria Emerson. Gloria once did an important book on Vietnam. Although I don't know her, Susan and also my friend Karen have told me how special her talent is, and it was immediately apparent to me in this piece. More important, the piece was crucial to me in that it detailed something I have had a great deal of trouble explaining to people: what happens to you in the kind of situation many face—in Nicaragua and El Salvador, Guatemala, Lebanon, and so many other places—until they go completely mad.

Emerson is speaking of several war photographers: "When Harry Mattison thought he had gone over the edge, after his first hallucination, it was Meiselas who gently persuaded him he was not going insane. He had been working hard for some months before the March 1982 elections in El Salvador, even spending Christmas there, and after returning from four days of combat in Suchitoto he came back to his room at the Hotel Camino Real and found it inhabited.

" 'Vultures were filling the entire place, jumping around, burping and farting and vomiting and picking at things,' he said. 'This lasted a second or two. I went out, worked some, and came back. The vultures started picking at me, at my body, I could feel it.' He found Meiselas and told her he would rather be dead than lose his mind. But she told him not to worry, it had happened to her in Nicaragua, and then once more. 'Susan gave me the knowledge that she had already passed down this road, suffering combat fatigue,' Mattison said. 'Susan was the only person I could go to, someone else would have probably said, "Oh, crazy Harry!" There weren't any men I would have trusted.' "

My own experience has points of contact. In Managua, in the

late spring of 1983, I suddenly began imagining the crime committed on a Salvadorean revolutionary leader, who had been hacked to death by one of her own security guards, as possibly awaiting me. It was not a dream, for my eyes were always open. Always. Indeed, I could not close them; I couldn't sleep. And it repeated itself, this experience, night after night after night.

Around that time the hallucinations began. I remember the most vivid included a displacement in time—not of days or months, but of centuries. I was driving my car past the Nineteenth of July Plaza and I had to stop, amazed and troubled by what I saw. In the middle of the huge square men were hitching four great white horses to the four extremities of a man about to be torn to pieces by their opposing movement. I knew I was in the eighteenth century, and that the man was Tupac Amaru. But of course I also knew that I was in Nicaragua, and that it was 1983. Just as I knew, during the dream-reality sequence suffered at night, that what I feared was not likely to occur.

The psychologist I saw was extraordinary. She had a profound history of dealing with this kind of problem, with herself and with others. I felt fortunate to have half a dozen sessions with her, particularly because she was then almost forced to give up her practice. She was dying of a muscle-degenerative disease and was attempting to use all the time left to her in as active and useful therapy outreach as possible. We used my current manifestations, born of anguish, stress, and near total emotional and psychic exhaustion, to reach back and try to address more deeply rooted problems. It became one of the most useful and privileged experiences of my life.

But Tony—for her name was Tony—told me that the only real cure for what I was suffering would be time. Time and space. Rest. An absence of pressure. When we began to speak of the possibility of my returning to the States, she was supportive of that. She told me that I would need about two years, without whirlwind tours, without intense work situations, to be able to come up through the pain and function in a totally supportive way.

I couldn't take the luxury of those two years. Like everyone else I know, I have to try to make a living. I have to work. I must not lose time, I constantly feel, in carving for myself a future in which I can do the work I know I am called to explore. So immediately upon arriving in the States I began to arrange for readings, a tour, then another. When I knew I wanted to stay, could I teach a class at UNM? One? More than one? How much, again, how much could I carry, without breaking?

I remember now the pain of that first tour: when I travelled the midwest and east this past spring. I measured my successes by how well I could get through some social situation following a reading (meeting people, talking to them, listening, keeping my concentration from wandering to spaces I couldn't then and cannot now speak about). I measured my progress by the white spots, or their absence: as my mind stopped dead in the middle of a lecture fewer and fewer times, I realized I was getting better.

And, what is getting better?

That's what I wonder today, as I flip a TV dial from station to station, vainly trying to find out what's happening in the world. Or bounce from a paragraph on Nicaragua to one on El Salvador and back to one on Nicaragua all jumbled together in a typcial Albuquerque *Journal* article, asking myself for the hundredth time: Why can't they at least dignify a nation by treating it as a self-contained place?

Or as I make a mental note that we need ketchup and toilet paper, and then suddenly receive the wrenching identification with people I have left behind—like some sort of slow-motion knife to the gut. And then immediately center on a class I must prepare for the following day, moving from one to another of these realities as if they bear equal weight in the universe, and then hating myself because that has become, somehow—perhaps for my survial—my sense of it.

Is "getting better always, simply, an adjustment?

Remaining Option

I
My temperature goes up
and "who can measure the heat and violence
of the poet's heart
when caught in a woman's body?"
Virginia Woolf asked that question
and went to sleep in her cold river.
Sexton and Plath, Santamaria and Parra
left abruptly

breaking the barrier of heat
as someone or something called
in a voice louder than the heart.
Sexton started me down this road today
telling me
Anne Frank was the Joan of Arc of Amsterdam.
A different kind of death.
And Ronnie Gilbert, singing
"The water is wide... I cannot cross."
It *is* wide
but I *can* cross,
am crossing now, falling against the waves,
hoisting myself aboard the craft again, going on.
We but warmed to this place
where a lagging heat
divides and pulls me together
once more.

II
On the silver road last night
I stopped my car
Stopped and pulled over, pulling my body
into its own curve,
hugging arms, thighs, ribs.
A shoulder was caught in the silent blade
of my windshield wiper.
The night was calm.
Fingers splayed against glass
and the ancient bridle
of an 18th-century mount
was crushed beneath the front wheel
when I emerged
desperate for air.
These are the fingers of war, the shoulders of war,
the bridle of unjust death,
fragments of fear.
These pieces of my mind
that will not stay behind
nor wilt.

III
Temperature and music
make room for the heart.
Memory presses against canyon walls
chipping the dark side of flight.

I am crossing now. Oh yes,
I am crossing.

20

Every night it goes below freezing, and every morning there is a
light white frost on the earth, the houses and trees. On the cars.
On the car windows. I go down and start the engine. Slowly. As
the car warms up, I listen to one of two stations that come with
me when I drive—the local classical music station or the local
"never less than three and up to six songs at a time" country and
western station. Mostly it's the latter, but when the lyrics to the
hackneyed pieces get too much for me, I switch to classical. Then
opera might appear, and I'll move back to country and western.

Work on the house is like magic. Faster than I could have
imagined it rises up off that frosty hillside. The thick door and
window frames are now stark against the brilliant sky when I've
managed to sneak up to see it during some rare break between
meetings or classes, between chores of one kind or another, and
obligations to be interviewed for that class, or meet with so-and-
so.

21

Our Thursday night class was wonderful. People had read the
Gladys Baez and the Mothers and Daughters chapters of *Sandino's
Daughters,* and since the underlying theme of both those sections
is the mother/daughter—daughter/mother relationship, I decided
to try to develop that in the group. We paired up, two students
going off in a corner together or out into the hall, to explore, with
each other, the mother/daughter roles. Stereotypes. Expectations.
Needs. Personal history or social science. I told them they could

get as intimate, or keep things as literary, as they wanted. We could take a half hour or so to explore, then come back to a full circle and share what had come up.

It was extremely interesting because everyone in the class really went to it. One couple composed of two male students said they had such a difficult time getting through to how they imagined women would see and feel this, that they couldn't get to the issues. That, in itself, was worth sharing. One woman whose mother is a lesbian while she herself is not, and another woman who is a lesbian and whose mother is not, got together—I don't know if they happened to be sitting together when the exercise began, or if they sought each other out from prior knowledge. The straight woman has felt abandoned by her mother in her mother's coming out; the lesbian woman is afraid to tell her mother she is gay for fear of being abandoned by her.

One woman, my friend Annie Esturoy, is the first daughter to leave home in five to six hundred years! Home is the Faroe Islands, a community deeply entrenched in traditions that date back to the Norse, a society where it is dark half the year and light half the year, where people do all kinds of things—a fisherman may write poetry and it is seen as entirely natural—and the world of television has not yet erupted on the scene.

December

1

This morning Anna, the almost-eighty-nine-year-old woman living next door, died. She had been getting weaker this past month or six weeks, retaining a lot of liquid in her body, and becoming prey to infections as her immunities diminished. She seemed to get smaller and smaller. Last week when I stopped to visit with her for a while, she spoke animatedly about everything: her old friends in San Francisco, her life, the people she had met here in Albuquerque. She enjoyed everything so much; the simplest things gave her real pleasure. I felt guilty and sad that I had not visited her more often—she loved people so!

But on that visit I noticed her clear and enthusiastic sentences occasionally trailed off, her mind seeming to cloud; I could almost see her brain struggling against too little oxygen. I recognize the problem, having had it so often myself when a bad attack of asthma leaves the brain light and airless. The confusion resulting from that. I sensed, then, that Anna would soon be gone. She sank into a kind of peaceful semi-sleep about a day ago, and died this morning while Diana was bathing her on the couch. I vividly remember something Anna said to us one night when she came for dinner: we were talking about her fifty-four years in a cork factory, and she insisted: "everyone always like me! I can't remember anyone not liking me a lot!" Nice to have been able to say that.

2

Tomorrow I will be forty-eight. It's strange: my innate sense of immortality (that always-sense that everyone or almost everyone has as they grow up, as they look into successive mirrors and simply don't imagine themselves growing old, that sense of eternal youth that is such a large and sturdy part of the first quarter of one's life, at least) has been spliced these last twenty years or so with a conflicting sense of early death. Early death when I lost my kidney. Early death in more recent times when my mind seemed to give way in great shimmering slices beneath the weight of too much death all around. Then, at one and the same time, there is the regeneration, the sense of nurturing, of being able to nurture what still may grow, the sense of replacing exhausted cells, very much the regeneration Meridel seems to be talking about when she speaks of the new energy of later life.

Since my return to Albuquerque, almost a year ago, I have wanted to stop and enter the First National Bank Building, the tall white building uptown, which in my youth was way out on the edge of the desert. My old friend, Alice Garver, a large and beautiful woman, an amazing artist, a woman somehow different from the rest of us, painted a mural in that building some twenty-four or twenty-five years ago. Alice was just beginning to get some commissions from the then incipient art-appreciative Albuquerque community. And she painted the mural and did a few other things. Then she died. Just like that. No one ever really knew how or why. She left a grieving husband—grieving because they had separated, she had left him a short time before, and grieving because she was dead. And she left two small sons. I have made it to forty-eight, I have thought more recently, and Alice never made it past twenty-eight. I wanted to see the mural, and every time I passed that tall white building I thought about stopping.

Today I did. I was with my friend Jane Caputi, and we parked and went in. On the first door a secretary at some firm or other wouldn't even answer our question. "I have to answer the telephone," she said, leaving us standing there. Someone who had just come into the lobby asked what we needed, we mentioned the mural, and she told us to try the second floor: "Ask at the Hinckle Corporation," she said, "if anyone knows, they will."

So we went up to the second floor. And repeated our question at the receptionist's desk. The woman was small and elegant and dressed in a bright red two-piece suit. When I broached the subject of the mural, her expression became at once familiar and pained. "You won't believe it," she began, "but they painted it over!"

Her voice held a sadness, even as her demeanor hardly evoked someone interested in mural painting. "Yes, they painted it over. It seems it was flaking, falling apart, and rather than have it restored they just painted over it." There was nothing more to be said. I told her a bit about Alice, and she seemed sincerely sorry. And we left. Jane and I didn't talk much going down in the elevator. Outside Jane put fifty cents in the New York *Times* machine, and when she opened the glass door we each took a paper. Then we walked silently to the car.

The Beginning Again
"the beginning for me is
never an idea"
—Leonor Fini

The beginning is dust
swirling,
a color charging
or rearing.
A notion of time
or of timelessness.

The beginning makes sense
instantly.
We hold it
and our fingers splay out
our palms become heavy

300

with patience
and wonder.

I am going home now.
I am listening
for my name
among the keen sounds
and the low.
              People's words
climbing upon each other's backs.
Wind. Juices.

I follow the sound
of my name
on all these years,
exploding.
Running to the beginning again.

It is three-thirty in the morning. All that cuts through the still-
ness and the blackness are the single lamp shining over my left
shoulder and the high-pitched sound of these electronic keys as I
hit them in the night.

3

The colors attached to numbers float just behind my eyes right
now. *Forty* is a deep purple-blue-black, the color of plums or
certain nights, as they fall over a very clear horizon. *Seven* is a
pale grey, sometimes a pearly grey, sometimes smokey or almost
silver, depending on the day. Life at forty-seven oscillates
between the uncertainty of smoke and the settledness of rich
pearl, but it's always got the strength of that blue-black-purple—
an anchor—the tone the Indian potters turn to black in their careful dyes. *Eight* is red. It's a good number because it's a strong, rich
red: sunrise, pulsation, blood, hope, a light to make you stop and
think, meditate, lips, ribbons, fiestas, joy (although the word
"joy" is a pale green). So forty-eight is a good number, a good
age, a good combination of midnight and dawn, dark blue/black
and bright rich blood.

4

There are a dozen shades of grey, brown-grey, grey-blue, dust, sand, soft purple, and intensifying blue, outside this second-story studio window as I write. In the distance strings of fading city lights still shimmer in the seven o'clock dawning. The demarcation line between earth and sky becomes more delineated even as I begin these lines. Earth, shapes of houses, windows and doors, a parking lot, and occasional bare-branched trees, become darker as the sky pales. Large-winged gull-like birds, dark in color, move now and then across the window space.

Ximena was supposed to have come in late Sunday night. But she called around midnight to say that she was in Ciudad Juarez, and there wasn't a continuing bus until the following morning. She was spending the night there and would come on the next day. Yesterday morning I was thinking of her on that bus, when I got a phone call from her at the El Paso Immigration Office. They were holding her and questioning her due, apparently, to some poetry (hers) and some photos (mine) about—as the woman Immigration Officer with whom I spoke explained—"the lifestyle in Nicaragua . . . people with guns."

When Ximena finally did arrive in Albuquerque late yesterday afternoon, she told a story of having been interrogated from around 7:30 a.m. to almost 11:00. Her luggage was thoroughly searched, and the poetry, the photos, and her personal address and telephone book were photographed. She herself was body-searched (though not undressed) by a woman official she described as "mean and brusque." A male official began the interrogation and treated her badly throughout; he shouted at her repeatedly, asking if she knew the meaning of a word which at first—when telling me this—she couldn't even remember. "Something like *piricuaco*," she said, trying to find it in her memory. (*Piricuaco* is a derogatory term for Somoza policemen, used mostly during the dictatorship.) Ximena finally settled on the word having been *milico*, a term used in Mexico and I believe in several other Latin American countries for cop, a word she was not familiar with. And so she kept telling this official she didn't know what it meant.

The same official asked her where she was born, and when she said Mexico, he said he didn't believe her. He asked her to describe the colors in the Mexican flag, and when she at first became confused and said "blue..." he began shouting: "See, she's not a Mexican...I told you she was lying..." (Ximena speaks only Spanish, but understands a few words of English.) This male official continued to harass her, demanding answers to his questions and, when she answered them, not believing her.

Then a woman official came. She was the "good" one. Her treatment of Ximena was entirely different, she asked a good many questions but in a friendly and consoling manner. Ximena tells me she was pretty calm throughout, sure of herself and of the fact that she was telling the truth, but also indignant—especially where the rude male official and the police-like body searcher were concerned—and also confused and frightened. She asked how long this was going to take, and how long she would be there, and was told by the "bads" a very long time.

The questions concerned her life in Cuba, her life in Nicaragua, and her life as a student in Mexico. Her friends, what kind of things she had done, whether or not she had belonged to any kind of communist organization, if she had received military training. Many questions were asked about me, including where I worked in Cuba and in Nicaragua, what kinds of things I did, how I had entered the United States, what kind of passport I had, what citizenship I have, when and where I met Floyce, when we got married, what I do now.

Ximena was told she would be interviewed by officials of the FBI, and indeed two of them came, identified themselves to her, and said they wanted to ask her some questions. She says they concentrated on her background and life, but also asked a few questions about me. Finally the woman official—the one who had treated her nicely—told her that the decision as to whether or not she could enter the States would have to be made by the head of Immigration for the whole border. About twenty minutes later she was told she would be allowed in.

5

My first semester of teaching ends, and fades into Christmas vacation. I have stopped the classroom experience for the semester, as this is closed week. During the last Third World Women session three of the students put on a music and dance program based on research about Domitila: they read about the musical instruments

303

and the dress, the feeling of the quena, women's struggles and solutions, and they expressed it all in their own choreographed movement. I must have all my grades in by the fourteenth.

This grading process is of course something few of us are comfortable with, but I have managed to work my way through its ins and outs by this time, moving from wanting to give everyone who came regularly an A to understanding that there must be some fair way, or close to fair way, of acknowledging people's individual efforts and results. So, this will be a week with a lot of heavy thinking. On Thursday night our Literature of Identity and Commitment class will have a potluck at my parents'. On Friday, the Third World Women class will have an end-of-course dinner at a local seafood restaurant.

6

What I had expected would be a tedious stretch of hours—reading and evaluating each of the final exams and/or project papers from my students in both classes—proved, once more, to be exhilarating. Seeing how much they each got out of the class experience, coming up against certain of their ideas in black and white, their findings, expressions. A young Hispanic woman from a farming family in Espanola (the same woman who went to college on money she made by showing a bull at the county fair—one she had nurtured to local stardom) wrote at the end of her paper: "This class has taught me a lot. It has made me more aware of women's lives in Third World countries. I had not realized before now how important it is to get involved, that our participation even in small ways can make a difference. I didn't think I knew much about the topics we discussed in class. But now that I think about it, I learned a lot from listening and enjoying. Thanks for a great class!" This woman realized that the experience had been a learning one for her; she still isn't aware, I don't think, of how much she herself gave to the class.

7

My most extraordinary responses were to some papers by students in A Literature of Identity and Commitment. The one that moves me most is from an older Apache woman. She is very quiet, studious and careful, but rarely able to express herself in class. In response to the question, What does identity and commitment mean to you?, she wrote: "At the present time I am having trouble with the identity part because I'm trying to decide what area of university study to major in, however I am quite satisfied with being who and what I am, in relation to my ethnic background. I am proud of my heritage as a Native American who has survived in spite of the many abuses inflicted upon my people. My pride in my heritage is confirmed when I find that in the various disciplines I have studied, there are many levels or parallels that are equivalent to the dominant society.

"For example: in Biology, the DNA molecule which is identified with the essence of life has an equal meaning in the native ways, even though we may be ignorant of the technical aspects of the molecule, we can recognize the structure, which resembles a whirlwind, as one of the symbols of the forces of life. In Geology, the term associated with landforms or various land structures such as the dike, a granitic composition that stems out from the core of the earth, has an approximate equal. This structure is know to my people as 'the backbone/spine of the earth.' These and other examples I have encountered mean to me that we as Native Americans are equally intelligent as the dominant culture, and are capable of adapting to a changing world in order to survive.

"Commitment: to me this means fighting for a cause, but I have yet to find a cause. When I do I'm sure I can be a real fighter. An area that could use such a person would be Native American feminist issues, since this is a relatively new field. And there is much work to be done."

8

One young woman, a film student and a very good writer, wrote: "Identity and commitment wrap around each other, connecting like strands of a net; the search for an exploration of a self-identity demands a commitment to that search, while the realization of a commitment (to a belief, ideal, cause, etc.) gives the searcher more information as to the kind of person she/he really is. Identity and commitment (words added to the list of those which have become nearly meaningless in this culture—next to 'new and improved,' 'revolutionary,' 'radical,' even 'matriarchal') are among the most important concepts in my world. Identity is a continuously, subtly-changing answer to an ongoing process, a long process of self-examination and affirmation, and a willingness to deal with the truth, however, difficult, complicated, or painful it might be. Again, this process depends on the depth of commitment to it. It often means, for me at least, alienation and loneliness, as part of the price I have to pay for my refusal to be a sheep, but to, instead, take certain comfort in knowing that I am honest with others, and more importantly, with myself."

9

Another of my Literature of Identity and Commitment students turns to Alice Walker's comments about Black women writers such as Lucy Terry, Phyllis Wheatley, Nella Larsen, and Zora Neale Hurston. To their having lived and died largely at the margin of any kind of recognition, or even personal fulfillment. And my student writes: "I thought about each one of those black writers, those women, and I also recalled all the other women artists and writers who had died, if not in poverty and obscurity, then often by their own hands. Unlike Walker, I cannot refuse to be pessimistic about any of them. I find Walker overly cheerful as she reclaims the past for black women in a convocational speech to a predominantly white upper class graduating from Sarah Lawrence. Nineteen seventy-two was not, as Walker announces, 'a great time to be a woman' (if I remember that year correctly) and I'm not so sure that it was an especially great year to be a black woman, either.

"In 1972 I was working in a west Texas city on the night crew of a county hospital. Most of my colleagues were black women: no one of us was particularly delighted to be a working woman, black or white, in a grisly, grossly understaffed and beleagured surgical ward. But then my co-workers at Bexar County Hospital did not go to Sarah Lawrence nor did they have the time to read Alice Walker. Reading Walker now, knowing what I knew then, I wonder at the discrepancy. I wonder at the discrepancy not just as it appeared in San Antonio but also a few years later in Newark where I was also a co-worker on an otherwise black woman crew.

I doubt that any of us would look back to that year and announce it was a great year to be a woman, black or white. We would have agreed on a lot of things: that there wasn't enough money for rent and the other bills, that working at night was killing our brains and our physicality, that our kids were causing us more grief than any other year of our lives, that Newark, New Jersey had to be the absolute pits for human beings. And we might disagree on a lot of things, too. But not about it being a 'great year.' "

When grading my final exams and projects from both classes, I missed one from one of my best students. I had given her an A in the course, because she has not only done every other project to perfection, but handed in dozens of unasked for papers, come to my office with ideas for teaching, and contributed to the class in many other ways. It wasn't until after all my grades were in that I found her paper, neatly typed and enclosed in a bright green plastic binder, and pushed beneath my office door. It had been pushed so hard that it had found its way behind the door, and into a far corner of the tiny office space. In addition to the exam, this woman appended a commentary which teaches me some of what I feel I need to know:

"I took a class back in the late '60s or early '70s at UNM—Women in Literature—offered through the English Department, and a forerunner, I believe, to Women Studies courses. Class format included lecture, discussion and 'creative' projects—creative to me as a student whose main college background up to that point involved undergraduate science courses requiring straight memorization of systems. There was no taking issue with xylem and phloem, veins and arteries, and chemical bonding patterns, so a class that asked what I thought about was something novel.

"There were a few men in the Women in Literature class, which surprised me, but I assumed they were there to learn, and that class dynamics would be such that we could all freely explore and comment on the images of women portrayed in the books.

"Instead the men quickly took over: always being the first to comment, always verbalizing their assessment of female class members' logic in making a point, and feeling free to roll their eyes or let out a noisy stream of air if a woman got on the soapbox or made a stinging comment. I looked at the instructor to rescue us, but this did not happen. (Was she her sisters' keeper?)

"I find my thoughts turning to the ways in which men take over space and make it their own. I consider how the discussion focus often turns subtly to the male experience. I remember how new labels are put on old patterns, clouding the issues in the latest jargon: conversations at the child-care co-op which turned to 'quality time not quantity' when men became the caretakers; laundromats which ceased to function as havens from male scrutiny and judgment when men took up the washing . . . another place to have to say 'excuse me' as the men took up the aisles while reading the paper or folding the clothes; a school for handicapped children—founded by mothers, run by women—which, when floundering, hired an office manager (male) who put his finger on the problem right away: 'you lack a division between management and workers.'

"Men in A Literature of Identity and Commitment—with mixed feelings did I regard their presence, I whose husband was among them. At times I perceived the comments of some of the men as critical in such a manner as to close avenues for further discourse. In listening to what some of the men had to say, I felt that my own level of knowledge about political and economic systems, particular histories and current events would be inadequate to enter into an exploration of the points they were making. I felt my emotional perceptions of the same issues would not be of use in responding to their comments. And at times when men of the class were silent, left early, or didn't show, I wondered what they were thinking and feeling. Were they uncomfortable? Bored? Confused? Taking this class with Tom has been enriching in a number of ways. We talked for years of doing such a thing, but we never got around to it. While I recognize that I possess good speaking and writing skills, I feel my style is too parochial at times. I had reservations about being in a Women Studies class with my male partner who has great talent in thinking on his feet and phrasing things clearly and concisely. But plunging ahead, I found I was able to respond in class in my own way without the sky falling in, and whatever myth was at work has been dispelled.

"Gaining comfort with our respective communication styles has given me encouragement to explore more seriously the possibility of our working together in the future. I feel, through the experience of this class, the value of each of our styles of communication and can see how they can both serve us well in the work world.

Although I've known him for seventeen years and feel I can, at times, predict what he will say under a particular set of circumstances, I found some new angles about him. Altogether, the experience of taking this class with Tom has strengthened the bonds of our relationship."

Having been prey to the same interrelationships with men in my life, becoming enmeshed in the same kinds of traps, but having worked through them (at least as far as I have) in a very different cultural and political context, I feel I often need to be reminded of the kinds of responses still engendered here—when women and men interact in, say, this kind of a classroom situation.

The semester has ended. My first semester of teaching. The two strongest criticisms I have for myself are that I was not structured enough in my classes, and that I did not demand enough of my students.

10

Trisha called me and told me the Lobo's Women's Basketball Team was playing Hardin Simmons at the Pit (a huge below-the-level-of-the-earth arena added to UNM's facilities in the last decade or so). I had been wanting to make some pictures of women in sports, and aside from liking to watch basketball, I thought this would be a great opportunity to do some photography. But I wondered: would I still be able to get a ticket? (I remembered accompanying my father to a basketball game last season, when the Lobo men played a team from out of state, and there were close to 20,000 spectators there, most of them with season tickets.)

Trisha just laughed at me on the phone, and told me they'd be by to pick me up at 7:15 for a 7:30 game. When we got to the Pit, the parking lot was empty. Inside, the enormous bleachers had, stretching it, 100 people. "Family members and dykes," was Trisha's description of who goes to these games!

The women were wonderful, and it was a pretty close contest. I kept reminding myself, over and over again: this isn't Cuba. This isn't Nicaragua. Here it makes a huge difference whether it's men or women playing. But I felt angry. It's a constant challenge to your sanity to grow up in a world where you work as hard as a man at something, and have to expect that no one will much give a shit—as if that were a natural part of life. When the men play there's a cheering crowd of 20,000. When the women play, less than 100.

UNM's Women's Lobo Basketball Team plays to empty bleachers.

11

The top headline in the Albuquerque *Journal* a few days back informed us that the Reagan government is finally admitting that it's not only Nicaragua's supposed foreign policy, but the nature of its internal system that is unsatisfactory to the U.S. And reason enough to stop at nothing to bring the Sandinistas down.

A Cappuchin priest and friend of mine, Jim Feltz, writes from his war-torn parish of Bocana de Paiwas in Zelaya, Nicaragua. Bocana de Paiwas is north of Matagalpa, where the departments of Matagalpa, Chinandega and Zelaya meet—deep in isolated mountain territory which is, of late, very much infiltrated by roving bands of contras. Jim describes, among other things in his letter, ''how the first free elections in the history of Nicaragua took place in this remote area. The people participated joyfully and massively in spite of the threats by the contras. The only signs

310

of fraud were on the part of the U.S. embassy which tried to convince two more parties on the right to boycott the process. Its efforts backfired. The people, with a percentage of participation much higher than that in the U.S. elections two days later, elected Daniel Ortega and Sergio Ramirez president and vice-president, both members of the FSLN. They sent sixty-one Sandinistas to the Constitutional Assembly, sharing the power of that body with thirty-five representatives of the other six parties. The parties to the right of the Sandinistas took twenty-nine seats, showing that the elections were just that and not a plebiscite as the U.S. government tried to claim in its efforts to discredit the elections it had ironically been insisting on for the past five years. Reagan may have won the elections in the States but he lost them in Nicaragua.

"His only alternative was to cover over the election results by scaring the American public with the exaggerated panic over the arrival of a Soviet ship, supposedly bringing supersonic MIGs to the port of Corinto on the Pacific Coast. It turned out that the boxes were too small for MIGs but the media blitz had done its job on the elections. Personally, I hope that the ship (twelve Soviet

Christmas is special in New Mexico, where the dried corn and red chile ristras hang with "Season's Greetings."

ships arrive every week to U.S. ports and nobody says anything!) brought food and light bulbs for this war-torn economy. In any case, Nicaragua has the right to defend itself however it can. Right now it has no way to control the airlift to the contras out of U.S.-controlled Honduras."

Now that Christmas is almost on top of us, record crowds storm shopping centers, the perennial Christmas cards flood the mail system, and everyone seems to have his or her own way of celebrating the painfully commercialized holiday. Yesterday I received a xeroxed letter from some friends of my parents—people who engage in the habit of sending a yearly letter, this season informing their friends and acquaintances of births and deaths in their immediate family, how well their new Chrysler Laser made a trip across country, and the individual accomplishments of each and every one of their grandchildren. These are good people, outgoing and generous, involved in religious and community outreach. Yet there wasn't a single mention of any event of collective importance in the world, not a note about Central America, Afghanistan, Poland, or even Chicago's south side or New Mexico's poverty-stricken north country. We are informed that both senders of the letter continue to be healthy and active. But this letter only made Jim Feltz's sound harder and deeper.

12

Look Me in the Eye is an amazing book by Barbara Macdonald with Cynthia Rich. Barbara is a woman who was sixty-five in 1978. She is a lesbian and a feminist. "Do you remember me?" is one of the first of her essays in the volume—the book is made up of a number of essays by Barbara, and some by Cynthia, her twenty-year-younger companion and lover—and it is, for me, the strongest.

In it, she names herself. She begins by naming her origins, the shape and size of her body, the space she occupies in the world. She names her mother's expectations for her, and her expectations for herself. She names the house she lives in, the apartment with two or more above it, and by naming those living in the other two, she defines the emotional space left for her.

Then she moves beyond the home sphere, and walks the streets of Cambridge, where she lives. She defines herself by the way others look at her, how they act with her, what gestures her presence produces in their manner and words. She enters the women's bookstore, and a women's restaurant and bar. She is always the oldest woman, the only *really* old woman around. Then she begins to wonder where everyone else is.

What happened to all those women with whom she interacted in one way or another through the years? Where are the women who drank with her in the Seattle pubs in the '20s, or with whom she made love in the '30s, the women who engaged in the same struggles she engaged in, or even those whose struggles were different. When she strikes up a conversation with another woman her age, out come the pictures of the grandchildren, "as though all the answers could be found there, among the living."

A pivotal moment in the essay is this: "My feeling of having been spared is confirmed in the way that no one seems to be expecting me anywhere. Even if I go into a local shop to buy clothes, I am always greeted with the question, 'Is this for yourself?' as though I must be buying for someone else, as though I didn't buy clothes for myself, as though I must have some supply somewhere in an old trunk, left me by my mother, there waiting for me to wear when I reached the right age."

13

Although aging, for me, has always been much more closely and immediately associated with a changing mind, a changing set of values (or values that firm themselves up, somehow—*becoming stronger as they at the same time become less rigid*), I can understand how in this way of life we have created for ourselves, THINGS do become palpable signs of change. The clothing I wanted as a young woman is no longer important to me. Gadgets only clutter my life. My focus is much more centered. More and more I spend time trying to understand the so many moments or passages that I once let pass me by in relative abandon.

Memory has a great deal to do with age. In fact, the two words, memory and age, occupy a space in relation to one another. As I grow older my memory changes. It is too easy to say it gets worse. I forget a great deal, but I also remember things I was not able to remember before. My reasons for remembering have changed.

A great deal of what has changed in me, and I find continuing to change, is my relationship to others. Certain relationships are immensely important. And their importance has much less to do with expected ties (parents, children, sisters, brothers) than it does with affinities—affinities of thought, of value, of vision.

Solitude is also more important—and more comfortable—to me. I have learned to be alone inside my skin and it seems that it took a very long time for me to learn this the way I know it now. No matter who I am with, no matter what the circumstances, conversation, stage diagram, it seems to me now that I am almost always alone. Alone in a way I cherish.

Forty-eight is not sixty-five, nor is it eighty-five or ninety. But there are physical changes as well. In her book Barbara Macdonald mentions the brown spots of aging. I have them too, all over my arms and legs and chest. The flab, the stoop, the slowing down of certain movements. The grey hair I now want so much (after having allowed myself to be enticed into coloring my hair back to its original brown for several years—finally I simply said to hell with always covering that line where it begins to grow out, I will broaden the line, and live with the two-tone consequences, until my hair is entirely my own again. Now it has grown out to just below my ears, and when I pull it back and up and tuck the ends under with a clasp, I am grey once more).

The lines no longer speak of accepted beauty standards or their lack. They tell me about my own tensions, where the pain was located, where and how I didn't do anything about that. They are a wonderful gage or measure, telling me where and how I stopped short in my tracks, and also that I have another chance, another opportunity to learn to be who I am.

The things we did to willfully hurt ourselves, to throw away this body given us only once, to shorten our lives, those things also seem much more absurd to me now. Smoking. Drinking. Doing dope. Becoming fat and slovenly on junk food (but always able to divest oneself of fat and slob, always until one grows older). As the second chances are eliminated, one's attention is more strongly pulled to a sensitive appraisal of one's body. As one begins to really assimilate what happens to other human beings throughout this world of ours—torture, imprisonment, premature age and death, misery, hunger, sub-human existence—one learns to value one's own body and mind, and the obligation one has to one's sisters and brothers. Anything less oscillates between stupor and crime.

14

Something happened in the lobby of the San Francisco Palace of Fine Arts the afternoon before I left San Francisco, after *Risking a Somersault in the Air* came out: I had had an extraordinarily heavy day at the end of a heavy weekend, doing readings and being with friends, relating to different sorts of people. That day alone I had been on the radio live on a call-in talk show in the morning, then gone over to La Pena for a big reading, and ended up at the lobby of the Fine Arts Palace where a big Nicaragua affair was about to begin. I couldn't stay for it, because I had to be on a 5:54 plane, but I was there signing books as long as it was humanly possible to do so and still make my flight. My friend Miranda came over and asked me if I wanted to go with her to see a backdrop she and others had painted that weekend, a backdrop for the event about to take place. And I had said no. I didn't want to go. It wasn't that I didn't want to go; I couldn't go. I just couldn't take into my mind and/or body another emotion, not another single one. Reading the Guatemala poem and the poem about Anna had taken so much out of me that weekend.

But I was haunted by my refusal, haunted by it on the plane and on my return to Albuquerque, haunted by it ever since. Almost every day it has come back to me. Miranda, who gives so much, Miranda who absorbed so much of my output that weekend, Miranda who only asked me, once, to "come see what I've been doing..." And I didn't go. That's happened to me a number of times in my life. And when it happens it's hard to get rid of.

15

TV coverage in the United States, TV entertainment or recreation—for that's what it is for the majority of the American people who watch it 7.5 hours a day—is a carefully orchestrated design of mind- and body-shaping ideological input ranging from blatant to subtle. From the bare racism in a series such as "Hotel" to the much more enticing—because it's often humorous, with likeable characters—"M.A.S.H." From the overpowering classism of "Dallas" to the crude sexism of "Paper Dolls." From the well-calculated patriotism of Reagan-era shows, to the advertisement of the American Way of Life which is "Jeopardy." And always there is the image of The Man, the fine, outdoors, strong, god-fearing, woman-dominating, everything-is-possible, American Man, appearing in his varied suits of clothes on "Trapper John," "Quincy," "Superman."

But a show that takes first place for all-out up-front face-to-face conservative dogmatism-made-saleable, is a Saturday night obscenity hosted by a freak called Wally George. Wally George is a white, born-again Christian, Reaganite, California-based hack man who sits at a table before a backdrop composed half of Reagan from his cowboy-movie days and half of a missile-blast anchoring the words "U.S. #1." He faces a select audience of trained booers and squawkers, cued to respond when the need arises. And of course he faces, as well, the hundreds of thousands—or millions—in the TV home audience who sit riveted to his show for any one of a variety of reasons: total approval and agreement, or that fascination and/or mesmerization that comes with being appalled but lethargic.

Wally George brings a series of guests to what he calls the hot seat, and proceeds to insult and humiliate them until he either boisterously and physically has them removed from the stage, by a couple of strongmen employed for the purpose, or until it's time for one of the spot-commercials sponsoring the show. His big crusades are America First, Anti-communism (communism for him, being anything left of the Girl Scouts), Down with Sex, Drugs. A conservative brand of Freedom, Racism, Sexism, and Reagan. His shows are studded with commercials for the Reagan government, and all that goes with it: America Strong in the World, a Containment of Socialist or of Different Ideologies, a repeal of any and all abortion rights, women's and gay rights.

Last night his show was an attack on heavy metal and punk rock; he put a couple of its exponents in his hot seat and primed his audience to chime in with sneers of "vermin...pigs...sick sick sick," and so forth. Two outrageously dressed and made up, as well as extremely articulate rock singers subjected themselves to a quarter hour of attack on their sexuality, ideology, humanity. This kind of Wally George show is perhaps the most interesting because—amid all the slander and horror—the values espoused on both sides have their complexities, and it's interesting to observe the management of provocation of each. Wally George is a fanatic and a fascist, in every sense of those words. His guests

316

and his audience, in the name of entertainment, subject themselves to the grossest kinds of abuse.

16

Marilyn Young has long been an anchor for me, an anchor in seeing and understanding certain important ways we move with one another, and what that creates in and of its own meaning/weight. She writes: "I received a letter from a friend who has spent many years in Appalachia, working and doing field work in anthropology. She is about to take a group of college kids on a trip to Appalachia. She talks about what happens to Appalachian migrants when they leave their place—the hills which store their collective past, present and future in landmarks such as crumbling old chimneys that point to an old family place long gone but not forgotten. People also have to leave the hills themselves which are a kind of timeless presence to life. Then there is leaving the place where stories fill the air (or *are* the air) like one continuous piece of art. Stories both give images (cultural context) and more importantly are a constant testimony that talk and meaning are possible.

"Then they come up here to a place which they call a place of nothing—a great swallowing silence. Later she says that on the trip she and the group of students will talk to people about what it means that others have left. 'When people leave they take pieces of the place with them in their memories and bodies. The others are left with holes, little empty spots, in odd places. Worse, their leaving opens up the world to loss. Suddenly the place has an end, an edge, and it's sharp. People can fall off or be impaled. So you are abandoned, passive, if you *stay in place* (place as history and context has been reduced to this) or you are . . . endangered by the void if you leave.' I was reminded in this of one of the students you wrote about, who had left *a place*."

When people leave they take pieces of the place with them in their memories and bodies. The others are left with holes, little empty spots, in odd places. Worse, their leaving opens up the world to loss. Suddenly the place has an end, an edge, and it's sharp. People can fall off or be impaled. So you are abandoned, passive, if you stay in place (place as history and context has been reduced to this) or you are endangered by the void if you leave.

This seems like a kind of key to me. What I have felt about leaving, about letting a place go, slip through my fingers, never again to feel its presence on my skin in exactly the same way; and about coming, arriving, picking up on a place whose recent history (or entire history, at moments in my life) has not been known by me, has not been etched in me, a part of my self. That is why, in the re-entry experience here in Albuquerque, there is always a sense of double exposure, or triple and even quadruple exposure: the place exists in terms of its history (in me), it exists in terms of its interval of absence (in me), and its present encounter (with me, me with it) reflects both those presences and absences as well as its own current dimension of meaning.

17

Ann Nihlen, Ximena and I drove up to Santa Fe last night to go to the Posadas, a yearly Christmas enactment of Mary and Joseph searching for their inn. It takes place around the city's main square with candles, songs, and lots of people. Also lots of cold. Lucas—Ann's seven-year-old son—had been up there, skiing with a friend of theirs, Sally, for a couple of days. We had a great time, eating and talking, gave up on the Posadas rather early on, and ended up in Sally's hot tub before driving back to Albuquerque. Just that short time immersed in the moving water, with space and trust to allow relaxation of one part of my body and then another, gave me a walloping sense of how very tense I have been these last few months. As the feeling returned to each muscle and nerve, it was as if a part of myself was returning—a becoming whole.

18

Christmas was always important in my family. I remember setting an apple before the fireplace long after my sister and brother and I knew there was no Santa. It was part of the tradition, expected each year. In my family there was always an attempt to break with the consumerism of the moment—at whatever level it manifests itself in our class and culture—and gifts one made oneself were always appreciated more than the store-bought kind. We wrote poems to one another and my mother is still especially good at writing funny ones, for particular occasions. The traditional turkey dinner was always shared with the immediate family once removed: parents, sisters and brothers and finally sisters and brothers and their offspring, as well as grandparents and uncles and aunts until most of them were no longer around, or lived too far away.

Christmas this year was joyous: being home, having Ximena and Anna here (although in some ways their wonderful presence only served to emphasize that neither Sarah, nor Gregory and Laura, are here). For me, I guess, the most painful part of this Christmas consists in what's happening in Central America, the Caribbean, and so many other parts of the world where terror reigns, death is like eating and breathing, the traditional festivities—wherever they may be—are saddened by blood. I think of Nicaragua, of the Purisimas, the Christmas mass at Uriel's church, the homes that are forever different because of a bomb, a land mine, a sniper.

Ximena and Anna at Ann Nihlen's house on Christmas day.

319

19

Floyce, Anna, Ximena and I went to Ann's house in the early afternoon—Trisha was there as well, and Becky, and we all shared Ann's Swedish glug and exchanged a few homemade or otherwise meaningful gifts. Then our contingent transported itself to my brother's and sister-in-law's house, for the family Christmas dinner. There was a good feeling, wonderful food—mostly made by Joanna—plenty of dogs and electronics (it's notable how, in the middle and upper classes in this country, kids live in an electronic world).

Shanti, my brother's son, and even Lucas, Ann's son—who is considerably less besieged by current fads and/or consumer pampering than any other kid I know here—both spent most of yesterday absorbed in their latest electronic toys. Shanti's toy is an amazing operation, capable of doing a real-life lie-detector test and solving all manner of complex problems. Lucas has a robot-like figure which, to be put together, requires learning what to me seems to be an impressive amount of electronics! Among the gifts exchanged in my family, as well as in Ann's, the emphasis was on things people had made. (In our family I think we have avoided measuring love by the size or cost of a gift. But we have not been free of the distortions a commodity-oriented society inflicts. Sometimes, for me, the joy is dulled by an insistent "you shouldn't have done it," as if some great hand might reach down and prevent that particular act of giving. We have not been totally free, either, from giving in the context of speculation about what will be given to us. How I hate these distortions! Sometimes I have preferred to give gifts to those I love entirely removed from these expected occasions for giving. Just to disconnect it, somehow, from the more hypocritical aspects of the custom.)

20

I can still hear Anna's voice, and see the expression on her face as she told me: "I blame you for letting me go out with that guy. . .and get pregnant!" She was referring to the relationship in Nicaragua which resulted in the pregnancy she then aborted in New York. After a visit of several days, with lots of warmth and closeness, this morning was the time for articulating some of what she's been working through with her psychologist. It includes a vivid memory (dominating most else, right now) of Robert and me in a knock-down drag-out fight in Cuba, a feeling she has that a part of her childhood is missing, and not recuperable; the recrimination that she has long felt that she was doing things not because she wanted or needed to, but because they were expected of her; and the difficulty now, of her life in New York—a less than good living situation, having to work almost full time and study—all at the age of fifteen.

Ximena soon joined us. And soon joined the recriminations. A memory strong in her past is of me telling her she must "do a good job" at something. "Make me proud of you" is the way she remembers me saying it. It is meaningless that I do not remember the scene, or do not remember it the way she does—nor, obviously, with the same emotional charge. Just as it is meaningless for me to remind Anna that I talked to her a number of times about her relationship with the guy who made her pregnant, asking her if she was sleeping with him (which she denied at the time), begging her to either wait or to get some sort of birth control.

Reality, between mothers and their daughters (or sons), includes a chain of hammering incidents, remembered by each as each was affected by it. Recriminations are a part of that, a part of one's own working it out.

Today we have gone over and over reasons for one thing or another. Reasons have taken on a brilliance throughout this day. Why did we leave Mexico? Why did *you* leave? Why did you say such and such? Why did you do this or that? Among the assurances, has been that guilt-edged assurance: "I blame you both!" Meaning me and whoever the particular father was: Robert or Sergio. We share in the blame, and that is supposed to make it somehow how better, fairer, more palatable. And then I hear myself answering: yes, it was both of us, and it was you, it was all of us. That was the way it was, and there were reasons, some of which I can remember, some of which I can tell you and you'll understand, others you probably won't. And sometimes I break down and tell Ximena and Anna that perhaps they will understand some things better when they are older and as women have these kinds of relationships, these kinds of responsibilities, must make these kinds of decisions. Or perhaps they won't.

I mean perhaps they won't understand all that much better. Perhaps our experiences *are* worth something, in that they do not always have to be repeated from generation to generation. Actually, I hope that's the case. I would give a great deal for all my daughters to possess the strength and self-esteem with which they could avoid much of what I have lived in relationships with men.

Today both Ximena's and Anna's anguish turned on me. I have tricked or wronged their respective fathers. And they must speak out their rage. O.k.

21

Dream: I am in a town or community. There are friends, but their faces are not ones I know. They are not hostile, but equally they are not known, familiar. I am somehow searching for Jane Goldman, but her name is Alice. Alice Goldman. As I write this, it comes clear: Jane Goldman was a woman I knew slightly; I knew her husband Herb better. He was a sculptor. It was Albuquerque, late 1950s. Herb taught at the university, and I became friendly with him on my own—although he and his wife were also friends of my parents—because I modelled in one of his sculpture classes.

She was to be the first of many many women I would know in my life, whose existences revolved around their domestic sphere in an agonizing way. I would see her struggling with her children, even at a party not at her home; she would be the one tugging at wet mittens or putting the kids to sleep in someone's back bedroom, sprawled and toppled with coats. Her physical appearance seemed a screaming advertisement of her overloaded misery. Herb Goldman was—as was his wife—of the local artists' colony, supposedly a liberated man, yet he did nothing visible to alleviate the constant responsibility loaded on this woman who was his wife.

Alice Garver was another friend of mine from those years. A big woman, beautiful, imposing. A painter. A muralist. They were her murals Jane Caputi and I had tried to see at the Albuquerque National Bank Building. Alice was somehow the opposite of Jane. She, too, was married—to a man named Ken Garver—and had two small boys, I think. I suppose Ken was no less individualistic in his way than Herb. But Alice was certainly very different from Jane. She instantly demanded recognition when she entered a room. She carried herself as few women in those days did. She stunned with her presence. It was larger than life. And then her life was over. Mysteriously. One day she was alive. Then she was dead.

In last night's dream, the name of the woman was Alice Goldman, and as I write this I suppose the names combined to produce a whole image in my memory. The woman I searched for in my dream was described by others, as "a model." Someone to be emulated. Alone and occasionally with others I wandered through a town, a community, a lifetime. Looking for Alice Goldman. At times I caught a momentary glimpse of her, moving through a crowd, or sitting at the far end of a room full of people. She had light hair and a clear, purposeful face; her build was more like Jane Goldman's: slight, wiry, unimpressive. But her face was not the face of a long-suffering woman. It was not the radiant face of Alice Garver. No. It was a face in which one had to search hard to find the answers, but on first encountering her one knew at once that the answers were there. Slightly hidden. Quiet. But there.

January

1

Ximena and I left at 3:30 yesterday morning for the Grand Canyon. It takes eight to ten hours to drive, depending on the highway conditions, and we were there by 11:00—even with a rather long stretch of fog on the highway, and patches of ice on the road into the park. I can't remember having been here in the winter before this; it's quite a different experience.

The canyon affects me as few other places do. There is a living energy there, beyond the sum total of whatever is describable of its beauty, its history, or the spell it is expected to cast. There is a kind of three-dimensional magnetism. Magnetism as in real, physical, pull. I feel this same pressure when sitting in the main room of the Mexican Museum of Anthropology, the room where the Calendar Stone and the altars and the statue of Coatlique are. I felt it at Machu Picchu, in Peru (though I can't be sure, because I was there such a very long time ago, and I don't know if I am imagining the feeling in retrospect, or really felt it at the time). I used to feel it along a brief stretch of road in Nicaragua's *meseta de los pueblos* area, a kind of luminous valley, when returning to Managua after having been in Diriamba, Diria, San Marcos, Catalina, those towns.

I could sit at the edge of the Grand Canyon for hours, lost in its layers and shadows and highlights and ravines until I was no longer staring but meshed somehow with the place. It is a very definite sense of *place*, of feeling place so intensely that one is no longer separate from it and looking at it, but is more truly a part of it. But that doesn't say it either. And I began to feel it again, on our way back from the canyon, when we decided to turn off on the road to Acoma and visit the sky city before returning to Albuquerque. It was almost dusk, and the amazing mesas stood out pink and gold in the rapidly blazing then diminishing light. Suddenly, the setting sun was on the road just before my eyes. I felt that I couldn't go on, and knew that it was useless to continue in any case, for we would have gotten to the pueblo much later than one is allowed in. So we turned back, and made tentative plans to go there, on a special trip, the following day.

The Grand Canyon, then, was what it has always been for me, and this trip was good for many reasons: being with Ximena, doing something together, just the two of us (and realizing, with no little pain, that I have never really travelled anywhere, for pleasure, with any of my kids). Talking with her, in that setting. The two of us enjoying a wonderful little cabin at Bright Angel Lodge, right on the canyon's rim. Loving the countryside. Sealing a coming together that has been important for us both.

2

It was enough to be with Ximena, listen to her stories and feelings, love her, respond to her needs. There was a time, last night, when the canyon suddenly turned frightening, sour or poisoned, mysteriously grim with a strange but mad kind of beauty. It was still light, but a hoard of dark grey clouds had moved in and taken possession of the lower levels on one side of the chasm. Those clouds moved back and forth, becoming thicker, somehow holding their own in an unspoken battle with what was left of the winter sun, still lighting the other side of the expanse.

Those dark grey, almost-black clouds were terrible—they

The Grand Canyon is like that great room at the Mexican Museum of anthropology—there's a magic there, an energy that recharges your soul.

The Colorado River, at the bottom of the Grand Canyon.

seemed vaguely reminiscent of a forgotten dream, or an unfulfilled need, an idea that died before it could give birth to itself as event or as history, a life broken at the root. I stood and looked at those clouds, their color and density, and I felt like sobbing. I didn't want to try to understand whether it was omen, or waste which had been exorcised and expelled. And so we went to our cabin, and to sleep. I slept from seven to seven, twelve solid hours. That soup of almost-black cloud substance, churning in the canyon depths, reminded me of all the parts of all the dreams I forget when I awake, the parts that will never come back, never be remembered, never come clear.

It is 1985 now. A new year. The old one died and this new one was born with a minimum articulation where we were. I had thought there might be some party or event, but there wasn't, and nothing on the car radio but news of drunken highway deaths mixed with parades, football games, and a roundup of the year's highlights. Floyce celebrates his birthday on the thirty-first, but we had observed it a day early in order for Ximena and me to be able to go to the canyon. It was a tiny affair, I baked a cake, brought out a hidden gift, and a couple of friends came over. Floyce is forty-six. The years themselves are a year older.

3

Waking brings with it a handful of gloom, as if the night had been inhabited by omens and heavy bits and pieces of misplaced extremities—small ones, like fingers and toes, but disarticulated pieces of one's own body nonetheless. I remember waking at about 1:30. I had the sensation that Floyce had just come to bed, but he was already asleep. Or seemed to be. I, gradually, was more and more awake. As I lay there trying to recapture sleep, my head filled with disjointed images: one would begin and develop only to be cut off and have another takes its place. A growing sense of despair, and an urgency to somehow set things right.

I felt that some parts of my real body were more exhausted than others, and wondered, momentarily, whether I should exercise those parts that seemed rested, so that they would tire like the rest, or rest those parts that were tired so I might wake refreshed and whole. I couldn't seem to find an answer to that, and I eventually fell back to sleep. The next hours were vivid with dreams. All sorts of luscious fruits festooned a large room or series of rooms. Grapes hung in clusters from the ceiling. Corners were garlanded with bananas and pineapples, mangoes just at their point of ripeness, peaches and apricots. Friends and their children were helping with the decorations. Some were in costume. Floyce seemed detached and grumpy. Later I discovered, through a friend, that he was that way because someone had stolen his credit card in the middle of the night. For some reason he hadn't wanted to mention it.

Meanwhile, some sort of a nursing home or halfway house was being set up in one corner of our house. A middle-aged woman came to the door. It seemed I had never seen her before, but immediately we began to talk. I explained the operation to her, and she smiled and told me: "I know all about it; why I'm the Sister in charge of the priests on the next floor!" Then I noticed that she was pregnant and about to give birth. I hurried her into a receiving room, where two volunteers immediately began preparing her for delivery. Four small neighborhood children had also been at the door when I let the sister in, and now I went back to where they waited and urged them, too, to enter. "A baby is being born," I told them, "hurry! It's a wonderful experience to see life coming!" They shyly inched their way down the hall—which seemed too long for the house, at that point—and came upon the scene in time to see the happy mother welcoming the head of her baby.

In this same dream, or in the fragments of many dreams which flooded my night, I discovered I had cancer of the stomach. The thought I would soon die saddened me, but not as much as I somehow thought it should. I remember thinking: now nothing about the Immigration and Naturalization Service (INS) is important. My body has moved beyond their decision-making process.

4

Suddenly I am besieged by the image of the Dutch Cleanser wrapper—the woman in her bonnet on the can, and the can with the image of the same woman in the bonnet holding a can with the same image and on and on into the tiniest tunnel of infinite

These two abandoned gas pumps on the road to Acoma reminded me of two decaying gas tanks on a broken-down wharf in San Carlos, on the Great Lake of Nicaragua.

Acoma.

sequence/distance. I am driving down Central Avenue, here in Albuquerque, and I am caught up with that image and suddenly I understand its meaning. It is not stylized and pat, some perfect commercial catch-all. No. It is something which grows of itself, naturally, like the women and men linked through this journal, how they comment on and move off from each other's observations and my own, from our dreams and needs.

Meridel LeSueur writes: "Your notes...I don't see how you have time to do it but they must clarify your ideas." She's right. But it is like a conversation. Perhaps it is a conversation on a different plane, and in a different tempo than when one faces another human being and speaks words which then register on that person who in turn speaks back. No, this is different. There are long spaces. And silences. The words, ideas, arrive at isolated moments. They come folded in envelopes, are retrieved from mail boxes or from under doors, are read late at night when time is somehow one's own. Chance—is it chance?—plays a part in when the pages come, in what is happening in the life of the recipient, how what I have seen or done or thought or imagined feeds the overloaded circuits or empty holes in her or his life. And all this is multiplied by twenty or twenty-five. A tremendous web is woven.

In the Indian pueblos, like in Latin America, there is always a stray dog.

5

Ximena and I wanted to go to Acoma, the sky city where one of
the Pueblo cultures has existed since 1000 B.C. We had tried to go
on the way back from the Grand Canyon, but the late afternoon
light exploded across the desert, illuminating great mesas, red and
gold rock, the bare branches of trees and the scrubby pinon and
chamisa. Everything became suddenly very brilliant, glowing,
and then the light failed quickly. We would not reach Acoma in
time to visit with sun, and we turned back and went home. We
had been left with the urge to see this mesa. The next day we
returned. I remember having been there as a child, with my own
parents. And now I was taking Ximena.

This woman sold pottery at Acoma village.

The experience turned out to be both beautiful and painful. A
modern tourist center now sits at the foot of the mesa, and everyone who comes must enter and pay a fee for visiting, another fee
for whatever type of camera you are using, a fee for the guided
tour—and that's the only way one can now visit the pueblo. We
had some fry bread while waiting for the next tour. The tortuous

pathway I remember from my childhood has given way to a paved road, carved from the side of the great rock in 1940 when a film crew was making a movie and had to have a way of getting its equipment to the top.

I respect the Acoma people's decision to make visitors pay to see their village, to tell tourists what they may and may not photograph, and even to insist upon accompanying everyone who visits the top. What I was not prepared for, is the fact that nobody really lives atop the mesa anymore. Our guide told us that only about seventy-five people actually reside there, because there's neither water nor electricity. Most of the Acoma people now live at Acomita or McCarty, two villages at ground level nearby. On top of the wind-swept mesa I saw only four or five people—women—each emerging from her home as we walked by, each standing beside a tiny table on which she had pottery for sale.

6

The light. I have always been fascinated by the light. Wherever I have gone. I remember, when first learning how to make pictures, in Cuba, listening to my teacher talk about Cuban light. Its particularities, its intensity and texture. It was then that I realized that light is different, in different places. And I began to see those different lights, to search for them. They became an important part of whatever landscape surrounded me. Of which I was a part. Driving up the mountains this afternoon, I immersed myself in the light. And in the shadows, yawning and receding across the peaks as I approached them.

I must have stopped the car a dozen times to photograph those changing contrasts on the snow-speckled slopes. Behind me the sun was lowering in the west, and when I turned to that, there were broad sweeps of soft light, shafts, falling from luminous clouds to the dull, even greyness of the city. When I drove down again the experience was even more intense. The light had become a bright gold, and gradually a deep dusty bronze. The bare branches of the winter trees along Central Avenue seemed etched against the smooth walls of the university buildings, giving back the intensity of that light. At that moment light itself seemed a link with all my times.

Never exactly the same, every moment absolutely its own, it was nevertheless the light that took me back to those walks across the desert in my mid teens—when I'd push myself to a place where I could reclaim an "original life" and weave a fantasy of what I supposed that to be. It threw me, as well, to walks along Havana's seawall in the late afternoon, the particular way the leavening light touched the water and transformed it. To Managua's strange *pistas* (transit arteries connecting various parts of that scattered city), when the swallows dip and rise at five-thirty in the afternoon.

Paris, in the fall, where light seemed linked to temperature, and cold air turned luminosity brittle till it shattered in my arms. New York, where light can be dirty or clean. Southern California where it always seems slightly artificial. Or on that recent road to Acoma, the first time Ximena and I travelled it, where the light was magic and its secrets penetrated our clothing and our memories. I have an image of the Enchanted Mesa, that holds that light on its face.

There is total whiteness, interrupted only by the perpendiculars and verticals of buildings, tree trunks, scattered chimneys—everything horizontal or approaching horizontal is covered with snow. There is no division between earth and sky. No visible division. The light is dull, intense but dull. And the snow continues to fall, slowly, steadily. My friend Debbie Vetterman wrote across a piece of paper: "form is revealed in the moment of light." We had seen the same luminous brilliance on the walls of the university buildings several afternoons before, the same deep blue sky behind them, the same play of bare branches against them. I want to write: I am hovering above my life. But I realize I don't really understand what such a phrase might mean. Is it an idea, or a sense of something, just around the corner?

7

Outside it is dull, a unifying hardness in the air, a brittle cold. The dullness of snow as it dirties. Inside, my heart sings. Extraordinarily important and good communication with people lately. Jane back from her Boston Christmas of work with Mary Daly on their *Wickedary*; Debra Vetterman letting me explore the recesses of her drawings which link nature and woman's body in a new way.

One luminous afternoon, driving from the city up to the Sandia Mountains.

The Enchanted Mesa, in the late afternoon light.

And her ideas about art. Although my attempt to get her to co-teach the Women and Creativity class with me seems to have failed, she will be taking the class as a student, and I look forward to great interaction and stimulus there. Communication through correspondence also arrowing in, straight and clear.

Meridel writes: "Albuquerque to me is the most violent reactionary colonial city in the Americas. It drove me out. I lived there during the Alianza uprising which brought all the reactionary middle-class oil interests, military, stripped naked. I was also there during the university struggle when they took over the cafeteria and marched down town, hundreds in the streets. They cracked down on the university. . . indian and women studies. . . indian studies, the indian leader was murdered. . . blacks, indians and chicanos were open game. The cops killed them like rabbits. The mothers made one demonstration of thousands in the streets before the court house. They sent Tijerina to prison where he was chemically changed. The Alianza is underground and you can hardly find anyone who will admit remembering it, or talk about it . . .

"The women involved in the Alianza were amazing. It was a small revolution. They took over the land. They started a clinic which was burned by the interests in the north. There were no hospitals for hundreds of miles. They published a paper called *El Grito*, published mostly by women, which was marvelous. They were framed for murder, tried, and Tijerina sent to jail. They went underground and I am sure they are still there. From the old guerrilla bands called the white hats they will always be there. But they are underground now. The silence is terrible. . ."

8

I've been reading the *Letters and Journals* of Paula Modersohn-Becker, wonderful draftswoman and painter of that German school at the turn of this century. They are tremendously moving to me. On January 15, 1901, from Berlin, she wrote to Otto Modersohn (her on-again off-again lover and husband): "I feel strongly that everything I previously dreamed of for my own art was not nearly experienced enough inwardly. It must go through the whole person, through every fiber of one's being." It touches me with a great intensity that this woman, of such a different life and time than my own, should have had this feeling, so close to mine. What consumed her eighty-four years ago consumes me today. Paula died of an embolism weeks after giving birth to her only daughter, in 1907. There is, clearly, a repetition of woman-power in all of us who would search it out. Or work to let it enter us.

Adrienne Rich has a poem about Paula Becker. It is a poem in Paula's voice, and she speaks to Clara Westhoff—Rilke's wife—a potter, her friend, and the other female person in that foursome. This poem has moved me perhaps in a more intimate way than anything I've taken in hand this year. It seems, in fact, a turning point:

Paula Becker to Clara Westhoff

Paula Becker 1876-1907
Clara Westhoff 1878-1954

became friends, at Worpswede, an artists' colony near Bremen, Germany, summer 1899. In January 1900, spent a half-year together in Paris, where Paula painted and Clara studied sculpture with Rodin. In August they returned to Worpswede, and spent the next winter together in Berlin. In 1901, Clara married the poet Rainer Maria Rilke; soon after, Paula married the painter Otto Modersohn. She died of a hemorrhage after childbirth, murmering, *What a shame!*

The autumn feels slowed down,
summer still holds on here, even the light
seems to last longer than it should
or maybe I'm using it to the thin edge.
The moon rolls in the air. I didn't want this child.
You're the only one I've told.
I want a child maybe, someday, but not now.
Otto has a calm, complacent way
of following me with his eyes, as if to say
Soon you'll have your hands full!
And yes, I will; this child will be mine
not his, the failures, if I fail
will all be mine. We're not good, Clara,

at learning to prevent these things,
and once we have a child, it *is* ours.
But lately, I feel beyond Otto or anyone.
I know now the kind of work I have to do.
It takes such energy! I have the feeling I'm
moving somewhere, patiently, impatiently,
in my loneliness. I'm looking everywhere in nature
for new forms, old forms in new places,
the planes of an antique mouth, let's say, among the leaves.
I know and do not know
what I am searching for.
Remember those months in the studio together,
you up to your strong forearms in wet clay,
I trying to make something of the strange impressions
assailing me—the Japanese
flowers and birds on the silk, the drunks
sheltering in the Louvre, that river-light,
those faces. . . Did we know exactly
why we were there? Paris unnerved you,
you found it too much, yet you went on
with your work . . . and later we met there again,
both married then, and I thought you and Rilke
both seemed unnerved. I felt a kind of joylessness
between you. Of course he and I
have had our difficulties. Maybe I was jealous
of him, to begin with, taking you from me,
maybe I married Otto to fill up
my loneliness for you.
Rainer, of course, *knows* more than Otto knows,
he believes in women. But he feeds on us,
like all of them. His whole life, his art
is protected by women. Which of us could say that?
Which of us, Clara, hasn't had to take that leap
out beyond our being women
to save our work? or is it to save ourselves?
Marriage is lonelier than solitude.
Do you know: I was dreaming I had died
giving birth to the child.
I couldn't paint or speak or even move.
My child—I think—survived me. But what was funny
in the dream was, Rainer had written my requiem—

337

a long, beautiful poem, and calling me his friend.
I was *your* friend
but in the dream you didn't say a word.
In the dream his poem was like a letter
to someone who has no right
to be there but must be treated gently, like a guest
who comes on the wrong day. Clara, why don't I dream of
    you?
That photo of the two of us—I have it still,
you and I looking hard into each other
and my painting behind us. How we used to work
side by side! And how I've worked since then
trying to create according to our plan
that we'd bring, against all odds, our full power
to every subject. Hold back nothing
because we were women. Clara, our strength still lies
in the things we used to talk about:
how life and death take one another's hands,
the struggle for truth, our old pledge against guilt.
And now I feel dawn and the coming day.
I love waking in my studio, seeing my pictures
come alive in the light. Sometimes I feel
it is myself that kicks inside me,
myself I must give suck to, love . . .
I wish we could have done this for each other
all our lives, but we can't . . .
They say a pregnant woman
dreams of her own death. But life and death
take one another's hands. Clara, I feel so full
of work, the life I see ahead, and love
for you, who of all people
however badly I say this
will hear all I say and cannot say.

—Adrienne Rich

The voices. Over and over again I hear Paula Becker, the words reach out and circle me. I need them, desperately. These days I find it harder than usual to listen to the words of convention, those that are spoken out of custom or in laziness, almost without meaning, or oblivious of the meaning they possess. In a heavy discussion in days past, the statement "I cannot know how a Guatemalan peasant feels because I am not a Guatemalan peasant" cuts so deep. The pain is only now beginning to recede, but stays lodged in my body—which alternately feels extraordinarily tired or on the cutting edge of new life.

More and more I understand, with an understanding that is necessarily also risk, that we cannot deny the Guatemalan peasant within us, the painter who yearned all the years of her life for new forms and who died with her days-old child in her arms, the Vietnamese slandered now once more in our press, the South Africans splitting apart the confines of history, the Nicaraguans, the Salvadoreans, the lesbian lovers whose bodies pull apart in the presence of "straight" society, the invisible, the real, those who struggle. We are in every real way part of them all, we are one and the same, to deny it is to deny ourselves, our place, our time.

This week, on the eighteenth, I will have been home a year.

Myself, Regrouping

These are my hands. Here they are.
Good hands, large
and strong.
Hands that have written poems,
brought children to the world,
made love
and war.
In dreams they sometimes race
trying to keep up
or grow beyond their boundaries.
In dreams they have been Black
as well as cold.

These are my feet. Also large.
Spread flattened for years
in crude sandals.
Lately, through re-entry,
shod with intimidating boots.
I like the intimidation.
It balances the smiles.

This is my smile. Sometimes
it fears exposure
but more often it breaks and tumbles
beyond the confines of my mouth.
In your mouth's upturned corners
it has found a friend.
Tongue to tongue. Tooth to tooth.
When your smile comes small
and suddenly stops
mine longs to move up close,
hold and complete
your process.

I have strong legs, thighs that seize
and clasp, broad hips belly and breasts
marked by babies and by age.
Elbows that never wait by windows anymore
but often stump against a silent keyboard
or are caressed by their own body's fingers
holding myself.

My fingers. They are light-sensitive
and live in history's mouth.
My nose has been called patrician
by some,
elephant snout by a boy in seventh grade
whose taunt
I am only now forgetting.
My hair has been braided, dark brown,
teased in the hesitant years,
dyed for a while in the bridging years,
now reclaiming its soft grey
fire.

I have been told my eyes can see
and yes, they can.
They see and see and sometimes do not close
even when I will them to.
A third eye opens and shuts around my neck,
my camera's lens, extension of my own,
ready and waiting on my skin.

I have two voices, two tongues
with which to ask
and say.

Sometimes my Latina high
lilts against the guttural deepness
of my Jewish shadowland.
The questioning Spanish "no?"

moves restless
through reclaimed English:
Seville, Mexico, Havana,
Lima, Hanoi, Managua,
Paris, Scarsdale, Lower East Side,
Albuquerque, everywhere.

My ears are less than perfect,
inherited with love from my father
(as are my gums).
My memory is shredded.
Memory...the hardest part.
So easy to lose. So distanced or so close.
Lately I spend half my life trying to remember.

I have four children
a son and three daughters
extensions of myself
though not now possessed
nor held by me.
Their own eyes and hands,
their own feet
travel them out
and they return
completing my voice
a circle
turning.

This is the skin I shed
and the new one
pulling against my bones.
This is my pain.
I claim it too
and offer it along with deepest love
as gift   and remedy.

*Photo of Margaret Randall on page 341 taken by Colleen McKay.

9

When my young student in today's poetry workshop told me that this campus is larger than any town he has ever lived in, and his gesture radiated a kind of shy hesitation towards life, I told him to hold on to his eyes as long as he possibly could, to look at his surroundings and know he was seeing them in a way others could not. I told him his eyes would grow old, and soon enough, but that he could set out on a marvellous journey of chronicling this experience, if he wanted to. He smiled and then looked at me with a sort of disbelief.

In this journal I have spoken of what I have seen and felt. The maps that have come apart in my hands. And those I have traced, moving.

Not everything is recorded here. It is important to remember that. Not everything can be said.

10

In Managua, not too many lives ago, I was forced to stop my car and pull over to the side of the road in that huge Nineteenth of July Square. In the exact center of its vast asphalt, four blistering white horses waited impatiently as they were hitched to the proud extremities of an eighteenth-century freedom fighter, Tupac Amaru. My body shook. I knew I was witnessing something that was not, in fact, "happening." Not then, or there. It was happening behind by eyes. It was as if my eyes had turned in their sockets, weighted with the weariness of pain and the tension of death.

I leaned forward over the steering wheel, cradling my face in the crooks of my elbows. I closed my eyes. When I raised my head again, and looked, the horses were still there, still impatient. I knew they would be. I knew I had nothing to fear. I knew that if I so desired or needed, I could turn the ignition key once more and drive through the middle of that image. It was not real—not in the sense society accepts or rejects in its computerized halloween. But it taught me that I needed to come home.

343

My dear friend Susan Sherman.

Colleen McKay

11

What most comes full circle for me, on this new January 18, is the coming home to women. Women who are close to me here, and the reality of a women's community, the strength and power there, the gift. Of course this also means coming full circle to myself, as a woman. Telling me something necessary about my own condition as woman, handing me back tiny pieces of a shared history.

Trisha Franzan

This must be something like what Blacks felt when they first understood that Black is Beautiful; or Native Americans when, however briefly, Wounded Knee became again their nation; or the Hispanics of this state during the Tierra Amarilla land take-over which Meridel mentions in her letter; or lesbians and gay men during those first amazing Gay Pride marches after Stonewall. It is a coming together with one's identity that has no substitute.

Debra Vetterman, by the bank of the Rio Grande, Albuquerque.

12

Some three hours from Albuquerque, going west and then north, on the highway to Grants and then through a scattering of houses called Thoreau (and pronounced Through), there is what's left of a twenty-mile badlands called the Bisti. Deb knew the place, but she remembered it being to the right of the dirt road that winds down into it, rather than on the left which was where we found it, after asking directions of a Navajo family in a truck. The younger of two extraordinarily beautiful women indicated clear signals, while the man, who had been driving, got out and in partial English made sure we understood. Deb told me then, "Sometimes I hate being white." I was flooded with memories of my earliest Latin American years.

Image As Intruder / The Bisti

All the images were huge, shale, contained
within your sense
of up and down.
All the images but one.

In the middle of the roll
after a lacy bush against the earth
before the rock tensing the sky
is the picture you didn't make
the body you didn't see
etched in silver on your film.

A soft vision. Shadows climbing
from the tray.
Touching your face. Pulling you
backwards and forwards in the same stroke.
Nothing gives
yet everything leans and sways.
Gentle against dry eyes, tight lips.

Who made the photograph, you want to ask,
but another question rises in your throat
from a time not yet explored,
a mind not yet your own.

Feathers.
Knowledge.

The Bisti Badlands, in northern New Mexico.

Rubbing memory.
Cave.
Faint triangle alive on a paper face.
Come on, it says, please come.
Only the dead of soul will stay behind.

The Bisti Badlands. This is what they are taking away from us.

The Bisti is being stipped, undoubtedly for some sort of ore, and to build a better road. As we walked away from where we left Deb's car, climbed up into the great soft erosions towering into amazing shapes and deep gullies, I could see chain after chain of truck cabs hauling several construction cars each. The industry of capitalism is destroying this place. "They've already taken my mountain away," Deb said. "I knew they would." But we walked and climbed, and I shot four rolls of film. If anything is New Mexico, this is it. If anything speaks of earth as a body, soft, pliable, yet immense, endless, strong, this is it. Entering.

On October 2, 1985, the Immigration and Naturalization Service denied Margaret Randall resident status, stating: "Her writings go far beyond mere dissent, disagreement with, or criticism of the United States or its policies." She was given twenty-eight days to leave the country. A first challenge to that decision was heard by an INS judge on March 17, 1986.

In support of Margaret Randall, the Center for Constitutional Rights and a group of American writers—including Alice Walker, Norman Mailer, Grace Paley, and Kurt Vonnegut—have filed lawsuits seeking to reverse the INS decision, and also challenging the constitutionality of the sections of the immigration law which allow the INS to exclude or deport foreigners for their political opinions.

Rounds of appeals and legal challenges could delay the outcome of her case for some years.

Printed in Canada